Understanding Amsterdam

understanding AMSTERDAM

Essays on economic vitality, city life & urban form

Léon Deben, Willem Heinemeijer, Dick van der Vaart
(editors)

Het Spinhuis 1993

CIP-DATA KONINKLIJKE BIBLIOTHEEK, DEN HAAG

Understanding

Understanding Amsterdam : Essays on economic vitality, city life and urban form / Léon
Deben, Willem Heinemeijer and Dick van der Vaart (eds.). - Amsterdam : Het Spinhuis
Zes lezingen in het kader van de Wibaut-lezingen cyclus. - Met lit.opg.
ISBN 90-73052-74-2
NUGI 652/671
Trefw.: stadssociologie ; Amsterdam / Amsterdam ; sociale geografie.

Cover: Jos Hendrix
Layout: René de Ree
Printed and bound in the Netherlands

Het Spinhuis Publishers, Oudezijds Achterburgwal 185, 1012 DK Amsterdam The Netherlands

Contents

Introduction

Léon Deben, Willem Heinemeijer and Dick van der Vaart

In 1987 – the year in which Amsterdam was entitled to call itself the 'Cultural Capital of Europe' – the city organized a conference on the subject of 'Capital Cities as Achievements'. In doing so, Amsterdam let it be known that it also numbered the pursuit of science amongst its cultural riches.

The theme of the conference was well-chosen: as a capital city, the organizer was a member of the species under study, and its achievements were thus also the subject of extensive discussion in various papers. The title of the conference also provided evidence of the city administration's pretensions. As the cultural capital, Amsterdam had something to offer which other cities in the Netherlands did not possess, and the organizers were keen to broadcast this fact. Capital cities – and hence also Amsterdam – had not only an interesting past, but also a promising future.

The development of the city was already showing signs of recovery. Suburbanization had passed its low point, and the capital's population was growing in numbers once again. And on the employment front, after the industry had closed down, the service sector had taken over the dominant position with the number of jobs increasing at a spectacular rate. The enormous success of Schiphol Airport meant that the decline of the port was quickly forgotten.

Nor was the integration of Europe perceived as a danger: the blurring of independent states meant that the importance of the regions was expected to increase, and the capital metropolises should be numbered among the speech-making centres as they had been in the past. To express it even more strongly: because all large cities are coming to resemble each other more and more closely, there is a bright future for capital cities in particular, as the home of cultural elites, as a melting pot for minorities and as a playground for experiments in the 'global village'. These are all notions which fit in with the festive mood of a 'cultural capital' of Europe.

To make much of any doubts about how well the city was working would not have been polite in that festival year. But didn't that celebratory mood lead to a restriction of self-criticism? Were all those positive expectations really based on accurate calculations and predictions? Wasn't Amsterdam, with its imbalanced population mix, its massive unemployment, its ageing housing stock and its lack of investments in infrastructure, in the process of moving out onto the periphery of Europe? Nobody touched on these questions during the conference.

Afterwards, however, they did. The city proved to be more than just a festival site, and on 'the morning after', it embarked on some serious self-study. After all, cities operate within a system of political, cultural and economic relationships, in which self-criticism and the pursuit of science also have a place. This was true in the past, and it is still true today. In the days of a waning Spanish empire, aided by its extensive maritime expertise and sophisticated exploitation of sources all over the world, Amsterdam was able to develop as a metropolis. Today, Amsterdam's strengths are based on its position as the capital city of a small, wealthy country with a high level of linguistic skills, education and services, and a superb airport site which in turn is the product of a phenomenal tradition of town and country planning.

These ingredients of urban welfare are not really so different from those of a few centuries ago. Cities change unintentionaly, but they do follow some kind of pattern. Every great city, including Amsterdam, has at least five characteristics which demand continuous attention. Curiously enough, these characteristics have remained the same for hundreds of years:

1. Cities are characterised by the clustering of a large number of people from diverse social-economic and cultural backgrounds. Together, they have a significance for an area which transcends urban and regional boundaries.

2. The population is distributed among districts and neighbourhoods on the basis of these diverse social-economic and cultural backgrounds. There is always a certain amount of segregation and differentiation

3. The city is divided up into functions such as industry, business services, administration, shopping, recreation and housing. Consumption and production are linked to the big city, although the nature of this link may be constantly changing.

4. The city is the centre of division of labour, with increasing numbers of people working as specialists within a system of complex technology. The links in this chain expand and contract cyclically: production moves out towards the edge of the city, to the hinterland or to countries with low wage rates, while the population moves in to the cities from rural areas or from the Third World to start a next stage of development and innovation.

5. Many traditional relationships on the economic, political and social fronts move onto a professional footing in the city, and the structure of social life

changes. The social control provided by family, class, profession and neighbourhood seems to have been replaced by an individual perspective of competition and presentation on the urban stage.

To put it into more modern jargon, big cities are not only centres for mobilization, experimentation and refuge, but also socio-economic and cultural meeting points.

In a nutshell, these are the cornerstones of the research programme which is carried out by urban economists, geographers, sociologists and historians, as was also demonstrated in that festival year of 1987. The collaboration that was launched by the conference on 'Capital Cities as Achievements' was so successful that the University of Amsterdam decided to take the title of 'City University' from then on, and for its part the City of Amsterdam decided to make every effort to promote metropolitan research.

That was not the end of it; actions were also initiated. Inside the University, people began increasingly to recognise that economists, geographers and sociologists were carrying out related urban research in different faculties and institutes without being fully aware of what each other was doing. A better structure for collaboration was put in place. A research centre was set up to promote collaborative urban research between three different faculties. The passage of a few years proved this collaborative approach to be successful and durable. The University of Amsterdam can now boast of a sizeable research institute: the CGO Centrum voor Grootstedelijk Onderzoek (Amsterdam study centre for the Metropolitan Environment), which has a great variety of expertise on metropolitan issues and is well-respected both nationally and internationally.

The City administration was equally active. Bonds between urban politics and academic urban research were reinforced. A fund to pay for visiting professors was set up, and preparations were made to establish a special chair at the university which would focus on metropolitan issues with particular reference to Amsterdam.

During the wait for this special chair to be established, renowned foreign researchers were invited to spend some time in Amsterdam. Their assignment was to investigate the situation at that point, and to give lectures in which aspects of the current state of affairs in Amsterdam were woven together with their own specific subject knowledge and a review of the literature. This was a task which seems simpler than it actually is. After all, the visitors' lack of knowledge about the local situation could easily cause them to resort to commonplaces, climb onto their hobbyhorses, or hide behind general observations. Nor would it have been surprising if the visiting professors had limited themselves to a few cautious additions to previously published results. However, in many cases the guests produced surprisingly interesting manuscripts. Each of the lectures was published in a modest series of yellow pamphlets, the first of which appeared in 1989. These publications found an eager market, and most sold out.

Now that the Wibaut special chair in 'Metropolitan issues with special reference to Amsterdam' has been established, this intensive programme of visiting professors has reached its conclusion. To mark the occasion of the inaugural speech by the formally appointed holder of the special chair, a number of these earlier publications which have retained their readability, topicality and accuracy have been selected for reissue. This selection has been supplemented with recent material which has not previously been published. Taken as a whole, the book provides a fascinating picture of the best that urban research has to offer.

Although all the lectures are of high quality, nevertheless we must shield the authors to some extent. They all produced their manuscripts as an edited version of a series of lectures at the University of Amsterdam. Inevitably, the texts are to a certain extent designed for the occasion, and would not have been written in the same way if the authors had been told in advance that they would be included in a collection with other lectures. Clearly, too, the more the authors comment on details of local characteristics, the greater the risk that their observations may fall wide of the mark. Bearing in mind the brevity of their few weeks' stay, their acquaintance with the city and with the issues which were current at the time was also selective.

Bearing all these factors in mind, it is nevertheless surprising to discover that the articles do provide high quality reading matter, and it does appear to be worth bundling the lectures. These well-informed visitors describe Amsterdam from a certain distance, within which their enthusiasm can clearly be heard without their losing sight of their knowledge of the state of affairs elsewhere in the world, and hence their ability to put things into perspective. All in all, a mosaic has unintentionally been created in which different scientific approaches and a variety of urban facets supplement each other wonderfully well to yield a kaleidoscope of urban research.

With a little goodwill, it could even be said to look as if there had been a tightly directed programme. The different contributions show a certain degree of coherence; what is more, they complement each other in terms of scale and discipline. Global developments are analyzed, in the course of which the focus zooms in slowly but surely on Amsterdam. After a number of observations on the city and on urban culture, the theme is expanded and supplemented with a historical component.

In the first essay, *European Cities, the Informational Society, and the Global Economy*, the changes in the economy on a global scale are examined, with Manuel Castells concentrating on developments which are of importance to European cities. Next, in *Between Sheffield and Stuttgart*, John O'Loughlin details the political and economic geography of these developments. Based on an extensive study of the literature, he succeeds in identifying links between global developments and the position of Amsterdam.

Armed with this knowledge, the reader next encounters Edward Soja, who provides an exceptionally lively view of the culture of metropolises in *The Stimulus of a Little Confusion*, beginning with the view from a window, and ending with an interesting comparison with the city which is probably the most extreme contrast to Amsterdam in terms of its urban character. Then Lyn Lofland introduces us to the creation of cosmopolitans in *Urbanity, Tolerance and Public Space*. She concentrates on the quality of public space in the city, which in the case of Amsterdam has international qualities. In *Thinking about Culture in Cities* and *Cities as Windows on the World*, Ulf Hannerz continues by making a connection with the changing social basis of urban culture, migration and ethnic groups. Rather than a decline in the importance of cultural diversity, he sees new possibilities for cultural diversity in the global village.

In *The Cultural Dimension in Restructuring Metropolises*, Paul Claval explores the theme of cultural restructuring in modern cities still further. He establishes a link between urban geography and the non-material aspects of the culture, and points to the perpetuating effects of the cultural identity of metropolises. Finally, Donald Olsen identifies yet another link between culture and cities, in the area of cultural heritage. A look at the buildings of Amsterdam yields a readable history of the city, which is interpreted as a sort of 'Gesamtkunstwerk in 'Time and the City' and 'Urbanity, Modernity, and Liberty.'

The inauguration of the Wibaut special chair marks the end of a period in which a variety of visitors had the opportunity to call upon Amsterdam. In coming years, the chair will be held for extended periods by Dutch researchers. Together, the professor holding the chair and the foreigners who, it is hoped, will continue to be invited in the future, will undoubtedly produce a surprising and interesting combination of urban research, in which the city administration, the University of Amsterdam, and the Centrum voor Grootstedelijk Onderzoek / Amsterdam study centre for the Metropolitan Environment will all be involved.

Amsterdam, July 1993

Léon Deben, Willem Heinemeijer, Dick van der Vaart

European cities, the informational society, and the global economy

Manuel Castells

Urban sociology, today

An old axiom in urban sociology considers space as a reflection of society. Yet, life, and cities, are always too complex to be captured in axioms. Thus, the close relationship between space and society, between cities and history, is more a matter of expression rather than of reflection. The social matrix expresses itself into the spatial pattern through a dialectical interaction that opposes social contradictions and conflicts as trends fighting each other in an endless supersession. The result is not the coherent spatial form of an over-whelming social logic – be it the capitalist city, the pre-industrial city or the a-historical utopia – but the tortured and disorderly, yet beautiful patchwork of human creation and suffering.

Cities are socially determined in their forms and in their processes. Some of their determinants are structural, linked to deep trends of social evolution that transcend geographic or social singularity. Others are historically and culturally specific. And all are played out, and twisted, by social actors that oppose their interests and their values, to project the city of their dreams and to fight the space of their nightmares.

Sociological analysis of urban evolution must start from the theoretical standpoint of considering the complexity of these interacting trends in a given time-space context. The last twenty years of urban sociology have witnessed an evolution of thinking (including my own) from structuralism to subjectivism, then to an attempt, whatever imperfect, of integrating both perspectives into a *structural theory of urban change* that, if a label rooted in an intellectual tradition is necessary, I would call Marxian, once history has freed the Marxian theoretical tradition from the terrorist tyranny of Marxism-Leninism.

I intend to apply this theoretical perspective to the understanding of the fundamental transformations that are taking place in Western European cities

at the end of the second millennium. In order to understand such transformations
we have to refer to major social trends that are shaking up the foundations of
our existence: the coming of a technological revolution centred on information technologies, the formation of a global economy, the transition to a new
society, the informational society, that, without ceasing to be capitalist or
statist, replaces the industrial society as the framework of social institutions.

But this analysis has to be at the same time general and structural (if we
accept that a historical transformation is under way) and specific to a given
social and cultural context, such as Western Europe (with all due acknow-
ledgement to its internal differentiation).

In recent years, a new trade mark has become popular in urban theory:
capitalist restructuring. Indeed it is most relevant to pinpoint at the fundamental
shift in policies that both governments and corporations have introduced in
the 1980s to steer capitalist economies out of their 1970s' crises. Yet, more
often than not, the theory of capitalist restructuring has missed the specificity
of the process of transformation in each area of the world, as well as the
variation of the cultural and political factors that shape the process of economic
restructuring, and ultimately determine its outcome.

Thus, the deindustrialization processes of New York and London take
place at the same time that a wave of industrialization of historic proportions
occurs in China and in the Asian Pacific. The rise of the informal economy
and of urban dualism takes place in Los Angeles, as well as in Madrid, Miami,
Moscow, Bogota, and Kuala Lumpur, but the social paths and social consequences of such similarly structural process are so different as to induce a
fundamental variegation of each resulting urban structure.

Therefore, in these lectures I will try to analyze some structural trends
underlying the current transformation of European cities, while accounting
for the historical and social specificity of the processes emerging from such
structural transformation.

The thread of the new history: major social trends affecting European cities at the dawn of the 21st century

Urban life muddles through the pace of history. When such pace accelerates, cities
– and their people – become confused, spaces turn threatening, and meaning
escapes from experience. In such disconcerting, yet magnificent times, knowledge
becomes the only source to restore meaning, and thus meaningful action.

At the risk of schematism, and for the sake of clarity, I will summarize what
seem to be the main trends that, together and in their interaction, provide the

framework of social, economic, and political life for European cities in this particular historical period.

First of all, *we live in the midst of a fundamental technological revolution,* that is characterized by two features:

a) As all major technological revolutions in history, their effects are pervasive. They are not limited to the industry, or to the media, or to telecommunications or transportation. New technologies, that have emerged in their applications in full strength since the mid-1970s, are transforming production and consumption, management and work, life and death, culture and warfare, communication and education, space and time. We have entered a new technological paradigm.

b) As the industrial revolution was based on energy (although it embraced many other technological fields) the current revolution is based upon information technologies, in the broadest sense of the concept, that includes genetic engineering (after all, the decoding and reprogramming of the codes of the living matter).

This technological informational revolution is the backbone (although not the determinant) of all other major structural transformations:

- It provides the basic infrastructure for the formation of a functionally inter-related world economic system.

- It becomes a crucial factor in competitiveness and productivity for countries, regions, and companies throughout the world, ushering in a new international division of labour.

- It allows for the simultaneous process of centralization of messages and decentralization of their reception, creating a new communication world made up at the same time of the global village and of the incommunicability of those communities that are switched-off from the global network. Thus, an asymmetrical space of communication flows emerges from the uneven appropriation of a global communication system.

- It creates a new, intimate linkage between the productive forces of the economy and the cultural capacity of society. Because knowledge generation and information processing are at the roots of new productivity, the ability of a society to accumulate knowledge and manipulate symbols translates into economic productivity and political-military might, anchoring the sources of wealth and power into the informational capacity of each society.

While this technological revolution does not determine per se the emergence of a social system, it is an essential component of the new social structure that characterizes our world: *the informational society.* By such concept, I understand the social structure where the sources of economic productivity, cultural hegemony, and political-military power depend, fundamentally, on the capacity to retrieve, store, process, and generate information and knowledge. Although information and knowledge have been critical for economic accumulation and political power throughout history, it is only under the current technological, social, and cultural parameters that they become directly productive forces. In other words, because of the interconnection of the whole world and because of the potential automation of most standard production and management functions, the generation and control of knowledge, information, and technology is a necessary and sufficient condition to organize the overall social structure around the interests of the information holders. Information becomes the critical raw material of what all social processes and social organizations are made. Material production, as well as services, become subordinate to the handling of information in the system of production and in the organization of society. Empirically speaking, an ever growing majority of employment in Western European Cities refers to information processing jobs. The growing proportion of employment in service activities is not the truly distinctive feature, because of the ambiguity of the notion of 'services' (e.g. in Third World cities a majority of the population also works in 'services,' although there are indeed very different kind of activities). What is truly fundamental is the growing quantitative size and qualitative importance of information processing activities in both goods production and services delivery. The contradictory, but ineluctable emergence of the informational society shapes European cities as the onset of the industrial era marked for ever the urban and rural spaces of the nineteenth century.

The third major structural trend of our epoch is the formation of a *global economy*. The global economy concept must be distinguished from the notion of a world economy, that reflects a very old historical reality for most European nations, and particularly for the Netherlands that emerged as a nation through its role as one of the nodal centres of the 16th century's world economy. Capitalism has accumulated, since its beginnings, on a world-wide scale. This is not to say that the capitalist economy was a global economy. It is only now becoming such.

By global economy we mean an economy that works as a unit on real time on a planetary scale. It is an economy where capital flows,. labour markets, commodity markets, information, raw materials, management, and organization are internationalized and fully interdependent throughout the planet, although in an asymmetrical form, characterized by the uneven integration to the global system of different areas of the planet. Major functions of the economic system are fully internationalized and interdependent on a daily basis. But many others are segmented and unevenly structured depending upon functions, countries, and regions. Thus, the global economy embraces the whole planet, but not all the regions and all the people in the planet. In fact, only a minority of the people are truly integrated in the global economy, although all the dominant economic and political centres from where people depend are indeed integrated in the global economic networks (with the possible exception of Bhutan...). With the disintegration of the Soviet Empire, the last area of the planet that was not truly integrated in the global economy, it is restructuring itself in the most dramatic conditions to be able to reach out to the perceived avenues of prosperity of our economic model (China already started its integration in the global capitalist economy in December 1979, while trying to preserve its Statist political regime).

This global economy increasingly concentrates wealth, technology, and power in 'the North,' a vague geopolitical notion that replaces the obsolete West-East differentiation, and that roughly corresponds to the OECD countries. The East has disintegrated and is quickly becoming an economic appendix of the North. Or at least such is the avowed project of its new leaders. The 'South' is increasingly differentiated. East Asia is quickly escaping from the lands of poverty and underdevelopment to link up, in fact, with the rising sun of Japan, in a model of development that the Japanese writers love to describe as 'the flying geese pattern,' with Japan of course leading the way, and the other Asian nations taking off harmoniously under the technological guidance and economic support of Japan. China is at the crossroads of a potential process of substantial economic growth at a terrible human cost as hundreds of millions of peasants are being uprooted without structures able to integrate them into the new urban-industrial world. South and South East Asia struggle to survive the process of change, looking for a subordinate, yet livable position in the new world order. Most of Africa, on the contrary, finds itself increasingly disconnected from the new, global economy, reduced to piecemeal, secondary functions that see the continent deteriorate, with the world only waking up from time to time to the structural genocide taking place in Africa when television images strike the moral consciousness of public opinion and affect the political interest of otherwise indifferent policy makers. Latin America, and many regions and cities around the world, struggle in the in-between land of being only partially integrated into the global economy, and then submitted to the tensions between the promise of full integration and the daily reality of a marginal existence.

In this troubled world, Western Europe has, in fact, become a fragile island of prosperity, peace, democracy, culture, science, welfare, and civil rights.

However, the selfish reflex of trying to preserve this heaven by erecting walls against the rest of the world, may undermine the very fundaments of European culture and of democratic civilization, since the exclusion of the other is not separable from the repression of the civil liberties and the mobilization against the alien cultures. Major European cities have become nodal centres of the new global economy, but they have also seen themselves transformed into the magnets of attraction for millions of human beings from all around the world who want to share the peace, democracy, and prosperity of Europe in exchange for their hard labour, and their commitment to a promised land. But the overcrowded and aged Western Europe of the late twentieth century does not seem to be as open to the world as was the young, mostly empty America of the beginning of the century. Immigrants are not welcome, as Europe tries to embark into a new stage of its common history, building the supra-national Europe without renouncing to national identities. Yet, the cultural isolationism of the paneuropean construction is inseparable of the affirmation of ethnic nationalism that will eventually turn not only against the 'alien immigrants' but against European foreigners as well. European cities will have to cope with its new global economic role while accommodating to a multi-ethnic society that emerges from the same roots that sustain the global economy.

The fourth fundamental process under way in European cities is *the process of European integration*, into what will amount in the 21st Century to some form of Confederation of the present nation states. This is an ineluctable process for at least 15 countries (the current 12 EC countries plus Sweden, Austria, and Switzerland) regardless of the fate of the symbolic Maastricht Treaty. If, as it is generally accepted, the European Community is heading toward a common market, a common resident status for all its citizens, a common technology policy, a common currency, a common defense, and a common foreign policy, all the basic prerogatives of the national state will be shifted to the European institutions by the end of the Century. This will certainly be a tortuous path, with the nostalgics of the past, neo-fascists, neo-communists, and fundamentalists of all kind, fighting the tide of European solidarity, fueling the fears of the ignorance among people, building upon demagogy and opportunism. Yet, whatever difficult the process, and with substantial modifications to the current technocratic blueprints, Europe will come to existence: there are too many interests and too much political will at stake to see the project destroyed after having come this far.

The process of European integration will cause the internationalization of major political decision making processes, and thus it will trigger the fear of subordination of specific social interests to supranational institutions. But most of these specific interests express themselves on a regional or local basis rather than at the national level. Thus, we are witnessing the renewal of the role of regions and cities as locuses of autonomy and political decision. In particular, major cities throughout Europe constitute the nervous system of both the economy and the political system of the continent. The more national states fade in their role, and the more cities emerge as a driving force in the making of the new European society.

The process of historical transition experienced by European cities leads to *an identity crisis* in its cultures and in its people, that becomes another major element of the new urban experience. This identity crisis is the result of two above mentioned processes that, whatever contradictory among themselves, jointly contribute to shake up the foundations of European national and local cultures. On the one hand, the march to supranationality blurs national identities and make people uncertain about the power holders of their destiny, thus pushing them into withdrawal, either individualistic (neo-libertarianism) or collective (neo-nationalism). On the other hand, the arrival of millions of immigrants and the consolidation of multi-ethnic, multi-cultural societies in most Western European countries, confronts Europe head on with the reality of a non-homogeneous culture, precisely at the moment when national identity is most threatened. It follows a crisis of cultural identity (with the corollary of collective alienation) that will mark the urban processes in Europe for the years to come.

More to the point: major cities will concentrate the overwhelming proportion of immigrants and ethnic minority citizens (the immigrants' sons and daughters). Thus they will also be at the forefront of the waves of racism and xenophobia that will shake up the institutions of the new Europe even before they come into existence. As a reaction to the national identity crisis we observe the emergence of territorially defined identities at the level of the region, of the city, of the neighbourhood. European cities will be increasingly oriented toward their local culture, while increasingly distrustful of higher order cultural identities. The issue then is to know if cities can reach out to the whole world without surrendering to a localistic, quasi-tribal reaction that will create a fundamental divide between local cultures, European institutions, and the global economy.

European cities are also affected by *the rise of the social movements of the informational society*, and in particular by the two central movements of the informational society: the environmental movement, and the women's movement.

The environmental movement is at the origin of the rise of the ecological consciousness that has substantially affected urban policies and politics. The issue of sustainable development is indeed a fundamental theme of our civilization and a dominant topic in today's political agendas. Because major cities in Europe are at the same time the nodal centres of economic growth and the living places for the most environmentally-conscious segment of the population, the battles for the integration between economic growth and environmental conservation will be fought in the streets and institutions of major European cities.

The structural process of transformation of women's condition, in dialectical interaction with the rise of the feminist movement, has completely changed the social fabric of cities. Labour markets have been massively feminized, resulting in a change in the conditions of work and management, of struggle and negotiation, and ultimately in the weakening of a labour movement that could not overcome its sexist tradition. This also points to the possibility of a new informational labour movement that because it will have to be based on women's rights and concerns, as well as on those of men, it will be historically different from its predecessor.

At the same time, the transformation of households and of the domestic division of labour is fundamentally changing the demands on collective consumption, and thus urban policy. For instance, child care is becoming as important an issue as housing in today's cities. Transportation networks have to accommodate for the demands of two workers in the family, instead of relying on the free driving service provided by the suburban housewife in the not so distant past.

Some of the new social movements, the most defensive, the most reactive, have taken and will be taking the form of territorially-based counter-cultures, occupying a given space to cut themselves from the outside world, hopeless of being able to transform the society they refuse. Because such movements are likely to occur in major cities, that concentrate a young, educated population, as well as marginal cultures that accommodate themselves in the cracks of the institutions, we will be witnessing a constant struggle over the occupation of meaningful space in the main European cities, with business corporations trying to appropriate the beauty and the tradition for their noble quarters, and urban countercultures making a stand on the use value of the city, while local residents try to go on with their living, refusing to be bent by the alien wind of the new history.

Beyond the territorial battles between social movements and elite interests, *the new marginality*, unrelated to such social movements, is spreading over the urban space. Drug addicts, drug dealers, and drug victims populate the back alleys of European cities, creating the unpredictable, waking up our own psychic terrors, and tarnishing the shine of civilized prosperity at the daily coming of darkness. The 'black holes' of our society, those social conditions from where there is no return, take also their territory, making cities tremble at the fear of their unavowed misery.

The occupation of urban space by the new poverty and the new marginality takes two forms: the tolerated ghettoes, where marginalized people are permitted to stay, out of sight of the mainstream society; the open presence in the core area of cities by 'street people,' a risky strategy, but at the same time a survival technique since only there they exist, and thus only there can they relate to society, either looking for a chance or provoking a final blow.

Because the informational society concentrates wealth and power, while polarizing social groups according to their skills, unless deliberate policies correct the structural tendencies, we are also witnessing the emergence of social dualism, that could ultimately lead to the formation of a dual city, a fundamental concept that I will characterize below, when considering the spatial consequences of the structural trends and social processes that I have proposed as constituting the framework that underlies the new historical dynamics of European cities.

The spatial transformation of major European cities

From the trends we have described stem a number of spatial phenomena that characterize the current structure of major metropolitan centres in Western Europe. These centres are formed by the uneasy articulation of various socio-spatial forms and processes that I find useful to specify in their singularity, although it is obvious that they cannot be understood without relating to each other.

First of all, the *national-international business centre* is the economic engine of the city in the informational-global economy. Without it, there is no wealth to be appropriated in a given urban space, and the crisis overwhelms any other project in the city, as survival becomes the obvious priority. The business centre is made up of an infrastructure of telecommunications, communications, urban services, and office space, based upon technology and educational institutions. It thrives through information processing and control functions. It is sometimes complemented by tourism and travel facilities. It is the node of the space of flows that characterizes the dominant space of informational societies. That is, the abstract space constituted in the networks of exchange of capital flows, information flows, and decisions that link directional centres among themselves throughout the planet. Because the space of flows needs nodal points to organize its exchange, business centres and their ancillary functions constitute the localities of the space of flows. Such localities do not exist by themselves but by their connection to other similar localities organized in a network that forms the actual unit of management, innovation, and power.

Secondly, the informational society is not disincarnated. New elites make it work, although they do not necessarily base their power and wealth in majority ownership of the corporations. The new managerial-technocratic-political elite does however create exclusive spaces, as segregated and removed from the city at large as the bourgeois quarters of the industrial society. In European cities, unlike in America, *the truly exclusive residential areas tend to appropriate urban culture and history, by locating in rehabilitated areas of the central city,* emphasizing the basic fact that when domination is clearly established and enforced, the elite does not need to go into a suburban exile, as the weak and fearful American elite needed to do to escape from the control of the urban populace(with the significant exceptions of New York, San Francisco, and Boston).

Indeed, *the suburban world of European cities is a socially diversified space*, that is segmented in different peripheries around the central city. There are the traditional working class suburbs (either blue collar or white collar) of the well kept subsidized housing estates in home ownership. There are the new towns, inhabited by a young cohort of lower middle class, whose age made difficult for them to penetrate the expensive housing market of the central city. And there are also the peripheral ghettoes of the older public housing estates where new immigrant populations and poor working families experience their exclusion from the city.

Suburbs are also the locus of industrial production in European cities, both for traditional manufacturing and for the new high technology industries that locate in new peripheries of the major metropolitan areas, close enough to the communication centres but removed from older industrial districts.

Central cities are still shaped by their history. Thus, *traditional working class neighbourhoods,* increasingly populated by service workers rather than by industrial workers, constitute a distinctive space, a space that, because it is the most vulnerable, becomes the battleground between the redevelopment efforts of business and the upper middle class, and the invasion attempts of the counter-cultures trying to reappropriate the use value of the city. Thus, they often become defensive spaces for workers who have only their home to fight for, becoming at the same time meaningful popular neighbourhoods and likely bastions of xenophobia and localism.

The new professional middle class is torn between the attraction to the peaceful comfort of the boring suburbs and the excitement of a hectic, and often too expensive, urban life. The structure of the household generally determines the spatial choice. The more women play a role in the household, and the more the proximity to jobs and urban services in the city makes central urban space attractive to the new middle class, triggering the process of *gentrification of the central city*. On the contrary, the more patriarchal is the middle class family, and the more is likely to observe *the withdrawal to the suburb*, to raise children, all economic conditions being equal.

The central city is also the locus for the ghettoes of the new immigrants, linked to the underground economy, and to the networks of support and help needed to survive in a hostile society. Concentration of immigrants in some dilapidated urban areas in European cities is not the equivalent however to the experience of the American ghettoes, because the overwhelming majority of European ethnic minorities are workers, earning their living, and raising their families, thus counting on a very strong support structure that makes their ghettoes strong, family-oriented communities, unlikely to be taken over by street crime.

It is in *the core administrative and entertainment district of European cities where urban marginality makes itself present*. Its pervasive occupation of the busiest streets, and public transportation nodal points, is a survival strategy destined to be present, so that they can receive public attention or private business, be it welfare assistance, a drug transaction, a prostitution deal, or the customary police care.

Major European metropolitan centres present some variation around the structure of urban space we have outlined, depending upon their differential role in the European economy. The lower their position in the new informational network, the greater the difficulty of their transition from the industrial stage, and the more traditional will be their urban structure, with old established neighbourhoods and commercial quarters playing the determinant role in the dynamics of the city. On the contrary, the higher their position into the competitive structure of the new European economy, the greater their role of their advanced services in the business district, and the more intense will be the restructuring of the urban space. At the same time, in those cities where the new European society reallocates functions and people throughout the space, immigration, marginality, and countercultures will be the most present, fighting over the control of the territory, as identities become increasingly defined by the appropriation of space.

The critical factor in the new urban processes is, however, the fact that urban space is increasingly differentiated in social terms, while being functionally inter-related beyond physical contiguity. It follows the separation between symbolic meaning, location of functions, and the social appropriation of space in the metropolitan area. The transformation of European cities is inseparable of a deeper, structural transformation that affects urban forms and processes in advanced societies: the coming of the Informational City.

The informational city

The spatial evolution of European cities is a historically specific expression of a broader structural transformation of urban forms and processes that expresses the major social trends that I have presented as characterizing our historical epoch: the rise of the Informational City. By such concept I do *not* refer to the urban form resulting from the direct impact of information technologies on space. The Informational City is the urban expression of the whole matrix of determinations of the Informational Society, as the Industrial City was the spatial expression of the Industrial Society. The processes constituting the form and dynamics of this new urban structure, the Informational City, will be better understood by referring to the actual social and economic trends that are restructuring the territory. Thus, the new international and inter-regional division of labour ushered in by the informational society leads, at the world level, to three simultaneous processes:

- The reinforcement of the metropolitan hierarchy exercised throughout the world by the main existing nodal centres, that use their informational potential and the new communication technologies to extend and deepen their global reach.
- The decline of the old dominant industrial regions that were not able to make successfully their transition to the informational economy. This does not imply however that all traditional manufacturing cities are forced to decline: the examples of Dortmund or Barcelona show the possibility to rebound from the industrial past into an advanced producer services economy and high technology manufacturing.
- The emergence of new regions (such as the French Midi or Andalusia) or of new countries (e.g. the Asian Pacific) as dynamic economic centres, attracting capital, people, and commodities, thus recreating a new economic geography.

In the new economy, the productivity and competitiveness of regions and cities is determined by their ability to combine informational capacity, quality of life, and connectivity to the network of major metropolitan centres at the national and international level.

Thus, the new spatial logic, characteristic of the Informational City, is determined by the preeminence of the space of flows over the space of places. By space of flows I refer to the system of exchanges of information, capital, and power that structures the basic processes of societies, economies, and states between different localities, regardless of localization. I call it 'space' because it does have a spatial materiality: the directional centres located in a few selective areas of a few, selected localities; the telecommunication system, dependent upon telecommunication facilities and services that are unevenly distributed in the space, thus marking a telecommunicated space; the advanced transportation system, that makes such nodal points dependent from major airports and airlines services, from freeway systems, from high speed trains; the security systems necessary to the protection of such directional spaces, surrounded by a potentially hostile world; and the symbolic marking of such spaces by the new monumentality of abstraction, making the locales of the space of flows meaningfully meaningless, both in their internal arrangement and in their architectural form. The space of flows, superseding the space of places, epitomizes the increasing differentiation between power and experience, the separation between meaning and function.

The Informational City is at the same time, the Global City, as it articulates the directional functions of the global economy in a network of decision making and information processing centres. Such globalization of urban forms and processes goes beyond the functional and the political, to influence consumption patterns, life styles, and formal symbolism.

Finally, the Informational City is also the Dual City. This is because the informational economy has a structural tendency to generate a polarized occupational structure, according to the informational capabilities of different social groups. Informational productivity at the top may incite structural unemployment at the bottom or downgrading of the social conditions of manual labour, particularly if the control of labour unions is weakened in the process and if the institutions of the welfare state are undermined by the concerted assault of conservative politics and libertarian ideology.

The filling in of downgraded jobs by immigrant workers tends to reinforce the dualization of the urban social structure. In a parallel movement, the age differential between an increasingly older native population in European cities and a younger population of newcomers and immigrants, builds two extreme segments of citizens polarized along lines of education, ethnicity, and age simultaneously. It follows the potential surge of social tensions.

The necessary mixing of functions in the same metropolitan area leads to the attempt to preserve social segregation and functional differentiation through planning of the spatial layout of activities and residences, sometimes by public agencies, sometimes by the influence of real estate prices. It follows the formation of cities made up of spatially coexisting, socially exclusive groups and functions, that live in an increasingly uneasy tension vis à vis each other. Defensive spaces emerge as a result of the tension.

This leads to the fundamental urban dualism of our time. The one opposing the cosmopolitanism of the elite, living on a daily connection to the whole world (functionally, socially, culturally), to the tribalism of local communities, retrenched in their spaces that they try to control as their last stand against the macro-forces that shape their lifes out of their reach. The fundamental dividing line in our cities is the inclusion of the cosmopolitans in the making of the new history while excluding the locals from the control of the global city to which ultimately their neighbourhoods belong.

Thus, the Informational City, the Global City, and the Dual City are closely inter-related, forming the background of urban processes in Europe's major metropolitan centres. The fundamental issue at stake is the increasing lack of communication between the directional functions of the economy, and the informational elite that performs such functions, on the one hand, and the locally-oriented population that experiences an ever deeper identity crisis, on the other hand. The separation between function and meaning, translated into the tension between the space of flows and the space of places, could become a major destabilizing force in European cities, potentially ushering in a new type of urban crisis.

Managing the transition to the informational city: the global and the local. Back to the future?

The most important challenge to be met in European cities, as well as in major cities throughout the world, is the articulation of the globally-oriented economic functions of the city with the locally-rooted society and culture. The separation between these two levels of our new reality leads to structural urban schizophrenia that threatens our social equilibrium and our quality of life. Furthermore, the process of European integration forces a dramatic restructuring of political institutions, as national states see their functions gradually voided of relevance, pulled from the top toward supranational institutions and from the bottom toward increasing regional and local autonomy. Paradoxically, in an increasingly global economy, and with the rise of the supranational state, local governments appear to be at the forefront of the process of management of the new urban contradictions and conflicts. National states are increasingly powerless to control the global economy, and at the same time they are not flexible enough to deal specifically with the problems generated in a given local society. Local governments seem to be equally powerless vis à vis the global trends but much more adaptable to the changing social, economic, and functional environment of cities.

The effectiveness of the political institutions of the new Europe will depend more on their capacity of negotiation and adaptation, than on the amount of power that they command, since such power will be fragmented and shared across a variety of decision making processes and organizations. Thus, instead of trying to master the whole complexity of the new European society, governments will have to deal with specific sets of problems and goals in specific local circumstances. This is why local governments, in spite of their limited power, could be in fact the most adequate instances of management of these cities, working in the world economy and living in the local cultures. The strengthening of local governments is thus a pre-condition to the management of European cities. But local governments could only exercise such management potential if they engage in at least three fundamental policies:

- The fostering of citizen participation, on the basis of strong local communities, that feed the local government with information, present their demands, and lay the ground for the legitimacy of local governments, so that they can become respected partners of the global forces operating in their territory.

- The inter-connection and cooperation between local governments throughout Europe, making it difficult for the global economic forces to play one government against the other, thus forcing the cooperation of the global economy and the local societies in a fruitful new social contract. New information technologies should make possible a qualitative upgrading of the cooperation between local governments. A European Municipal Data Bank, and a network of instant communication between local leaders could allow the formation of a true association of interests of the democratic representatives of the local populations. An electronically connected federation of quasi-free communes could pave the way for restoring social and political control over global powers in the informational age.

- Managing the new urban contradictions at the local level by acting on the social trends that underlie such contradictions requires a vision of the new city and of the new society we have entered in, including the establishment of cooperative mechanisms with national governments and European institutions, beyond the natural, and healthy, partisan competition. The local governments of the new Europe will have to do their home work in understanding their cities, if they are to assume the historical role that the surprising evolution of society could call upon them.

Thus, the historical specificity of European cities may be a fundamental asset in creating the conditions for managing the contradictions between the global and the local in the new context of the informational society. Because European cities have strong civil societies, rooted in and old history, and in a rich, diversified culture, they could stimulate citizen participation as a fundamental antidote against tribalism and alienation. And because the tradition of European cities as city states leading the pace to the Modern Age in much of Europe is engraved in the collective memory of their people, the revival of the city state could be the necessary complement to the expansion of a global economy and to the creation of a European State. The old urban tradition of Amsterdam as a political centre, as a trade centre, and as a centre of culture and innovation, suddenly becomes more strategically important for the next stage of urban civilization that the meaningless suburban sprawl of high technology complexes that characterize the informational space in other areas of the world.

European cities, because they are cities and not just locales, could manage the articulation between the space of flows and the space of places, between function and experience, between power and culture, thus recreating the city of the future by building on the foundations of their past.

Selected bibliography

Note: this bibliography does not provide specific references to the arguments presented in this text. The characteristics of these lectures did not seem to be appropriate for the standard procedure of references, since the analysis was deliberately placed at a general, theoretical level, based on the author's own elaboration of ideas and hypotheses. However, since no theory develops in a vacuum, the selected titles cited below refer the interested reader to further elaboration of the themes evoked in these lectures, either in the works of the author or in other recent, related writings, whose mention does not indicate anything other than the author's own intellectual interest.

Borja, J. et alter (eds.)
   1991   *Las grandes ciudades en la decada de los noventa*, Madrid: Sistema

Brotchie, J.F., P. Hall and P.W. Newton (eds.)
   1987   *The Spatial Impact of Technological Change*, London: Croom Helm

Campos Venuti G.
   1991   *L'urbanistica del riformismo*, Roma: Franco Angeli (new edition)

Carnoy, M., M. Castells, S. Cohen, and F.H. Cardoso
   1993   *The New World Economy in the Information Age*, University Park, PA: Penn State University Press

Castells, M.
    1983   *The City and the Grassroots: A Cross-Cultural Theory of Urban Social Movements*, Berkeley: University of California Press
    1989   *The Informational City*, Oxford: Basil Blackwell

Castells, M. and P. Hall
    1993   *Technopoles of the World*, London: Routledge and Kegan Paul

Hall, P. and P. Preston
    1988   *The Carrier Wave: New Information Technology and the Geography of Innovation, 1846-2003*, London: Unwin Hyman

Judd, D. and M. Parkinson (eds.)
    1990   *Leadership and Urban Regeneration: Cities in North America and Europe*, Newbury Park, CA: Sage

Kings D.S. and J. Pierre (eds.)
    1990   *Challenges to Local Governments*, London: Sage

Mollenkopf, J. and M. Castells (eds.)
    1991   *Dual City: Restructuring New York*, New York: Russell Sage

Portes, A. et alter (eds.)
    1988   *The Informal Economy*, Baltimore: The Johns Hopkins University Press

Sassen, S.
    1991   *The Global City: New York, London, and Tokyo*, Princeton, NJ: Princeton University Press

Between Stuttgart and Sheffield

John O'Loughlin

Introduction

My stay in Amsterdam (May-June 1992) coincided with the Danish referendum that rejected the Maastricht agreement and the intense debate of the future direction of the European Community in all the member states. Despite the hiccup towards the eventual merger of the 12 national economies of the current members of the Community and up to 10 more Eastern and Northern European states, there seems little doubt that the inexorable trend to an integrated economic union will not be stopped. Most of the hesitation in the member states centres around the feelings of Brussels central control and loss of national sovereignty and does not seem to be too concerned (with the exception of the United Kingdom) with the economic integration that had earlier designated 1992 as the end of the myriad of tariffs and regulations that cloud the European economic scene. No doubt the Danish vote and similar oppositions in all the member states will slow the race to develop a common currency with a European Central Bank as well as put a wrench into any plans to develop a common security and foreign policy. But the primary reason why governments, businesses and the majority of citizens are in favour of an economically-integrated Europe has not altered significantly; they all believe that it will eventually benefit all the constituent components of the sub-continent and make Europe an equal on the world economic-stage with the other great economic powers, the United States and Japan. Just as companies in the U.S. can take advantage of economies of scale, so too in an economically-united Europe, the individual national enterprises can expand their operations without hindrance or national regulation.

I deliberately opened this essay with a discussion of current European developments since it will be in Europe that Amsterdam's fortunes will rise or fall. Amsterdam is historically unusual since there are few other places in the world that have been so involved in international trade and communications for so long. Moreover, there are few other cities in the world that are as outward-orientated as this city. Yet, despite the willingness to compete internationally and the eagerness with which the European ideal is grasped by the vast majority of the Dutch population and especially by Amsterdammers, it is by no means certain that the city will prosper in a united Europe as it has as an international city in a region of national economies. In other words, there will be many more Amsterdam-like cities in the Europe of the future and the competition will intensify for the activities and enterprises that will both provide employment and place each community at the centre of the growth enterprises of a rapidly-changing world-economy and a new Europe. The jealousy and competition between Rotterdam and Amsterdam will pale in comparison to the struggle for European (and by extension, global) status and rank in the future as the bounds of national economies and debates will be eroded.

It should be clear that the political controls of national economies is no longer a matter of debate. Location theorists have had to adjust the raw materials, market and transportation costs formulas to recognize the limits and opportunites that states place on locational decisions. Despite decades of research that indicated that trade was growing much faster than any individual national economy and that the most successful local economies were export-orientated, it is still difficult to dispense with a mind-set that sees economic flows ending at the national borders. Governments, naturally, are in two minds about the internationalization of economies. On the one hand, they recognize the limits to autarky and inward-looking policies (even, the United States has deliberately embarked on a course of free trade bloc-building as a way of guaranteeing access to foreign markets) but on the other hand, they fear loss of control of economic policy and the consequences of the open borders for their domestic manufacturers.

In order, then, to understand the future development of Amsterdam's economy, we need to develop a perspective that integrates political and economic geography. Such a view is provided by world-systems theory. A broad question such as the future economic development of an international city in a rapidly-changing world economy, associated with new technologies and means of production, and in dramatically-changed political circumstances demands a broad historical theory. In this view, cities such as Amsterdam are the nodes in the networks that link the national and local economies of an integrated world-economy and the cities at the top of that urban hierarchy can be termed 'world cities' (Friedmann and Wolff, 1981: Friedmann, 1986). Because of the end of bounded national economies and their replacement by states that form the constituent blocks of the world-economy, it is easy to agree with Castells (1988) when he refers to the replacement of a 'space of places' by a 'space of flows.' In the language of geography, 'formal regions' are being displaced increasingly by 'functional regions.'

Scales and politics in world-systems theory

Implicit in the discussion thus far is the notion of the linking of scales in the study of the economic fortunes of a place. The major geographic contribution to the development of world-systems theory has been this linking. Though geographers are familiar with scales, they are less comfortable with the links between them. Instead, we speak of 'changing scales' and tend to operate at a scale-dependent basis, pursuing our various analyses at a local, national, regional or global scale, without considering the effects of scales above and below the one we are examining. One of the most exciting developments in modern geographic research is the revival of 'regional geography' by placing regions in their temporal and geographic contexts and by linking the regional scale of analysis to scales above and below. To understand the fate that has befallen cities as far apart as Detroit, Duisburg, Rochdale and Valenciennes, we need to examine the fate of their respective industrial bases. This requires a consideration of the shifting nature of manufacturing from core to semi-peripheral states, the role of government policy in allowing decline or in regional development policies, the alternatives available to the declining cities and local efforts, such as public-partnerships to stem the losses. Though there are a variety of unique conditions that contributed to the particular fortunes of a place, more importantly, there are common elements in the changing nature of industrial production and the associated new international division of labour that allow us to consider these places as representative of global developments. Similarly, in considering the Amsterdam case, we need to raise our sights beyond the city or region to the political developments across Europe that, in turn, are a response to the global economy.

Though up to 7 scales have been identified in the application and development of world-system theory, effectively the emphasis has been on just three levels. There is only one world-economy, into which all countries and communities have been gradually incorporated since the expansion of Europe in the 16th century. Taylor (1989) terms this the *'scale of reality'* and assigns it primary position in the relative importance of the scales. In his and Wallerstein's (1979) view, it is the changing nature of the world-economy that is responsible for setting the limits and terms for the individual national and local economies. In a world of economic uncertainty, it is the role of national governments to provide some security for their respective populations.

The national state lies at the *'scale of ideology'* since the national government can choose to follow (at the two extremes) either a free trade or autarkic policy. There are other options for the state, including encouraging replacement industries to locate where decline has occurred, worker re-training and other infrastructural programmes, etc. Despite a tradition in political geography that has stressed the examination of state roles and functions without regard to the global context, Taylor (1991a, 395) and other world-systems theorists like Chase-Dunn (1989) stress that 'states are prime institutions within the world-economy that are used by fragments of the system-wide classes in their competitions and conflicts.' The interstate system is an essential component of the world-economy as it provides capital with the option of moving between states and a freedom of manoeuver that is not possible in a unitary state. Governments can try to control capital mobility but in a world in which there are always alternative options, these efforts are usually doomed to failure.

The third scale of analysis is termed the *'scale of experience'* by Taylor. This is the metropolitan level in which the changes and developments, positive and negative, of the global economy are experienced. The movement offshore of production in a mono-industry town will have immediate and obvious impacts on the community and all sections of it. Beyond this obvious example, we can see how even gradual shifts in manufacturing locations and technological methods will have ramifications in localities, even in the cases where they are not directly involved in an industrial shift. All localities are now part of the global economy and some places will not escape its adverse effects while other places experience growth. One consistent trend has been the shift in manufacturing from high to low-wage countries in many different industries.

In addition to these three scales of the world-system, we need to consider other scales of analysis since the functional relationships at these additional scales add significantly to the rather sparse and rigid three scale model of the world-economy. They also give it less of an economic tinge and more of a broader cultural and political focus. Wallerstein (1979) and Taylor (1991a, b) have noted that *households* are the basic 'atoms' of the world-system where small income-pooling groups have significantly different budgeting plans and social aspirations. Little consideration of the households has been undertaken from a world-system perspective. A second addition should be the *neighbour-hood* scale. Though both Taylor and Wallerstein talk about the 'cultural status groups' that provide subjective identities to accompany the class identification engendered by respective capitalist or worker roles, this institution receives very little attention. Classes rather than peoples remain the focus of attention. Unlike the geographically-specific treatment of the three scales of analysis, the treatment of classes and peoples remains ephemeral and is not geographical-context specific. We can redress this imbalance through the addition of another spatial container, that of neighbourhood. It is obvious that in all societies, from wealthiest to poorest, there is a spatial sorting of peoples and classes within cities. While both kinds of neighbourhoods are found (the kind that is race-specific but class mixed, like black communities in the American cities, and the kind that is class-specific and race mixed, as can be found in some gentrified neighbourhoods though it is a rare phenomenon), the more usual circumstance in multi-cultural societies is a strong correlation between class and culture-race. This is especially true for the kind of rich society like the Netherlands that has experienced significant immigration but the American class-race model cannot be transferred unaltered to Europe (O'Loughlin, 1987). Nevertheless, we can give a spatial expression to the 'peoples' of world-systems theory in the mosaic of neighbourhoods that characterize all cities of multi-cultural societies as well as to the class-based living spaces of uni-cultural cities.

The last scale that we can consider is the one that opened this essay, that of the *continental block*. In the world-systems view, first developed by Wallerstein in the early 1970s, there was little consideration of any other political units except the nation-states. Recently, as a result of the growing competition between Japan, Europe and the United States, Wallerstein (1991) has briefly considered the changing alignment of the power blocs in the world-system but has failed to examine the consequences for the world-economy of the growing integration of the blocs. As I have already indicated, there seems little doubt that Western Europe will proceed beyond a free trade area to become an integrated economy in which national governments will have given up most of their autonomy and power to control local economic developments. In North America, the U.S.-Canada Free Trade Area is already in operation and there is agreement in principle to extend the zone to include Mexico. Further discussions with countries to the South continue but the U.S. has stated its wish to see these states too in the Pan-American bloc. Given the power of the U.S. and the dependence of these Latin American states on the American giant, there seems little doubt that this continental bloc too will coalesce into an economic zone within a generation. And that leaves the third zone, focused on Japan. Like the U.S., Japan has become dominant in its region. The countries of South and East Asia see increasing proportions of their trade with Japan, their currencies are increasingly aligned with the yen, they receive massive amounts of Japanese foreign direct investment and development aid, and many countries find that Japan is the most reliable purchaser of their exports in a world in which it is increasingly difficult to penetrate new markets. Malaysia has actually called for the creation of a Japan-led economic bloc in

Asia that would emulate the ill-fated 'Greater East Asian Co-Prosperity Sphere' of the 1940s. Should the 'yen bloc' become a reality, either through the indigenous efforts or as a response to 'Fortress Europe' and 'Fortress America,' we would in effect have the Pan-regional world of the 1930s German geopoliticians that was supposed to end imperialist competition by giving each core power an unchallenged sphere of influence and domination (O'Loughlin and Van der Wusten, 1990).

Table 1 Contlicts at the five scales of the world-system

	Blocs	States	Cities	N-hoods	H-holds
1 Blocks	6				
2 States	11	7			
3 Cities (regions)	12	13	8		
4 Neighbourhoods	NA	14	15	9	
5 Households	NA	16	17	18	10

NA: Not Applicable

Conflicts: 1=Intra-bloc; 2=Intra-state: 3=Intra-city; 4=Intra-neighbourhood; 5=Intra-household; 6=Inter-bloc; 7=Inter-state; 8=Inter-city; 9=Inter-neighbourhood; 10=Inter-household; 11=Bloc-state; 12=Bloc-city; 13=State-city; 14=State-neighbourhood: 15=City-neighbourhood; 16=State-household; 17=City-household; 18=Neighbourhood-household.

The outcome for our re-arrangement of world-systems theory is of 5 scales within the world-economy, bloc, nation-state, city (or more properly termed metropolitan area and region for non-urbanized areas), neighbourhood and household. Following Taylor (1991a), we can consider different kinds of politics between and across these scales and the result is a typology of 18 competitions or politics (see Table 1). Obviously, in this essay, it will not be possible to consider all 18 of these politics in detail, even with consideration only of Amsterdam but it is useful to list the kinds of competitions that could typically result in this framework and provide a brief example of each.

In this essay, it is type 1 politics that is the focus. It is one of a set of five intra-institutional politics and refers to competition between political units of the economic blocs. These units could be nation-states (interstate politics, which is formally type 7 or inter-city (regional) politics, also type 8). In our consideration of the fortunes of Amsterdam, it is type 8 that will take precedence as we examine the competition between places of the European bloc for new industrial investment and as service locations. It is also the case that while the nation-states seem pre-eminent now in both the European and the international arena, we would expect that future inter-state competition in Europe will wane as the relative power and sovereignty of the states themselves wanes and as more power is transferred to the regions. Inter-city or *intra-bloc* politics will be fundamentally about competition for investment, economic growth and governmental functions. We will see how Amsterdam is placed to pursue this competition in a restructuring world-economy that knows no regional bounds.

Intra-state politics is familiar to all as the domestic politics practised in the liberal democracies usually concentrating on the competition for votes and seats in legislative assemblies. In Third World countries, this level of competition is frequently associated with coups d'état and violent changes of government. Since both parties in liberal democracies and interest groups in peripheral states have well-defined geographic bases, this politics also assumes a territorial form. *Intra-city* politics is also about the territorial competition among the constituencies of the locality for control of the local state. While local government is severely constrained in its taxing and legislative functions in some democracies (including the Netherlands), in the U.S. a great deal of autonomy accrues to this level of power and urban politics assumes an importance that is unusual when contrasted with the European model of strong central state control. In Amsterdam, about 90% of the city's revenues comes from the central government in the Hague.

Intra-neighbourhood politics (type 4) will more likely be significant in mixed areas. In a homogenous neighbourhood, we would generally expect little internal debate but a united front against outsiders and especially to members of different cultures and classes. In the case of the European city, including Amsterdam, minority neighbourhoods are very mixed with large proportions of the majority population living with a diverse immigrant community. Therefore, there are many instances of local dispute frequently emanating from cultural value differences and norms. Though the level of spatial segregation may be low, the social distance between the cultural groups remains high. Finally, *intra-household* politics is a growing field of interest to feminist scholars, including geographers, and focusses on the key concept of patriarchy and the balance of career and family orientation.

Inter-bloc politics dominates the pages of business magazines and the bookshops are filled with speculations about the coming global competition between the three Panregions, Europe, the Americas and the Yen Bloc. Currently, the discussion is framed as the U.S.-Europe-Japan trade wars but with the expected cohesion of the blocs, the competition will be clarified as each of the core powers finalizes its control of the respective spheres of influence. Inter-bloc politics will constitute a new kind of international relations but it will be a logical successor to the kind of inter-state politics that has been the hallmark of international relations for about two centuries as new forms of territorial units replace or extend the familiar state system. *Inter-state* politics (type 7), as noted, is the stuff of international relations.

Inter-city politics (type 8) is changing its form rapidly. Previously, this kind of politics was intra-state in nature as metropolitan areas with a country vied for state funds or for investment from relocating businesses. The business magazines are filled with advertisements for site-specific tax and infrastructural benefits that would accrue to the company moving to that site. In the U.S., for example, the Sunbelt cities have been very aggressive in selling their competitive advantages (lower taxes and wage rates, climate, etc.). In our discussion, we extend the inter-city politics beyond the state boundaries to the rest of the bloc. If the scenario of declining state autonomy is correct, then the range of the competition will extend to all countries forming the bloc. The literature on Dutch cities, for example, frequently refers to the competition between Amsterdam and Rotterdam and often to the Randstad versus the rest of the country. Such local comparisons will appear increasingly trivial in the context of a wider and more significant bloc politics.

Inter-neighbourhood politics (type 9) is commonly referred to as 'turf politics' in the United States. Most of the issues generating the controversies relate to the neighbourhood character or to siting decisions. Neighbourhoods compete for salutary services (parks, recreation centres, etc.) will trying to mitigate the effects of the necessary provision of noxious facilities by trying to steer them away from the home area, the so-called NIMBY (not in my back yard) phenomenon. Though there seems to be comparatively little research on this topic in continental European cities, it appears that the strength of feelings and defense of turf is much stronger in Anglo-American, especially U.S., cities. Lastly, *inter-household* politics (type 10) revolves around local struggles for status in a competitive capitalist system which has now extended to all corners of the globe. Since households are viewed as income-pooling groups in a world-system perspective, there is a general attention to the strategies that households adapt to position themselves in the labour markets and to attain satisfactory levels of consumption. Interestingly, in the Dutch case, an increasingly-common strategy is for both partners to engage in part-time work as the ratio of men (25-65) working full-time is now about 66% while the ratio of women in the labour force is still very low by European and North American standards. While the labour market remains difficult, employers are much more willing to hire part-time and temporary help and this encourages couples to pool their wage resources. In a world of flexible production and decreased labour strength in the ongoing struggle with capital, the pooling of part-time employment wages will be expected to increase as inter-household competition intensifies in countries with labour surplus and large pools of reserve labour.

As well as the intra- and inter- politics, can create 8 more politics by looking across the scales. This is the real advantage of the geographic approach to world-systems analysis. *Bloc-state* politics (type 11) can be clearly seen in the recent Danish decision to overturn the Maastricht agreement. Immediately, the other 11 states certified their intent to proceed without Denmark, though it is not clear to what extent the governments' pursuit of Maastricht is supported by the respective populations. We can expect many similar discussions in the process of building the blocs and with the certain admission of at least 7 more states into the European bloc, intense debate and political strategy can be anticipated over such issues as common security and foreign policies, common monetary system, free movements of peoples, etc.

Bloc-city (region) politics is not seen very often at the present but we can also anticipate its development as the blocs gain in authority and power. Already it is clear that many individual cities and regions within Europe are unhappy with the prospects of growing centralization and loss of power to Brussels. For cultural-nationalist reasons, like Wales, or for specifically-ideological reasons like the rejection of the capitalist objectives that underlay much of the motivation for a united Europe, we can again anticipate some negotiations and compromises as the various component parts of the blocs are gradually pressured into accession to the ideal and the reality of a new political territorial unit. Just as various peripheral and/or minority-cultural areas have tried to certify their autonomous demands in the individual states of Europe, so too will these and perhaps other regions or metropolitan areas continue to reject the wider political framework. We can eliminate bloc-neighbourhood and bloc-household politics from consideration since the scale differences are so great that the relationships across them are barely existing.

State-city (regions) relationships have been noted as the type of national-local politics that has been the most violent and resistant to solution in Western Europe. Struggle for control of the nation-states by regionally-based groups has been a consistent feature of both European and non-European state building. *State-neighbourhood* (type 14) politics is perhaps best exemplified by the recent riots in Los Angeles which were in fact very neighbourhood-specific. Since the street activists were predominantly from two minority groups (blacks and Hispanic residents) and the segregation of the minorities is so intense in the American urban arena, the events of April 1992 were widely interpreted as a key test of state control of minority areas. In this instance, the state was not just federal or state authorities but also involved a significant amount of city politics. This shades over into type 15, *city-neighbourhood* politics in which, in the case of Los Angeles, local state power is firmly in the grasp of traditional white elites despite the fact that the city now has a majority-minority population of black, Hispanic and Asian residents.

The three remaining politics involve households. Type 16 politics, *state-households*, usually involves welfare issues and the access to governmental services by individual households in a world of very complex decision rules and access provisions. Type 17, *city-households,* is quite similar because the local state usually implements national welfare policies and procedures. A good example is the tension engendered by the arrival in Europe of large numbers of Islamic immigrants and the desire of many parents to see the children educated in Islamic, rather than in state schools. The issue has already produced widespread debate in the United Kingdom, France and Germany over the extent to which personal beliefs and practices take precedence over state requirements. For the last type of politics, *neighbourhood-household*, we can return to Los Angeles for an example where Korean shopkeepers fought gun-battles with the black and Hispanic majority residents of the same neighbourhood during the days of rioting. Inter-cultural tensions, long present in American cities, have historically produced such bitterness and resentment between neighbours.

We can finish our discussion of the relevant parts of world-systems theory by observing that a key notion of the theory impinges directly on the future prospects of Amsterdam. Over the past 200 years, the world-system has experienced four Kondratieff 50 year cycles, each with about a quarter-century and a quarter-century of decline. Currently, we are in the B (decline) phase of the fourth cycle (Taylor, 1989). While the cycles are well-defined, the particular circumstances giving rise to the growth and decline phases are not well-explained. There seems to be growing evidence for the innovation-production-overproduction explanation. In this view, each cycle corresponds to a new technology and to the products that spin off from it. Thus, the first cycle was generated by the steam engine and coal power, the second by the iron and steel revolution, the third by chemicals and the fourth by electronics in the 1940s. The geographic location of the innovation and the first manufacture of the resulting products will have an initial competitive advantage over all other areas and the result will be an industrial boom and a major surge in exports from that location. Gradually, the innovation diffuses to other competitive locations and eventually over-production results from the individual decisions of numerous manufacturers. Production shifts to low-wage locations especially during the decline phase as producers try to cut costs in order to keep adequate profit margins. Competition between businesses and locations intensifies in this phase and governments increase their efforts to protect and defend their domestic producers in the competitive world-economy. It is unclear what the new technology will be that will spur the fifth cycle but bio-technology looks most promising at this stage.

In Wallerstein's (1979, 1991) view, the sequence after the development of the new technology is that the state controlling its initial development will have a productive lead that will soon be translated into a trade lead as its products are in wide demand. The capital accumulating from the productive-trade lead is used to generate increased concentration of financial resources, in the leading city of the leading state. Thus, Amsterdam was a leading financial centre of the first hegemonic power (the Netherlands) in the seventeenth-century, London became the world city in the nineteenth-century and New York retains that role in the late twentieth-century. Just as hegemony is gained through the succession of research and development, production, trade and financial services leads, it is lost in the same sequence. Thus, it is clear that in 1992, the U.S. has lost the research and development, productive and trade advantage and is increasingly being challenged by Europe and Japan (London and Tokyo, respectively) for the financial services lead (O'Loughlin, 1993). The development of economic blocs is therefore an attempt at a logical geographic fix to the problems produced by the global competition in a Kondratieff decline phase.

World cities in the world system

As noted already, world cities are the key basing points in the myriad network of flows that characterize the modern world-economy. They play a dual role, being both points of distribution and control for both the national and the global economies and they perform both roles by acting as the interstices of the global and national networks. Friedmann and Wolff (1982) note that there are different kinds of world cities corresponding to the zones of capitalism (core, semi-periphery and periphery) defined by the core and peripheral processes of the contemporary world-economy. Thus, the core world cities of New York, London and Tokyo have more in common than the mixed bag of Tokyo, Singapore and Mexico City. Core world cities are similar to other core world cities and so on because the mix of functions are similar despite the enormous differences in culture, size and location that give each its special character. There exists a distinct hierarchy and Amsterdam (or more usually, the Randstad) is generally placed in the second rank of core world cities along with such cities as Frankfurt, Zürich, Milan, Brussels, Sydney, Toronto and Los Angeles.

In the writings of Friedmann and those of other writers (Hall, 1988; Castells, 1988; Kasarda, 1988) on the world city phenomenon, we can identify seven additional contemporary developments (since the hierarchy of world cities was first settled in the nineteenth-century) that will help to place Amsterdam in its contemporary context. First, they note the continued *de-industrialization* of the core cities as high-wage manufacturing jobs have migrated to the semi-periphery in the past 20 years of global economic stagnation. As we shall see, Amsterdam has been a classic case of this development. Second, they note the influx of *immigrants* from the global periphery and semi-periphery to the core cities. Most of the formal recruitment and open door reception of the immigrant workers were in the growth years of Kondratieff IV-A up till 1973 and since then, it has been increasingly difficult to get permission to enter the core cities. It has meant that the character of previously-homogenous cities like Amsterdam has been changed irrefutably as the immigrants and their families settle permanently. Third, they pay attention to the *government policies* that have fluctuated from free trade and recruitment of workers from abroad in a time of growth, productive leads and labour shortages to protective tariffs, attempted repatriation and building of trade blocs in a time of global economic stagnation.

In the fourth place, world city proponents and all the writers on the changing nature of the economies of the core countries have stressed the replacement of manufacturing by the *growth of service industries* (Dertouzos et al., 1989; Drennan, 1992; Fainstein and Fainstein, 1981; Hall and Preston, 1988; Jobse, 1987; Norton, 1992; Soja, 1991). Mollenkopf (1983) classified American cities into three types on the basis of their mix of manufacturing and service activities and their resulting economic fortunes. Decline was characteristic of Cleveland, Detroit and Buffalo in the traditional manufacturing heart of the Midwest while growth was the result of the development of high-technology industry and corporate services in Sunbelt cities such as Seattle, Tucson, San Jose and Boulder, CO. The third type had a mix of services and manufacturing and as a result experienced both growth and decline at the same time. The large East coast cities of New York, Boston and Philadelphia were in this group. New York City is archetypical. During the period, 1953-84, the city lost 600,000 manufacturing jobs but gained 700,000 service jobs (Castells, 1988). The result was the development of a 'dual city' in which Friedmann's 'citadel' and 'ghetto' are well-defined.

The key service sector is considered to be producer services, such as communications, banking, security brokers and agents, holding companies, business services, legal services, advertizing and film production. This sector grew by 9.5% per year in the United States between 1980 and 1990 with exports growing three-fold in the same period. 31% of exports went to Western Europe, mostly from the four gateway cities that generate 24% of the U.S. total of this sector (Drennan, 1992). What is most interesting about the new industrial sectors is the discovery of the old concept of agglomeration. Noyelle and Stanbach (1984), in what has now become a classic study, noted that services cannot be stockpiled and that they usually cannot be shipped so that typically they must be produced to meet special and immediate needs. They are found where accessibility to clients are maximized. Face to face contacts still remain of vital importance in that sector (Norton, 1992).

Large companies are characterized by vertical integration of services with back-offices located in cheaper wage locations and not as formerly where cheap female labour was available. Thus, Neodata a huge company in Boulder, CO. which fills magazine subscription orders, has back offices in Co. Limerick, Ireland for data entry and the files produced are sent to the headquarters in Boulder, CO. by satellite. Increasingly, companies such as this will move to Third World locations with India a favourite site because of the English-language skills of a large number of people there. Small companies contract out services, in turn generating a spawning of ancillary service operations. Service growth is not just an American phenomenon. In the European Community, 7% of total Gross Domestic Product is currently contributed by this sector and it is expected to grow fast so that it will be over 10% by 2000. The integration of the market after 1992 is expected to increase the concentration of the employment in the sector in London, Paris, Frankfurt and the Randstad.

A fifth contemporary development of the world city network is the *geographic stratification of the networks* into three sub-systems. The Asian one has Tokyo-Singapore as its major axis, the American one links New York, Los Angeles, Chicago and Toronto intensively and to South American less intensively and the European one retains its London-Paris-Frankfurt orientation with weak links to South America, the Middle East and to Africa. There are, of course, huge transfers of capital and services across the Pacific and the Atlantic but the more noticeable trend has been the intensification of the networks within the individual economic blocs.

The sixth contemporary development has the appearance of the *moving headquarters*. On the one hand, headquarters continue to centralize but on the other hand, they seem to have an increasing mobility as a result of a willingness to move. Declining urban services and quality of life in the large metropolitan areas of the Northeast and Midwest U.S. has lead many companies to shift their operations to the South and West. New York City, in particular, has seen the readiness of companies to move as a special problem and the city authorities have tried to retain them in Midtown and Lower Manhattan. In an integrated Europe, we would expect this phenomenon also to occur, especially if the disparities in office rents between high-cost cities (London, especially) and the cheaper Mediterranean locations persists and if regional incentives to move remain in effect.

The last phenomenon, that of a *dichotomized labour force*, has already been noted. Service jobs are not an undifferentiated category. We must distinguish especially between personal services, which are usually low-paying and on the margins of the formal sector, and the kinds of producer services discussed earlier. Even the back-office functions of the producer services category should give pause to anyone who views growing employment in this category as an unmitigated blessing. To quote Castells (1988: 96), 'New York City is the showcase of the process we are analyzing: a booming CBD, a growing gentrified Manhattan, and yet the persistence of rundown devastated areas are the spatial signs of a new process of growth that deepens its contradictions while showing extraordinary vitality.' Social polarization has been noted in cities all across the capitalist core as the traditional manufacturing jobs of the working class have moved offshore and the service jobs that have replaced them are either geographically-inaccessible in the suburbs or require skills that the working-class, especially the minority segments of it, do not have.

Friedmann and Wolff (1982) have developed a hierarchy of the chief economic functions of the world city that clarifies this polarization. At the top are the producer services defined earlier as well as research and higher education. In the second tier comes a cluster servicing the first of real estate brokers, construction activities, hotel services, luxury shopping, entertainment, private police and domestic services. Third is international tourism and the fourth level is falling fast, that of manufacturing. A fifth level is government services, which is many countries grew quickly in the crisis years of the early 1980s as states had to provide welfare services to a whole new segment of the population that had never known state dependence. The sixth, seventh and eight levels are the informal sector, the illicit economy and those on no steady income. Clearly, the relative size of the sectors will vary from place to place but the classification is useful since the emphasis is on the new type of services that drives city growth or decline.

As well as services, there are three other growth industries in the contemporary world-economy. High-technology industry is important not only for the employment that it generates and the export revenue that accumulates. Out of current high-tech ventures will likely come the next generation of products that will lead the world-economy out of the current slump. To remain far from the frontiers of science and technology is to remain far from the product development of the next wave. In the European Community, 5% of total GDP is generated by high-technology industry and it is growing at a rate of 15%

per year. It will be over 10% by 2000 (Commission of the European Community, 1991). Again agglomeration economies seem to be important here (Norton, 1992). There has been a rediscovery of Marshallian industrial districts where small batches of flexible production systems and key spatial linkages (networks or clusters of firms) gather. Thus, the Silicon Valley and Route 128 around Boston became the gathering places for computer firms, Houston became the service centre for the oil industry, New York became the capital of producer services and Boulder, CO. is leading the bio-technology agglomeration race. Since industrial decline is not the result of regional ageing but of product ageing, there is a constant need to invest in research and development of new products. Furthermore, even high-technology industries are subject to boom and bust cycles as can be seen in the fate of many companies along Route 128 and the resulting regional recession that resulted. In Europe, high-technology centres have been located in environmentally-attractive places, as in the U.S. The efforts of the French government have been rewarded with sparkling research and development centres in Sophia-Antipolis (near Nice), Grenoble and Montpellier while Cambridge (England) and Hannover-Göttingen offer alternative models of growth stimulation.

Distribution network centres also offers great opportunities for growth at the end of the twentieth-century. Central to this sector is leading communications and transport facilities. Because of mechanization and automation, the employment generated is not as high as might be expected in the transport sector with the notable exception of major airports. There, the airplane, freight and passenger services generate enormous numbers of jobs so that it is estimated that Schiphol (Amsterdam's airport) generates about 40,000 jobs and over 2% of Dutch GDP. The problem with the transport sector is that the restructuring of the global networks is far from complete and it is very uncertain how the future 'hub and spoke system' and the amalgamation of the airlines will play out in any individual city. If the U.S. experience is any guide for a Europe that is now taking tentative steps towards airline deregulation, the end result will be only a few mega-carriers and no more than 5 or 7 airline hubs on the sub-continent. Should Schiphol not be on the list of these hubs, the implications for its rapid growth over the past decade as an intercontinental and international hub would be very serious (De Smidt, 1991).

The final growth industry in industrial countries is that of tourism. As more and more countries experience a rise in leisure time and disposable incomes, international tourism is expected to continue to grow quickly. Already Northern Europe has seen a reversal of the traditional one-way flow of tourists with large groups of Spaniards and Italians travelling to cities such as Amsterdam. Unfortunately, jobs in the tourist industry (in hotels, food and services) are notoriously low-paying and though the amount of employment generated may be large, the number of skilled high-wage jobs is small.

A final aspect of the world city must be described. The spatial impress of the economic restructuring processes has led to an intensification of long-term trends in the United States. Castells (1988) has summarized the pattern for the U.S. and already we can see some signs of similar developments in British and French cities. At the core of the metropolitan area, the CBD is increasingly concentrated in directional activities and is being emptied of retail, commercial and residential land uses. This is Friedmann's 'citadel' and is visibly seen in the enormous high-rise office buildings and hotels, all reflecting glass and polished steel, that are to be found in most big American cities. It is the centre of political dominance, economic growth and cultural centrality. Nearby are the homes of the 'new elite,' the lawyers, brokers, managers and financiers of the citadel in gentrified sub-areas. In these up-scale neighbourhoods are found the expensive restaurants and other entertainment functions of the elite.

Next to the CBD is the 'ghetto' or 'urban reservations' as Castells calls them. Populated by destitute workers – almost all of minorities in the U.S. – they are the scene of greatest misery and a downward trajectory of hope and social malaise. If there is an underclass in Western societies, this is where it is found. In these minority areas and scattered throughout the city are pockets of vitality, produced by the newly-arriving immigrants from Asia (Koreans, Filipinos, Indians, Vietnamese, and Chinese), Europe (Russians, Poles and Jews), the Middle East (Israelis and Palestinians) and Latin America and the Caribbean (Colombians, Salvadoreans, Cubans, Puerto Ricans and Haitians). Many are engaged in small-scale entrepreneurial activities and demonstrate a remarkable resilience in the face of economic adversity. Beyond the city limits, suburban sprawl is changing its face. On the one hand, it is showing signs of concentrating business services and other office and retail functions into 'Edge Cities,' economic sub-centres that are often larger and busier than the downtown. They are often found near motorway interchanges and are, like the rest of the area beyond the city, accessible only by car. Finally, the residential areas of the suburbs are increasingly diversified and targeted to specific lifestyle groups, such as couples without children, young families, tennis-oriented individuals, etc. The homogenous suburb of Levitttown has long gone.

When we discuss Amsterdam, we are making comparisons with other core, especially American, cities. In semi-peripheral and peripheral world cities, the gaps between the citadel and the ghetto are even greater and the comparison to Amsterdam is less apt because of the different global economic role that these cities play. Clearly, the kind of nightmare scenario portrayed so well by Mike Davis (1990) for Los Angeles is nowhere on the horizon for Amsterdam, yet the American urban experience has salutary lessons for any city entering the kind of restructuring that U.S. cities have seen for the past two decades. It may not be so far from Manhattan to Rio de Janeiro after all.

The Dutch national context

As we have noted, the role of the national government in the restructuring world-economy has assumed great importance in political geography. Even the most free trade-orientated states try to interfere with the activities of MNCs, both those based at home and the foreign ones operating in the state. Though there are differences between the opposite ends of the political spectrum in the cumulative activities of governments, effectively each government in capitalist states, either left or right, act as promoters of capital accumulation (Habermas, 1973; Fainstein and Fainstein, 1981). The state especially acts as a mediator between capital and labour and provides services such as national planning and coordination as well as benefits to the workers to keep them loyal to the accumulation process. In the struggle between capital and labour since the end of the nineteenth-century, it appears now that the struggle is essentially over. With capital's win even in formerly state socialist countries, the close support of governments world-wide for capital is challenged even less.

The Netherlands is one of a group of small, rich Western European states that are defined by a national politics that has been called 'democratic corporatism' by Katzenstein (1985). The Netherlands ranks highest of the OECD (Organization of Economic Cooperation and Development) states in the proportion of the national wealth controlled by either the top 20% or the top 40% of the population. It has achieved this rank by the most active programme of wealth redistribution in order to reduce social inequalities and, of course, paying for them with high tax rates. The top marginal rate of personal tax was reduced to 60% from 72% in 1990. The country is famous for the size and length of its unemployment benefits, its still-active social housing construction and renovation policy, resulting in the highest ratio of social housing in the world as well as the laxity of its qualification rules for disability and other governments programmes. Though there is now general agreement that the scale and range of the welfare state will have to be curtailed in the face of a continuing national debt, the resulting policies will still be much more generous than most liberal democracies.

In trying to understand this Dutch consensus of national policy, Katzenstein (1985) compares the country to the other 'democratic corporatist' states (Austria, Switzerland, Belgium, Denmark, Norway and Sweden). Their politics is characterized by 'consociationism' and 'amicable agreement' with prolonged bargaining among interest groups with something for everyone in the end. To use the cliche loved by American business executives, the groups strive to produce a 'win-win' situation. The state is especially active in promoting compromise between capital and labour.

The state ideology has three key components, strongly entrenched in the Netherlands but shared to some extent by all of the 'democratic corporatist' states, according to Katzenstein (1985). In the international economic arena, free trade remains the unquestioned ideology. There is now no practical alternative since the Dutch economy has been open for so long. While there are various measures of openness, one of the most reliable is the consumption of imports and in this category, the Netherlands also sits at the top of the world rankings of imports per capita. An open economy needs access to other's markets and to resources. Since the Dutch industrial composition has such a high proportion controlled by large multinationals (Phillips, AKZO, Shell, Unilever, among others) and the country has been an integral member of the global core for decades, it is no surprise that the business community and the political establishment are one on the direction of foreign economic policy. The Netherlands has some of the lowest tariff barriers in the world and strongly supports the concepts and procedures to force other members of GATT (General Agreement on Tariffs and Trade) to do likewise. Katzenstein (1985) ranks the Netherlands consistently second to Switzerland in the internationalization of its economy.

The second element of the national ideology is a logical result of the first. Resulting from the free trade and economic internationalization principles is a national commitment to international cooperation. In the Dutch case, it can be seen in many instances, including the forming of the first effective multicountry economic bloc as the BENELUX during World War II, the rapid accession to NATO, the League of Nations and later the United Nations, the European Community, OECD, the West European Union, etc. Since the early years of this century, the Hague has been the meeting-place for the International Court of Justice while the Dutch population consistently show strong support for the institutions to which they belong. It was no accident that it was under the Dutch presidency of the Council of Ministers of the EC that the Maastrict agreement was signed by the heads of states.

Yet, while the Dutch remain strongly attached to the international organizations to which they belong, they have also been very active in trying to build international bridges, including the attempts to reduce the tensions of the Cold Wars in Europe. A commitment to detente and to peace-making and peace-keeping principles is not really a matter of national debate but this attachment has been interpreted by some conservative commentators as 'hollanditis' or the 'Dutch disease,' which was supposed to be capable of infecting other West European states and undermine NATO's capabilities. A final indication of this international cooperation of the Netherlands is the consistency with which the country meets (with Norway and periodically other 'democratic corporatists') the 0.7% of GDP target of the United Nations for development aid.

The third leg of the national ideology is the necessary compensation that must accrue to the domestic groups hurt by the internationalization commitment. The most obvious counter the harmful effects of free trade while other programmes are more competitive in orientation, like the wage policy that kept national wage demands under rigid control until 1963 in order to maintain a low-wage location in a rebuilding Europe after World War II. Of course, the low wages were compensated by the most ambitious social housing programmes ever attempted that set as a national commitment that all Dutch citizens should be adequately housed. The welfare state is not just a result of a cultural-religious belief, though that undoubtedly underlies the practices, but is another indicator of a national consensus that has managed to solve, or at least remove from any serious debate, all sorts of national divisions like the confessional divide of earlier years.

Over the past twenty years, since the beginning of the global downturn that we can identify as the Kondratieff IV-B phase, the Netherlands has been performing close to the OECD average. If we examine the productivity statistics, the evidence is consistent with others of a fairly successful economy that has managed to avoid much of the boom-bust character of other OECD member states. In labour productivity, the Netherlands increases at a rate 0.7% greater than the OECD average between 1962-73, at 1.4% better than the average between 1973 and 1979 and was exactly at the average over the past 12 years. For capital productivity increases, the pattern is similar with the Dutch rate of change at 0.1% better than the OECD average from 1962-73, at 0.6% better in 1973-79 and 0.2% better over the past 11 years. Other comparative statistics indicate the same trends.

The Netherlands has a sizeable trade surplus, equal to 4.5% of GDP in 1990. The major partner is Germany, which takes about one-third of the Dutch exports. This level is problematic since it means that the Dutch economy effectively prospers or stagnates depending on the nature of the imports demand in Germany. Though the guilder is effectively linked to the Deutsche mark through the ERM (European Rate Mechanism), there is still a nagging fear that too much of Dutch economic fortunes lie in the German basket. Dutch exports reflect the products of a core economy, with one noticeable exception, that of commercial garden products (flowers, vegetables, etc).

However, the Dutch economy has one major negative feature and that relates to the welfare state nature of the economy. With over 5 million residents dependent for their livelihood on the state (out of a population of about 15 million), the welfare state runs a deficit each year that equalled 5.3% of GDP in 1990 and 3.5% in 1991. The cumulative debt ratio (total debt/GDP) is .596 which is even larger than the much-discussed U.S. ration (.368) and the OECD average (.33) but it remains much smaller than Belgium (1.121) or France (1.03). Dutch unemployment payments have fallen dramatically from the black days of the mid-1980s and the national unemployment rate (6.1%) is still lower than the OECD average (7.1%). The unit labour costs of the Netherlands remain competitive and they have actually fallen in relation to the OECD competitors over the past 5 years.

The dependence on the Dutch state can also be seen in the economic composition of the country in relation to other EC states. The Netherlands is less agricultural than its neighbours (5% of employment compared to the EC average of 8%), less industrial (30% compared to the European average of 37%), near average in services (15 compared to the EC average of 17%) but much more dependent on the state (50% of employment [generating about 60% of GDP] compared to the EC average of 38%). Though the state share of economic activity is not growing as fast as it was in the 1970s, it is not yet reversing with only 3.5 million people employed in private activities. Of those working, the ratio of women in the labour force is very low compared to the other 'democratic corporatists' or to the other OECD countries. Of women aged 15-64, only 35% work in the Netherlands compared to the EC average of 49% while only 78% of men of the same age-group are working as opposed to an EC average of 84%. The ratio of men working is falling due to unemployment, disability and early retirement while the numbers working part-time are growing fast as is this category of women employees. It is claimed that the Netherlands has the highest ratio of part-time workers in the Western world, although this assertion is very hard to verify.

Amsterdam is unusual because it is rare that a small country like the Netherlands has domestic competitive cities. Primacy is the norm in those countries. The Dutch government has to promote more than Amsterdam (Rotterdam, the Hague and Utrecht, the other big cities of the Randstad all have special needs and advantages) and the rivalry between the cities, though subdued and polite, remains for investment from abroad and for government infrastructure support. Since 90% of the revenues of Dutch cities comes from the central government (Terhorst, 1992), this gives the government a lot of authority and ability to direct growth to targeted regions and cities. The national Physical Plans appearing about every 8 years (the last one was in 1988; Van der Veen, 1989) have been touted as the best strategic models of national planning; regardless of that, they allow the state a much stronger role in development than is normally the case in capitalist states. However, like all Dutch decision-making, there is something for every group and region in the plans. The latest stresses the desired goal of compact cities in the context of further internationalization of the economy.

Amsterdam's position in the European Community

There exists general agreement that whatever the new Europe will mean, it will mean a drastically-changed role for the nation-states that now constitute the units of the EC. One common hypothesis is that the various regions and metropolitan areas will come to exercise significant new powers and identities and that the real political and economic competition now existing between states will be replaced to some extent by a larger but more diffused regional form. In this new world, the issue of metropolitan competition will be foremost especially in the wider world-systems context of a dynamic East Asia, a reformed Eastern Europe and the continuation of the core and peripheral processes that have been evident for the past quarter-century. It is therefore important to examine how Amsterdam is currently placed in the existing rank-orders of the European cities with a view trying to anticipate the future prospects of the city in an economically-integrated Europe.

In the view of the Commission of the European Community (1991), the contests that will develop after 1992 will not be a free-for-all but more logically will proceed in a manner that will place each metropolitan area in competition with only those cities that share a similar economic profile. Large cities will no longer have unchallenged dominance in their home countries as rival cities reach into the territories of adjacent states in the expansion of trade and influence fields. This has already happened in an embryonic manner for Nice, Barcelona, Basel and Geneva and we will be looking at multi-state functional areas that have posed special problems in the U.S. for such sprawling areas as the New York, Philadelphia, Chicago, and Washington DC metropolitan regions. It appears that new political structures and territorial definitions will be needed to catch up with the new economic realities. Further projections by the Commission indicate that the major rates of economic growth will occur in medium-sized metropolises and that the largest city-regions (London, Paris, Randstad, Berlin, etc.) will remain fairly static.

Two recent studies have tried to come to grips with the difficult questions of which city-regions in Europe are most prosperous, what are the reasons for prosperity and which ones have the best prospects for success over the new generation. Brunet's (1990) study for DATAR, the French planning agency, considered both the profile and the economic fortunes of cities to develop an eight class rank-order. Amsterdam is placed in the third rank along with Madrid, Munich, Frankfurt, Rome, Brussels, Barcelona, but behind the first-ranked London and Paris and the second-ranked Milano. Sixteen indicators, mostly measuring size, are used to generate the rankings. The profiles are done by grouping the cities on the basis of over-weighted indicators so that Amsterdam is placed in the strong international and communications, moderately good on economic indicators along with Hamburg, Rotterdam, Antwerp, Düsseldorf, and Southampton. Perhaps the most interesting and important part of the study is the identification of a second axis of growth in Western Europe in addition to the traditional banana of prosperity from Northern Italy via the Lotharingian axis to Southern England. The new banana reaches from about Bologna through Northern Italy and Southern France to Madrid-Valencia (Cortie and Dignum, 1991).

The second set of studies, funded by the European Commission, has yielded a valuable data set on the comparative ranking of European cities. The study had limited objectives and did not try to find the best place to live in Europe, as is the usual circumstance of American city comparisons. Instead, Cheshire and his co-workers (Cheshire, Carbonaro and Hay, 1986; Cheshire, 1990) narrowed their examination to the economic fortunes of 'functional urban regions' (FUR) which are defined on the basis of aggregates of munici-palities in the area of dominance of the city under consideration. Thus, cities like Wiesbaden can have high rankings with other cultural, social and environ-mental characteristics that make some cities attractive places to live. The key index is composed of four measures, Gross Domestic Product per capita, in-migration rate, unemployment rate and more questionably, the ratio of hotel beds. In defense of the latter measure, Cheshire makes the point that the number of hotel beds is an elastic measure of business growth but the high ranking of such tourist centres as Florence and Venice should give pause to unqualified use of the index. Amsterdam's comparative rankings can be seen in Table 2.

The study covered the years 1971-88. Amsterdam has consistently ranked 8th to 12th over this period of the approximately 115 cities in the study. Cities ahead of Amsterdam are either West German cities or the tourist-centres of Italy. By any indicator, Amsterdam has an enviable rank in the comparison of European cities. The 1981-84 rankings show some interesting changes from

Table 2 Amsterdam's Comparative Ranking with Other European Cities

	1971-75	1975-81	1981-84	Change 1971-88	Residuals
1.	Munich	Frankfurt	Frankfurt	Brussels	Frankfurt
2.	Frankfurt	Venice	Venice	Frankfurt	Verona
3.	Venice	Brussels	Brussels	Verona	Valladolid
4.	Bonn	Munich	Munich	Bologna	Taranto
5.	Florence	Bonn	Bonn	Nice	Murcia
6.	Stuttgart	Wiesbaden	Florence	Bordeaux	Glasgow
7.	Wiesbaden	Düsseldorf	Stuttgart	Paris	Derby
8.	Brussels	*Amsterdam*	Wiesbaden	Antwerp	Bordeaux
9.	London	Florence	Düsseldorf	Rome	Bologna
10.	Düsseldorf	Stuttgart	Nice	Strasbourg	Nice
.	.	.	.	.	Bruxelles
.	.	.	.	.	.
12.	*Amsterdam*	.	*Amsterdam*	*Amsterdam*	
-					
19.	.	.	.	.	Rotterdam
-					
21.	.	.	.	.	Stuttgart
-					
24. .	.	.	.	.	*Amsterdam* (50th in log-linear model)

Source: Cheshire, Carbonaro and Hay, 1986; Cheshire, 1990

earlier periods with the arrival of the sunbelt city of Nice and the capitals of Bonn and Brussels in the top 10. Cities near the bottom of the lists are the old industrial centres of Britain (including Sheffield) and the peripheral cities of the Italian and Iberian peninsulas. If one groups the cities by country, the German cities are generally highly-ranked, the French cities have a middle profile, the Benelux cities have varying fortunes along with the Italian cities while the British and Spanish cities rank near the bottom.

The second part of Cheshire's work is more interesting for our consideration of Amsterdam's fortunes. In his recent work, Cheshire (1990) has been trying to account for the economic status of places. He has formulated a good fitting regression model that accounts for .80 of the variance in FUR scores. In order of importance, the predictors are size of city (larger is better), economic potential (location with respect to the economic heartland of Europe), percent employed in industry (lower is better), percent employed in agriculture in the service area of the FUR (lower better), coalfield location (poor), port location (poor) and rapid population growth, which is negative since it increases unemployment. Given the processes in operation during the past 25 years of global stagnation, with the de-industrialization of large parts of Europe, the consequences for unemployment as a result of changing technological and transportation development, the mechanization of traditional sectors and the continued core-peripheral disparities in Europe, the rankings and their explanation seem sensible.

Cheshire claims that the value of the residuals from the regression model are an indication of city performance, the quality of the policy decisions that cities make in pursuit of economic growth. Crampton and Evans (1992) have accepted that argument for London and believe that its near-bottom ranking on the list of residuals is fully deserved in light of the past decisions. While there is undoubtedly some (perhaps a large) element of policy-making reflected in the residuals (the value of the FUR score minus the predicted score on the basis of the indicators), Cheshire puzzlingly ignores random error and other statistical possibilities for the error terms. Amsterdam emerges more poorly in the residual scores than in the FUR scores. Its ranks of 24 in the linear and 50 in the log-linear model suggest that its policy choices have not been of the same quality as its natural characteristics. By contrast, Rotterdam, which might be expected to do poorly in the rankings and indeed ranks modestly, gets a residual score that places it in the 19th rank. Cheshire praises the city for moving away from the emphasis on social housing and the port facilities to trying to attract business services and diversifying the local economy. Amsterdam by contrast, while not hostile to business, has not made the same kind of industrial development effort that it has made on the social front.

By comparison with other European cities, Amsterdam is well-off. It is located close to the traditional heart of the continent and near the epicentre of the economic potential map. It has had strong transport and communication links with the three major powers within 150 miles (France, Germany and Britain). The advertisements of the Dutch industrial development agency placing the Netherlands at the geographic heart of Europe are, unlike most similar maps, not exaggerated. Strategic planning is usually the function of nation-states but like regional development agencies in the U.S., that role will be increasingly turned over to the local states. While the European Commission follows the usual prescriptions for development (adapt economic base to avoid mono-structures, increase transport and tele-communication links, educate a skilled workforce, enhance the quality of life through better cultural and environmental features, develop a coordinated strategy and cooperate with adjoining regions), very few city-regions are able to follow them wholeheartedly. Amsterdam, with its strong legacy of planning and governmental

Figure 1 Trends in 4 types of employment
Amsterdam, 1970-1990

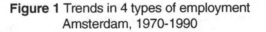

Trends in 4 Types of Employment
Amsterdam, 1970-1990

involvement in attempting to improve the lives of its residents, would seem
to be better-placed than most places in this policy-making process.

The changing economic profile of Amsterdam

In the discussion of the world-city earlier in this essay, I listed the sectors that
Friedmann and Wolff (1982) have identified as characteristics of their stereotypical world-city. It is impossible to gather adequate data on either the
informal or illicit sectors of the economy (there are strong indications that
Amsterdam has an active informal sector, especially in the area of personal
services, (Terhorst and Van de Ven, 1986) but we can group the employment
categories into meaningful groups in order to be able to document the
changing profile of Amsterdam over the past 20 years. The source for the data

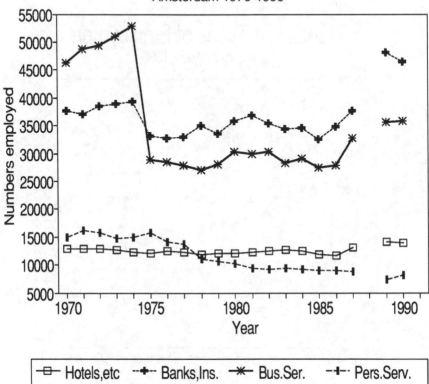

Figure 2 Trends in 4 types of employment
Amsterdam 1970-1990

is the annual statistical yearbook for the city published by the Amsterdamse
Bureau voor Onderzoek en Statistiek. While the yearbook concentrates on the
city of Amsterdam, it reports on an irregular basis on comparative trends in the
'omgeving' (surrounding area) of Amsterdam, with about 25 communities adjacent
or functionally-tied to the city. This allows some comparison in the identification
of city-suburb employment during the period under study.

If we group the dozens of SIC categories into four groups that follow the
Friedmann/Wolff formulation, we can see some obvious trends in Figures 1
and 2. On Figure 1, some confusion is introduced by the changes in definition
in 1974 and again in the mid 1980s but the overall trend is clear. Industrial
jobs are disappearing consistently from the city's employment profile, down
from 60,000 in 1970 to about 22,000 today. The trade and transport sector is
essentially static despite the rises and fall of the values in the curves due to the

Figure 3 Trends in service and non-service
Employment ratios Amsterdam, 1970-1990

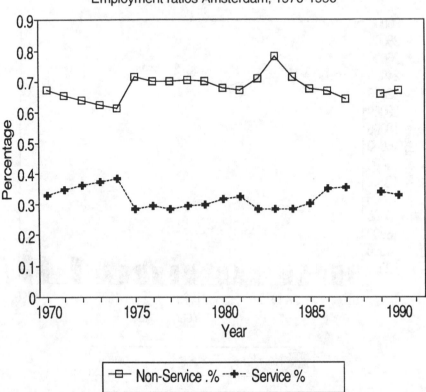

definitional changes. Construction mirrors the overall strength of the city's economy and it has been very flat since 1970. The real growth sector has been the public sector whose values in Figure 1 are partly a reflection of the inconsistency of the measure which has been changed to meet political exigencies.

The four sectors in Figure 2 are the core service sectors as the figure does not portray the public sector. Despite the huge increase in tourist numbers and in disposable income since 1970, the numbers employed in the hotels, restaurant and entertainment sector are stagnant. Personal services is also flat as individual service providers have found their roles mechanized or amalgamated into larger concerns, for whom personal services are a minority interest. We should note too the trend towards the 'informalization' of the personal services sector in all countries including the Netherlands (Terhorst and Van de Ven, 1986). Business services and banks, insurance, etc have seen strong

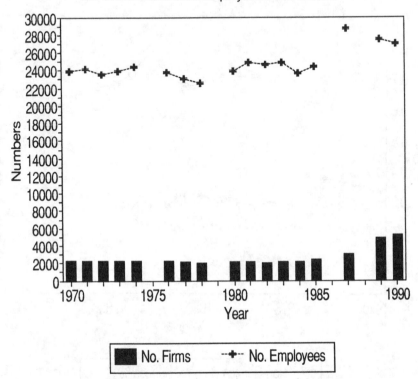

Figure 4 Trends in business services employment
no. of firms and total employment 1970-1990

growth since the end of the deep Dutch recession in the mid 1980s. After a decade of stagnation, 1975-85, these two sectors have added about 30,000 jobs over the past half-decade. This is a sizeable figure by Amsterdam's standards though of course, it pales in comparison to the values of the other large European service centres like London, Paris and Frankfurt. There is also still a question mark about these figures since the definitions in the yearbook were changed irregularly.

In order to attempt to remove the effects of the definition changes and to see the general long-term trends, the employments in the categories of both figures were summed and plotted on Figure 3. The service definition used in this instance is narrower than the usual term since it includes only non-public service employment. Since 1970, the overall pattern is one of consistency with private sector service employment hovering around 30%. The major development in the city has been the replacement of industrial jobs by public employment and the relative stagnation in the overall private service sector.

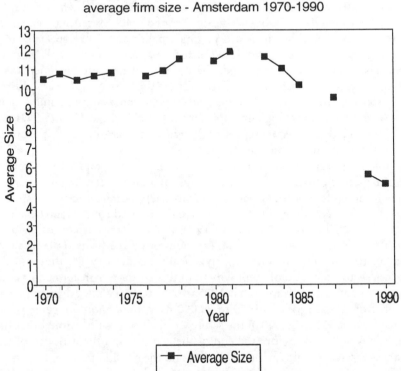

Figure 5 Trends in business services employment
average firm size - Amsterdam 1970-1990

Since there seems to be some confusion about the operational definitions of the categories, a specific SIS category, 84, *(zakelijke dienstverlening)* was chosen for analysis. In the yearbooks, this category is consistent and some data for the category are available for the Amsterdam region. In all accounts of the restructuring of cities, it is this sector that is considered to be critical. In any case of either decline or restructured growth, the business services sector should stand out. Date for both the number of establishments and employees were collected from the yearbook in Figure 3. The data are missing from some years but the overall pattern is clear. From 1970 to 1985, the numbers employed in business services in Amsterdam hovered about 24,000 and the number of establishments was about 2,000. Over the past half-decade, the number of employees has increased by about 5,000 while the number of establishments has shot up to about 4,000 (Figure 4). A large increase in the number of enterprises has not been matched by a parallel increase in the number of employees. In fact, the average number of employees per firm has fallen substantially from about 10-12 employees to about 5-6 (Figure 5). Flexibility is a trademark of this industry and the changes shown in Figures 4 and 5 probably reflect a boom in the number of employees setting themselves as new businesses. The firms are getting smaller and more specialized, a common characteristic of the post-Fordist service economy in all Western countries. While on the one hand, the number of new establishments is a strong indicator of flexibility and dynamism in the business services industry in Amsterdam, the low level of additional employment is a disappointment in light of the continuing huge unemployment figures (about 17% in 1991 get benefits) and the larger increases registered elsewhere in other European financial centres in the same period.

It might be argued that the figures portrayed in these graphs do not reflect the true picture of Amsterdam's economy. After all, the city is only a part of a much larger functional urban region, to use Cheshire's term. Despite a growth in total employment in the ring of cities around Amsterdam from less 100,000 in 1970 to over 200,000 in 1990, Amsterdam, despite losing over 35,000 worker in the same period, still accounts for three-fifths of the employment in the city-region. Looking specifically at category 84, the business services sector, the ratio of employment in this sector in Amsterdam has not changed much, down from 71% in 1975 to 60% today. While Amsterdam has grown from 23,000 jobs in 1975 to 29,000 now, the region *(omgeving)* has grown from 9,300 to 20,000 in the same period. There is little doubt that the trend lines will cross before the end of the century and the majority of the business services employment will be beyond the city limits.

There are important implications in these trends for the city of Amsterdam and the possibility of a repetition of the edge city phenomenon in the surroundings of Amsterdam is a real possibility. Coupled with the continued shrinkage of the employment of all sectors in the Centrum, a comparison with Detroit is not out of the question although Amsterdam's Centrum has far more residents and retail activities than Detroit's CBD, though the office employment profile is not too different. Recent studies by Hassels (1992) and Lie (1992) provide more evidence for the trends noticed in these figures. The fastest area of growth for the business services sector was in the suburban belts around Rotterdam and Amsterdam. Suburbs were preferred as locations because of the better office facilities available there. The Fourth National Physical Plan notes the importance of the business services sector to the Dutch economy with over 10% of the workforce now in the sector. Though business service employment grew by 3.5% in Greater Amsterdam in the 1984-88 period, this increase lagged the national average of 5.6% and the value for the Rotterdam area, 7.0%. The difference in the service composition of employment between Amsterdam and the whole metropolitan area has narrowed to such an extent that the ratios are now almost equal (59 and 53% respectively) (De Smidt, 1992b). Whether the Amsterdam city will continue to reap the benefits of the growth is debatable since the most desired business service location is not the Centrum but the World Trade Center area on the ring road in the south part of the city (Van de Ven and Westzaan, 1991). There, office rents are the highest but they are still only a fraction of the prices of London. For prime locations, the London value was 2,400 guilders per square metre per year compared to 1,470 in Paris, 1,090 in Madrid, 945 in Frankfurt and 360 in Amsterdam. Thus, Lie (1992) could rightfully claim that there were no prime locations for business services in Amsterdam. The differential in rents should continue to offer Amsterdam a comparative advantage in attracting mobile international business services but the recent glut of office space in London will change the picture greatly.

Amsterdam's future role in an integrated Europe

It is widely-agreed that Amsterdam lies in the second tier of European cities behind London and Paris. Also in this tier are such traditional business centres like Frankfurt, Zürich, Brussels, Milan, Hamburg, and new centres in Madrid, Berlin and Munich. Beyond Europe, cities such as Singapore, Sydney, Johannesburg and Toronto lie at the same world-level as Amsterdam. London and Paris are separated from the rest of the European urban network because of their size, their former roles as capitals of far-flung colonial empires, their long-standing headquarters functions, and their mix of governmental, cultural and business strength. Though both large cities have seen dramatic price increase in rents and high demand for office space, there seems to be little movement away from these centres to less-crowded and cheaper locations. As noted earlier, business services is one activity that requires face to face contact in the conduct of daily operations, despite the telecommunications revolution of the past decade.

If we try to make a balance sheet of the advantages and disadvantages that Amsterdam has at this stage of the inter-city competition in Europe, we can estimate what the future holds for the city. The discussion focuses on the city but clearly there are close connections between the activities in the city and those in the surrounding ring cities. The level of competition does not seem nearly as intense as can be found in most large U.S. metropolitan areas but the growth of office parks beyond the city and the decline of employment in the Centrum from 50% in the mid 1960s to 25% in 1989 (Van de Ven and

Westzaan, 1991) indicates that a similar decentralization is underway and the rivalry between the territorial units is expected to increase.

Amsterdam's comparative advantages are easy to identify and they emerge clearly in Cheshire's study and those of De Smidt (1992a). First is the city's central location near the core of the European Community. Traditionally stated as 'between Berlin and London' or as the percentage of the European population within 200 miles of Amsterdam, this locational advantage has given some special characteristics to the Dutch economy. With only 5% of the Community GDP, the Netherlands controls 5 times that ratio of the Community transport sector (De Smidt, 1992a). The Netherlands, especially Rotterdam, has acted as the traditional port for Northern Germany, especially the Ruhr industrial heartland and Schiphol has ambitions to become London's fourth airport in order to take advantage of the crowding in the London area. Intercontinental passenger traffic is up substantially at Schiphol and Amsterdam seems to be continuing its central character as an international transit point.

But there are two developments and one counter-development that throw the estimates of the future centralization of the Amsterdam node on the international trade and transport networks into some doubt. First, the European airline industry is de-regulating and the outcome for KLM (the Dutch carrier) and Schiphol is uncertain. Schiphol is very important not just for the direct jobs that it creates related to the passenger and freight traffic but also for the spinoff industries that it has generated in business services in its vicinity. If Schiphol is not on the list of the major hubs of the future airlines in Europe, severe repercussions could reverberate throughout the Dutch economy. Though KLM and British Airways had failed merger talks last year, the expectation is that it will eventually happen as part of a series of airline mergers across Europe that will produce a handful of mega-carriers as has happened in the U.S. The future of the national airline is closely bound to the future of the airport (now in the process of a large terminal expansion) and to the national economy.

The second possible negative trend is the shifting centre of gravity of the European Community to the South. As noted by Brunet (1989), the area of fastest growth is in the Mediterranean countries and especially the second banana along the coast between Florence and Valencia and inland to Milan, Lyon and Madrid. This trend places Amsterdam further and further from the Rhineland core and presumably would result in a gradual marginalization of its setting.

But this undoubted Sunbelt growth may be countered by a secondary development of the East and, especially, the German role there. All signs point to a renewal of the pre-war German dominance of the Eastern European economies and the growth of the Berlin-Hamburg area. If Eastern Europe prospers (this is a big if), especially within the framework of the European Community, we can expect the position of Amsterdam in the European network of trade and transport, and as a link to the wider world economy, to remain essentially unchanged.

The second comparative advantage that Amsterdam has is the international character of the city. The history of the city is a history of outward orientation and this has even been intensified by the development of the European Community. English is an comfortable second language for most Amsterdammers and the trend is towards a city that effectively is part of the Anglo-American business world while still maintaining contacts to the Germanic countries to the East. There is no dispute about the importance of foreign language education in the Netherlands and the ease with which the Dutch can maintain contact with the English-speaking world through television on both the Dutch stations, where the astonishing number of English-language programmes are sub-titled, and cable stations from Britain and the U.S., and through daily contact with tourists and businesspeople is quite remarkable even in a global communications age. Only Brussels, Singapore, Hong Kong and Miami come to mind as cities that equally span the cultures and international barriers as Amsterdam and all of these cities are driven by domestic cultural conflicts.

The third national advantage of the Netherlands and of Amsterdam is the quality of planning and the acceptance by all segments of society of the national plans after they are developed through careful negotiation and provision of something for all parties and interest groups. The Fourth Physical Plan, as already noted, stresses the international character of the Dutch economy and how local plans have to coordinate with the overall national policy to produce a flurry of business services activity as well as environmental protection and compact cities. Previous plans were not just dust-gatherers but were effectively implemented and we can expect the same of the current policy. Having identified the target, the state is now engaged in the necessary infrastructural developments to meet the goals. Though all European and other core and semi-peripheral states are trying to attract service industries, the Netherlands in general and Amsterdam in particular seems to have an unusual property of careful national plans in which the role for each city is well-defined.

A fourth comparative advantage is the national consensus identified by Katzenstein and others. Unlike other European states who all have internal or external social or political strife, the Netherlands is remarkably quiescent. In the past, religious, class and regional attachments were quite strong but they have effectively disappeared in the structure of 'democratic corporatism' that has been implemented for decades. For international businesses, such a peaceful setting is attractive in an increasingly-uncertain world in which the old certainties, including the national boundaries, are no more. Though Amsterdam is a conflictual city by Dutch standards, it is widely perceived as the capital of a tolerant, peaceful and successful society.

The fifth advantage that Amsterdam possesses has already been identified in the discussion of office rents. By international standards, rents are very low in the Amsterdam area and are especially low in the Centrum compared to the values of other centre-city locations in Europe. Dutch wage rates are also comparatively low while the level of education of the population is high. On the basis of the traditional locational decisions, Amsterdam ranks very high in any international comparison.

The small size of the Netherlands is a major advantage in the competitive struggles between the European states. From international relations, we know that a balance of power can be expected to develop in which a powerful state will face a coalition of less powerful countries. In the EC, the four major powers (Germany, France, Italy and the United Kingdom) have tried to place their impress on the Community with varying temporary degrees of success. In decisions about locations and community posts, there has been a tendency to compromise on candidates from smaller countries as the larger states block each other's ambitions. A good example is the debate over the siting of the European Central Bank, assuming that it will still happen after the Danish rejection of the Maastricht treaty. The current major candidates, London and Frankfurt, will probably cancel each other out, allowing Amsterdam to emerge as a compromise candidate. Similar decision-making circumstances could prevail in other locational debates to the benefit of Amsterdam and the Netherlands.

Compared to the list of advantages, it would appear that Amsterdam's disabilities are modest. First, its location in Northern Europe is a distinct disadvantage given the Sunbelt growth that is already evident in the member states of the European Community. The environmental circumstances driving growth in Europe along with the low-wage and active efforts of states to attract growth is very reminiscent of the situation in the U.S. in the 1950s and 1960s. Presumably the consequences will be the same and many cities in the North will see major population out-migration and relative economic decline. But just as not all Rustbelt cities of the U.S. have declined, so too the process will be selective in Europe and there is no reason to expect decline in Amsterdam as a general consequence of the movement South. A related disadvantage of Amsterdam is its relatively close location to Brussels. The European capital is expected to see a continued boom as non-European businesses continue to cluster close to the centre of European power. Given a choice of being at the centre of the activity (Bruxelles has a pro-active policy of attracting businesses) and Amsterdam, many companies are likely to opt for Brussels.

A second set of disadvantages relates to the perception of the city and its government. Both in the Netherlands and abroad, the city's strong socialist tradition is well-recognized. Already we have seen how, by Cheshire's reckoning, the policy choices of Amsterdam were far inferior to its locational and compositional advantages. The stress in city politics has always been on housing and social welfare distributions but there has been a greater willingness recently to place other items on the city agenda. This is similar to national discussions about the future of the housing market and the need to create more private housing. Public expenditure for housing is no longer the sacred cow that it once was and policies to encourage more owner-occupied housing are now the vogue (Dieleman and Van Weesep, 1986; Jobse and Musterd, 1992). Unlike the entrepreneurial roles of the American cities, Dutch cities have left such enterprises to the national state. Now, Amsterdam is belatedly getting into the act of encouraging public-private partnerships with specific visions for certain dilapidated areas along the docks and in specific sites in the inner-city. Compared to Rotterdam, however, the city is widely-perceived to be lackadaisical about economic growth and more concerned with income distribution.

There is a wider image of Amsterdam which Soja (1991) captures well in his description of the Centrum as a 'twenty-something' mecca. In the domestic and international images, Amsterdam is still a 'sinful place' as the Pilgrims called it nearly 400 years ago. It has an image as an entertainment and fun place for a specific subset of the population, young, educated, relatively-poor, childless and with many living on public assistance or on the margins of the formal sector. These are some of the new households that have formed in the past 10 years in Dutch (Engelsdorp-Gastelaars and Vijgen, 1990; Jobse, 19887; Musterd, 1991) Belgian (Kesteloot, 1990) and German cities (Friedrichs, 1985). The Centrum is not a stereotypical business district like the City of London, Lower Manhattan or the high-rise banking sector of Frankfurt. Offices are small, scattered, mixed with all other kinds of land uses and only along a few certain streets can a business air be identified. We have seen how in the literature on American cities, that the overall quality of life in a place is a powerful magnet to corporate officials. While the quality of overall services in Amsterdam is high by American standards, it must rank low compared to other European cities. There is a special air of public squalor not usually found in Europe, with the exception of British cities. This is visible in filthy streets, graffiti-ridden walls and buildings, large numbers of junkies and derelicts, and a general air of litter, petty crime and citizen nonchalance. The city has to be careful not to cross the threshold from the *'Stimulus of a little confusion'* (Soja, 1991) to an environment that makes the Centrum uncomfortable for families, businesses and other non-residents.

Amsterdam's future is closely-bound up with the composition of its resident population. The city has failed to attract or keep Dutch families, who have been at the forefront of the suburbanization movement for two decades and who have not been lured back into the city despite the city's pursuit of a balanced Centrum and city policy. It is estimated that two-thirds of the households in the city are either one or two-person households. Gentrification of selected parts of the Centrum has been done by over 35, childless, educated individuals with lots of disposable income (Jobse, 1987; Musterd, 1991; Jobse and Musterd, 1991). The housing market is quite split along public and private lines with over 80% of the stock in the public sector and strong rent, building and lease controls on the remainder. Housing costs are low and the average Amsterdammer spends more on food each month than on accommodation. The city policy of maintaining a mixed Centrum of housing, retail and office functions seems to be in jeopardy as the ratio of metropolitan employment in the centre has fallen from 50% to only 25% in the past 25 years. As job losses from the centre continue, the population keeps rising with about 2,000 more residents each year, almost all of the student and singles variety. Housing pressures still result in 52,000 *'urgenten'* (people on the waiting list for social housing) but many seem to be waiting to 'trade up' in the social sector to better or bigger accommodations.

A second concern is the minority-majority ratio in the city. The overall minority ratio is modest, about 28% and the level of residential segregation between the immigrant minorities and the Dutch population is very low by Western standards. The minority population is concentrated in the early 20th century housing zones and in some high-rise projects on the outskirts of the city and these are the areas of greatest dilapidation and need for renewal (Hoogvliet, 1992). The Dissimilarity Index stands at an overall rate of about 25 with a tendency in recent years for a decline. However, there are some clear danger signals towards separate societies. Half of the primary-age children in the city are minority and in 10 of the 18 *stadsdelen* (districts), minority children are in a majority. The reasons behind these figures have to do with the age composition of the Dutch population and there is little indication of white flight from inner-city schools. But if the age-specific segregation trends continue, then there will be little choice but to confront the issue of racial isolation in the schools. As Hans van Amersfoort (1992) has remarked, the Dutch and local governments have been a lot more successful in dealing with the provision of adequate housing than in the provision of adequate educational skills or occupations for the minority population.

Amsterdam's other flaw is the continuing very high level of official unemployment, now standing about 17%. While the rest of the country has seen a substantial drop from the peak unemployment figures of the mid-1980s, Amsterdam still continues to see lower full-time employment by men, more part-time employment by man and women, and a growth in the number of long-term unemployed. The reasons behind the surge in the unemployment figures in the 1980s were mostly demographic as a 1960s baby-boom cohort came into the market when the economy slowed. Amsterdam, of course, continues to have disproportionate numbers of this baby-boom and their relative lack of success on the labour market is reflected in the figures. There is a growing disparity between the big cities like Amsterdam with its large pool of uneducated and unskilled labour force, combined with the specific Amsterdam problem of enormous numbers of young job-seekers, and the rest of the country (Boot and Verart, 1987). The part-solution to the disjuncture of jobs and skill levels has been the growth of the informal sector and especially of part-time work.

Though Dutch economists decry the low level of women working, this combined with the flexibility of the labour force offers many options for employment than the Fordist one worker per family, 40 hours a week model. There is a real danger, of course, that the workers hired in an informal personal and formal business sector economy will not have the same security or wage benefits of the unionized force of the past. In this regard, the Dutch society needs to choose between the Swedish model where the ratio of women working is higher than the U.S. (more than 70%, contrasted to 35% in the Netherlands) and protection for the workers is written into law and the U.S. model where women on average get paid only 70% of men's wages and have few rights and protection in an essentially-private bargain between businesses and employees.

On balance, then, the indications are favourable for Amsterdam in the new Europe of the post-Fordist world. The biggest questions relate to the success of the city in keeping a mix of populations, including Dutch families. Otherwise, the city would have the appearance of Manhattan, with a large minority population sharing the island with yuppies and only a few white families. There is much more to New York City than Manhattan, of course; there seem to be fewer and fewer middle-class residential areas in Amsterdam and since the city's growth is bounded, any future developments will have to come *in situ*. It is this linking of global economic, European political and local social issues that makes Amsterdam such a special case in the contemporary political geography of the world economy.

Conclusions

If we consider future scenarios for Amsterdam, we can extend and modify Shostak's (1982) list. Nine options come to mind, some of which are very undesirable. The first scenario of a *conflict city* like Detroit with huge job losses in traditional sectors not replaced by other activities is very unlikely in Amsterdam because of the activity of the local state and the size of the service sector. The majority-minority issue, social malaise and dead downtown phenomenons are nowhere on Amsterdam's horizon. The second scenario of *imbalanced city* is more realistic and would make Amsterdam like Philadelphia or Baltimore or even New York City or Los Angeles. It features a prosperous centre, with a polarized community across racial lines and job security in the corresponding formal and informal sectors. It is Friedmann's world city. Whether it develops in Amsterdam is a function of the closeness of the relationship between the employment sectors and the racial groups.

A third scenario is Shostak's *wired city* where an empty and eerie downtown at night is symbolic of the real power in the city. The City of London, downtown Los Angeles, Washington DC and Wall Street show that these kinds of downtowns are not for people but for businesses. Given the residential attractions of the Centrum and the mix of activities there in addition to the offices, there again is little likelihood of its occurrence. The fourth scenario, that of the *neighbourhood city*, does not seem to be successful in Amsterdam. In this model, best-known in Pittsburgh in the U.S., neighbourhoods are well-defined by natural boundaries and by the residential composition. Attachment to place is very strong and stability is characteristic despite the change in social status. Amsterdam has tried to implement the formal aspects of neighbourhood definition with the 18 *stadsdelen* (districts) given local city halls, identifications on buildings and street signs and much publicity about the range of services available locally. But the missing element seems to be pride of place which is difficult to measure but is obviously missing in the districts of Amsterdam. As Hoogvliet (1992) notes, there is a lot of mobility in many areas and in these circumstances, neighbourhood attachment is difficult to create.

The fifth scenario, that of *tourist city*, is possible, but unwelcome, in Amsterdam. Venice, Miami Beach or Bruges would be archetypes of this scenario. It is expressed in an imbalance between residents and tourists at certain times of the year and the creation of a museum-like quality to the city as well as the spread of the global signs, boards and symbols of the international tourist. Already much of the Centrum, especially between the Central Station, the Leidseplein and the Dam, is filled with the tacky indications of mass tourism. At certain times of the week, there are more tourists visible than natives in much of the Centrum. Amsterdam's tourism strikes one as distinctly down-scale and the tackiness of its visible structures seems to match well the tackiness of the whole enterprise.

The sixth scenario, *the high-tech city*, seems to have missed Amsterdam. In the European context, Cambridge, Montpellier and Grenoble would be good models. Each of these had strong government involvement in setting up the initial research enterprises and university-private business links are the engines that fuel the continued growth. Despite its position as the centre of the Dutch university system, there seems to be only a belated recognition of the possible externalities of university research in the recent plan to develop a university research park in the east of the city. Since this decision comes late in the game, the comparative competitiveness of Amsterdam in high-technology development and manufacturing may already have evaporated.

Amsterdam as a *business services city* has already been discussed in detail. As noted earlier, the city sits in the second league of European cities and will likely remain there. The greater concern is that the service industry will continue to locate disproportionately in the suburbs and the edge city will have arrived in the Netherlands. To avoid this development, the city has to be aggressive in keeping existing business services in the city itself and by attracting new ones to projects like the WTC.

An eight scenario is a *slow decline city*. In this model, the population gradually shrinks through natural attrition, as was the case for West Berlin, Vienna and some German cities. More households but fewer children is characteristic of this model and foreigners come to comprise an increasing share of the population through the natural decrease of the natives. Housing shortages are exacerbated by the number of new households and the pervading air is the opposite of a vital dynamic city like Madrid. This scenario is a real possibility in Amsterdam and should be carefully guarded against through an aggressive policy of maintaining economic growth while keeping the traditional households in the city.

The last scenario, the *balanced city*, is the desired one and is the backbone of the official Amsterdam policy for the Centrum but should be extended to the city as a whole. There are no obvious models although Stuttgart and Tokyo come close. It requires action on a variety of fronts including the development of a high-tech manufacturing sector, the continued attraction of business services, the maintenance of a balanced demographic structure including families with children, upgrading urban services and appearance, and the active pursuit of programmes that would incorporate the minority population more fully into the formal economic sector. Amsterdam has a real chance to become such a model city. It would then offer a real choice to international businesses of a world city model, that of Los Angeles or New York with their citadel-ghetto frameworks or a humane city concerned with people, conjunctures and quality of life.

References

Amersfoort, H. van
1992   'Ethnic residential patterns in a welfare state: Lessons from Amsterdam, 1970-90.' *New Community* 18, 439-56.

Amsterdamse Bureau voor Onderzoek en Statistiek
yearly   *Jaarboek, Amsterdam in Cijfers* Amsterdam.

Bagchi-Sen, S.
1991   'The location of foreign direct investment in finance, insurance and real estate in the United States' *Geographiska Annaler B* 73, 187-97.

Boot, P.A. and M. Verart
1987   'The Dutch labour market'. *Tijdschrift voor Economische en Sociale Geografie* 78, 399-403.

Brouwer, H.J.
1989   'The spatial restructuring of the Amsterdam office market'. *Netherlands Journal of Housing and Environmental Research* 4, 257-74.

Brunet, R.
1989   *Les villes Européenes: Rapport pour la DATAR*, Montpellier: Groupement d'Invéret Public RECLUS.

Castells, M.
1988   'High technology and urban dynamics in the United States'. In: M. Dogan and J.D. Kasarda (eds). *A World of Giant Cities: (The Metropolis Era Volume 1)* Beverly Hills, CA: Sage, pp. 85-110.

Chase-Dunn, C.
1989   *Global Formation*. Oxford: Basil Blackwell.

Cheshire, P.
1990   'Explaining the recent performance of the European Community's urban regions'. *Urban Studies* 27, 311-33.

Cheshire, P., G. Carbonaro and D. Hay
1986   'Problems of urban decline and growth in EEC countries or measuring degrees of elephantness'. *Urban Studies* 23, 131-49.

Commission of the European Community
1991   'The development of the Community's urban system'. In: *Europe 2000* Luxembourg: European Communities, pp.138-50.

Cortie, C. and K. Dignum
1991   'Stedelijke welvaart en economische functies'. *Geografisch Tijdschrift* 25, 442-52.

Crampton, G. and A. Evans
1992   'The economy of an agglomeration: The case of London'. *Urban Studies* 29, 259-72.

Davis, M.
1990   *City of Quartz*. London: Verso.

Dertouzos, M.L., R.K. Lester and R.M. Solow
1989   *Made in America: Regaining the Productive Edge*. Cambridge, MA.: MIT Press.

Dieleman, F.M.
1986   'The future of Dutch housing: A review and interpretation of the recent literature'. *Tijdschrift voor Economische en Sociale Geografie* 77, 336-44.

Dieleman, F. and S. Musterd
1991   'Maatschappelijke veranderingen en de herstructurering van de Randstad'. *Geografisch Tijdschrift* 25, 490-501.

Dieleman, F.M. and J. van Weesep
1986   'Housing under fire: Budget cuts, policy adjustments and market changes'. *Tijdschrift voor Economische en Sociale Geografie* 77, 310-15.

Drennan, M.P.
1992   'Gateway cities: The metropolitan sources of U.S. producer services exports'. *Urban Studies* 29, 217-36.

Droogleever Fortuijn, J.
1990   'Emancipation and residential differentiation: A study of Dutch dual-income families'. In: L. Deben, W. Heinemeijer and D. van der Vaart (eds) *Residential Differentiation*, Amsterdam: Centrum voor Grootstedelijk Onderzoek, pp. 235-44.

Engelsdorp Gastelaars, R. van and J. Vijgen
1990   'Residential differentiation in the Netherlands: the rise of new urban households'. In: L. Deben, W. Heinemeijer and D. van der Vaart (eds) *Residential Differentiation*, Amsterdam: Centrum voor Grootstedelijk Onderzoek, pp. 136-63.

Fainstein, N.I. and S.S. Fainstein
1981   'Restructuring the American city: A comparative perspective'. In: N.I. Fainstein and S.S. Fainstein (eds). *Urban Policy under Capitalism*. Beverly Hills, CA: Sage, pp. 161-90.

Friedrichs, J. (ed)
1965   Die Städte in den 80er Jahren. Opladen: Westdeutscher Verlag.

Friedmann, J.F.
1986   'The world city hypothesis'. *Development and Change* 17, 69-83.

Friedmann, J.F. and G. Wolff
1982   'World city formation: An agenda for research and action'. *International Journal of Urban and Regional Research* 6, 309-44.

Hall, P.
1966   *World Cities*
1988   'Urban growth and decline in Western Europe'. In: M. Dogan and J.D. Kasarda (eds). A World of Giant Cities: (The Metropolis Era Volume 1) Beverly Hills, CA: Sage, pp.52-84.

Hall, P. and P. Preston
1988   The Carrier Wave: New Information Technology and the Geography of Innovation, 1846-2003. London: Unwin Hyman.

Heijden, G.J.L.M. van der and J.H.T. Kramer
1991   'Mainports en economische ontwikkeling: de Europese mainports vergeleken en hun betekenis voor de stedelijke en regionale economie'. *Geografisch Tijdschrift* 25, 453-61.

Hessels, M.
1991   'Zakelijke diensten: Winnende en verliezende deelmilieus in de Randstad'. In: S. Musterd and P. Hooimeyer (eds) *De Randstad: Balans van Winst en Verlies* Vol. 1. Utrecht: Stedelijke Netwerken, pp. 67-77.

Hoogvliet, A.
1991   'Winnende en verliezende woonmilieus in de vroeg-20ste-eeuwse zone'. In: S. Musterd and P. Hooimeyer (eds) *De Randstad: Balans van Winst en Verlies* Vol. 1. Utrecht: Stedelijke Netwerken, pp. 119-32.

Jobse, R.B.
1987   'The restructuring of Dutch cities' *Tijdschrift voor Economische en Sociale Geografie* 78, 305-11.

Jobse, R.B. and S. Musterd
1992   'Changes in the residential function of the big cities.' in: F.M. Dieleman and S. Musterd (eds) *The Randstad: A Research and Policy Laboratory* Dordrecht: Kluwer Publishers, pp. 39-64.

Jobse, R.B. and B. Needham
1988   'The economic future of Randstad, Holland'. *Regional Studies* 25, 282-96.

Kasarda, J.
1988   'Economic restructuring and America's urban dilemma'. In: M. Dogan and J.D. Kasarda (eds). *A World of Giant Cities: (The Metropolis Era Volume 1)*. Beverly Hills, CA: Sage, pp.52-84.

Katzenstein, P.J.
1985   *Small States in World Markets: Industrial Policy in Europe*. Ithaca, NY: Cornell University Press.

Kloosterman, R.C. and J.G. Lambooy
1992   'The Randstad: A welfare region'. In: F.M. Dieleman and S. Musterd (eds) *The Randstad: A Research and Policy Laboratory* Dordrecht: Kluwer Publishers, pp. 123-140.

Knight, R.V.
1990   'Knowledge and the late advanced industrial metropolis'. In: G. Gappert (ed) *The Future of Winter Cities*. Beverly Hills, CA: Sage, pp. 196-208.

Knight, R.V. and G. Gappert (eds)
1989   *Cities in Global Society*. Beverly Hills, CA: Sage.

Kesteloot, C.
1990   'Guestworkers' neighbourhoods in the current regime.' Paper, Instituut voor Sociale en Economische Geografie, Universiteit te Leuven, 19 pages.

Lambooy, J.G.
1991   'Europese hoofsteden: rivaliteit en suprematie'. *Geografisch Tijdschrift* 25, 434-41.

Mollenkopf, J.
1983   *The Contested City*. Princeton, NJ: Princeton University Press.

Marcuse, P.
1989   'Dual city: A muddy metaphor for a quartered city.' *International Journal of Urban and Regional Research* 13, 697-708.

Musterd, S.
1991   'Neighbourhood change in Amsterdam'. *Tijdschrift voor Economische en Sociale Geografie* 82, 30-39.

Norton, R.D.
1992   'Agglomeration and competitiveness: from Marshall to Chinitz'. *Urban Studies* 29, 155-70.

Noyelle, T.J. and T.M. Stanbach
1984   *Economic Transformation of American Cities* Totowa, NJ: Rowman and Allenheld.

O'Loughlin, J.
1987   'Chicago an der Ruhr or what? Explaining the location of foreign minority neighbourhoods in Continental European cities'. In: G. Glebe and J. O'Loughlin (eds) Foreign Minorities in Continental European Cities. Stuttgart: Franz Steiner Verlag, pp.
1993   'Fact or fiction? The evidence for the relative decline of the United States, 1950-1991'. In: C. Williams (ed.) The Political Geography of the New World Order London: Belhaven Press (forthcoming).

O'Loughlin, J. and H. van der Wusten
1990   'The political geography of Panregions'. *Geographical Review* 80, 1-20.

Shostak, A.
1982   'Seven scenarios of urban change'. In: G. Gappert and R.V. Knight (eds) *Cities in the 21st Century*. Beverly Hills, CA: Sage, pp. 69-93.

Smidt, M. de
1986a   'Labor market segmentation and mobility patterns.' *Tijdschrift voor Economische en Sociale Geografie* 77, 399-407.
1986b   'Von den industriellen Emanzipation zur Neustrukurierung: Die Niederlande als Industrieland in den vergangenen zwei Jahrzehnten'. *Geographische Rundschau* 38, 377-86.
1991   'De Randstad: Internationaal logistiek knooppunt en Europese metropool'. *Geografisch Tijdschrift* 25, 462-71.
1992a   'A world city paradox: Firms and the urban fabric'. In: F.M. Dieleman and S. Musterd (eds) *The Randstad: A Research and Policy Laboratory*. Dordrecht: Kluwer Publishers, pp. 97-122.
1992b   'Bedrijfsprofiel van de Randstad: Winnende en verliezende milieus'. In: P. Hooimeijer, S. Musterd and P. Schröder (eds) De Randstad: Balans van Winst en Verlies Vol.1. Utrecht: Stedelijke Netwerken, pp. 17-34.

Smidt, M. de and R. van der Mark
1991   'European metropolises in competition for offices: The functional network of cities and real estate market indicators'. *Geoforum* 24, 247-56.

Smith, N.
    1987   'Dangers of the empirical turn: Some comments on the CURDS initiative'.
              Antipode 19, 397-406.

Soja, E.
    1991   *The Stimulus of a Little Confusion: A Contemporary Comparison of Amsterdam
              and Los Angeles.* Amsterdam: Centrum voor Grootstedelijk Onderzoek.

Taylor, P.J.
    1989   *Political Geography: World-economy, Nation-state and Locality.* 2nd ed. London:
              Longman.
    1991a   'Political geography within world-systems analysis'. *Review* 14, 387-402.
    1991b   'The crisis of the movements: The enabling state as Quisling'. *Antipode* 23, 214-28.

Terhorst, P. and J. van de Ven
    1986   'The revival of personal services in cities: An expression of polarization'.
              Netherlands Journal of Housing and Environmental Research 1, 115-38.
    1990   'The territorial strategies of Amsterdam.' *Tijdschrift voor Economische en Sociale
              Geografie* 81, 267-79.

Urry, J.
    1986   'Locality research: The case of Lancaster'. *Regional Studies* 20, 233-42.

Veen, F.H. van der
    1989   'The Fourth Report on physical planning in the Netherlands'. *Tijdschrift voor
              Economische en Sociale Geografie* 80, 124-28.

Ven, J. van de
    1991   'Het Amsterdamse gemeentebestuur en het functieverlies van de Binnenstad'.
              Geografisch Tijdschrift 25, 502-09.

Ven, J. van de and M. Westzaan
    1991   'Amsterdam inside out? Conversion of office space into condominiums in the
              historic city centre of Amsterdam'. *Netherlands Journal of Housing and the Built
              Environment* 6, 287-306.

Wallerstein, I.
    1979   *The Capitalist World-Economy.* New York: Cambridge University Press.
    1991   *Geopolitics and Geoculture.* New York: Cambridge University Press.

The stimulus of a little confusion
A contemporary comparison of Amsterdam and Los Angeles

Edward Soja

On Spuistraat

> *All these elements of the general spectacle in this entertaining country at least give one's regular habits of thought the stimulus of a little confusion and make one feel that one is dealing with an original genius. (Henry James, experiencing the Netherlands in "Transatlantic Sketches," Boston, 1875, p. 384)*
> *What, then, is the Dutch culture offered here? An allegiance that was fashioned as the consequence, not the cause, of freedom, and that was defined by common habits rather than legislated by institutions. It was a manner of sharing a peculiar – very peculiar – space at a particular time...the product of the encounter between fresh historical experience and the constraints of geography. (Simon Schama, "The Embarrassment of Riches: An Interpretation of Dutch Culture in the Golden Age," Fontana Press, 1987, xi)*

In Amsterdam in 1990, I dwelt for a time on Spuistraat, a border street on the western flank of the oldest part of the Inner City. Squeezed in between the busy Nieuwezijds Voorburgwal (literally, on the 'new side' of the original settlement, in front of the old city wall) and the Singel (or 'girdle,' the first protective canal moat built just beyond the wall), Spuistraat runs roughly North-South starting near the old port and the teeming Stationsplein, where the Central Railway Station sits blocking the seaview, pumping thousands of visitors daily into the historic urban core. At half its length, Spuistraat is cut by Raadhuisstraat, the start of the main western boulevard axis branching off from the nearby Royal Palace (once the Town Hall or *raadhuis*) and Dam Square, where the city was born more than 700 years ago in a portentous act of regulatory tolerance (granting the local settlers toll-free use of the new dam across the Amstel River, Amstelledamme becoming Amsterdam).

After passing my house the street ends in what is simply called Spui, or 'sluice,' once a control channel connecting the Amstel and the older inner city canal system with the great bib of concentric canals that ring the outer crescent of the Inner City, or Centrum. The Spui (pronounced somewhere in between 'spay' and 'spy') is now a short broad boulevard lined with bookstores, cafes, a university building, the occasional open air art fair, and the entranceways to several popular tourist attractions, ranging from the banal (Madame Tussaud's) to the enchanting (the Begijnhof and just beyond, the Amsterdam Historical Museum). The 'city museum' offers the most organized introduction to the historical geography of Amsterdam, with roomsful of splendid imagery bringing to life what you see first upon entering, an exemplary model that sequentially lights up the city's territorial expansion from 1275 to the present. Just as effective, however, as a starting point for an interpretive geography of Amsterdam is the Begijnhof, or Beguine Court.

The Begijnhof is a small window onto the Amsterdam *mentalité*, that bewildering Dutch mix of the familiar and the incomprehensible that so attracted Henry James in 1874 and later inspired Simon Schama's brilliant interpretation of the 'moralizing geography' of Dutch culture in its 17th-century Golden Age, *The Embarrassment of Riches* (1987). One enters the Begijnhof through an arched oak door off the Spui, an innocently unmarked opening to an enticing microcosm of civic refuge and peaceful respite in a cosmopolitan Dutch world of ever-so-slightly repressive tolerance. Before you is a neat quadrangle of lawn surrounded by beautifully preserved and reconstructed 17th and 18th century alms-houses, nearly every one fronted with flower-filled gardens. A restored wooden house dates back to the 15th century, one of two survivors of the many fires which burned down the old city before the more substantial Golden Age. The other survivor is located in a different kind of refuge zone along the Zeedijk, today known as the 'boulevard of junkies.'

There are also two small churches, one dating back to 1392 but built again in 1607 and known since as either English Reformed or Scottish Presbyterian. Here the fleeing English Pilgrim Fathers prayed before setting sail on the Mayflower, comfortable in their temporary Dutch haven. On one of my visits, the church was filled with the concerted voices of the Loyola College choir from New Orleans, singing American spirituals to the passersby. The other church, a clandestine construction in 1665, was originally a refuge for Catholic sisters escaping post-Reformation Calvinist religious purges. One of its stained-glass windows commemorates the epochal 'wafer miracle' of 1345, an event that boosted Amsterdam into becoming a major medieval pilgrimage center and began its still continuing and far reaching internationalization.[1]

The Beguine Court was actually founded one year after the miracle as a sanctuary for the Beguines, a Dutch lay sisterhood that sought a convent-like life but with the freedom to leave and marry if they wished, an early marker of the many Dutch experiments with what might be called engagingly flexible inflexibility. Today, the Begijnhof continues to be home to *ongehuwde dames* (unmarried ladies) who pay a nominal rent to live very comfortably around the lawned quadrangle. Despite the flocking tourists, it remains a remarkably peaceful spot, a reflective urban retreat that succeeds in being both open and closed at the same time, just like so many other paradoxical spaces and places in the refugee filled Amsterdam Centrum.

I lived just around the corner in another of these artfully preserved places and spaces, a relatively modest variant of the more than six thousand 'monuments' to the Golden Age that are packed into the sustaining Centrum, the largest and most successfully reproduced historic inner city in Europe. With a frontage that seemed no wider than my garage back home in Los Angeles, the building, like nearly all the others in the Centrum, rose four storeys to a gabled peak embedded with a startling metal hook designed for moving furniture and bulky items by ropes in through the wide windows. I had visions of having to be hauled up and in myself when I first saw the steep stairwell (*trappenhuis*) to the first floor. Golden Age taxation systems encouraged physical narrowness and relatively uniform facades up front, squeezing living space (and expansive creativity in design) upward and inward from the tiny street- or canal-side openings. The patient preservation yet modernization of these monuments reflects that 'original genius' of the Dutch to make big things of little spaces, to literally produce an enriching and communal urban spatiality through aggressive social intervention and grass-roots planning, an adaptive feat on a par with the Dutch conquest of the sea.

Simon Schama roots Dutch culture in this moral geography of adaptation, an uncanny skill in working against the prevailing tides and times to create places that reinforce collective self-recognition and identity. 'Dutchness,' he writes, 'was often equated with the transformation, under devine guidance, of catastrophe into good fortune, infirmity into strength, water into dry land, mud into gold.' (1987, 25) In Amsterdam, perhaps more so than in any other Dutch city, these earthy efforts to 'moralize materialism' moved out from the polderlands to become evocatively urban, not through devine guidance as much as through secularized spatial planning and an extraordinarily committed civic consciousness that persists to the present. The canal house simulates this rootedness, enabling one to experience within it the very essence of a liveable city, the agglomeration of individuals into socially constructed lifespaces that open up new possibilities even as they tightly enclose, that are popularly designed to make density beautiful as well as accommodating, that flexibly enculturate and socialize without imprisoning, and that somehow add to one's regular habits of thought that entertaining stimulus of a little confusion.

To live in a canal house is to immediately and precipitously encounter Amsterdam, as my kind hosts from the University of Amsterdam's Center for Metropolitan Studies knew well in finding me such strategically located lodgings.[2] The past is omnipresent in its narrow nooks and odd-angled passageways, its flower-potted spaces and unscreened windows that both open and close to the views outside. Every day life inside becomes a crowded reminder of at least three centuries of urban history and urban geography being preserved on a scale and contemporary intensity that is unique to Amsterdam. At home, one is invited daily into the creative spatiality of the city's social life and culture, an invitation that is at the same time embracingly tolerant and carefully guarded. Not everyone can become an Amsterdammer, but everyone must at least be given the chance to try.

The prevailing atmosphere is not that of a museum, however, a fixed and dead immortalization of the city's culturally built environment. The history and geography are remarkably alive and filled with the urban entertainment that makes Amsterdam so familiar and yet so tolerantly incomprehensible, neat and clean and regular but curiously tilted, puzzling, an island of mud not quite entirely turned into gold but transformed enough to make one believe in the creative alchemy of Amsterdam's democratic city-builders. From my vantage point on Spuistraat a moving picture of contemporary life in the vital center of Amsterdam visually unfolded.

The view from my front windows affirmed for me what I continue to believe is the most extraordinary quality of this city, its relatively (the Dutch constitutionally refuse all absolutes) successful achievement of highly regulated urban anarchism, another of the creative paradoxes (along with the aforementioned and closely related 'repressive tolerance' and 'flexible inflexibility') that two-sidedly filter through the city's historical geography in ways that defy comparison with almost any other *polis*, past or present. This deep and enduring commitment to libertarian socialist values and participatory spatial democracy is openly apparent throughout the urban built environment and in the social practices of urban planning, law enforcement, popular culture, and daily life. One senses that Amsterdam is not just preserving its own Golden Age but is actively keeping alive the very possibility of a socially just and humanely scaled urbanism. Still far from perfection itself, as the Dutch never cease telling you, Amsterdam is nonetheless packed with conspicuously anomolous achievements. There is little or no boosterism, no effort to proclaim the achievements or to present them as a model for others to follow.

Instead, there is again, *pace* Schama, an unadvertised 'embarrassment of riches,' modestly reproduced as in the past on the 'moral ambiguity of good fortune.'

There are many ways to illustrate this peculiar urban genius. For now, the view through my Spuistraat window will do for a start. Immediately opposite, in a building very much like mine, each floor is a separate flat and each storey tells a vertical story of subtle and creative city-building processes. It was almost surely a squatter-occupied house and is probably one now, for Spuistraat has long been an active scene of the squatter movement. On the ground floor is an extension of the garage offices next door. There is a small 'No Parking' sign on the window but nearly always a car or two is parked in front. Our ground floor, in contrast, is a used book shop, one of the many dozens densely packed in this most literate of Centrums, the place where enlightened scholars from Descartes to Voltaire, Montesquieu, and Rousseau first found the freedom to have their works published and publicized.

One cannot avoid noticing that the automobile is an intruder in the Inner City of Amsterdam. Spuistraat, like so many others, has been designed and redesigned primarily for pedestrians and cyclists. Alongside the bike path there is a narrow one-way car lane and some parking spaces, but this accommodation to the automobile is tension-filled and wittily punctuated. The police are always ready to arrive with those great wheel clamps and the spectacle of their attachment usually draws appreciative, occasionally cheering crowds of onlookers. Traffic is nearly always jammed, yet (most of the time) the Dutch drivers wait patiently, almost meekly, for they know they are guilty of intrusion and wish to avoid the steel jaws of public approbation. I was told that the city planners have accepted the need to construct several large underground parking garages in the Centrum, but only with the provision that for every space constructed below ground, one space above is taken away.

On the first floor of the house across the way were the most obviously elegant living quarters, occupied by a woman who had probably squatted there as a student but had by now comfortably entered the job market. She spent a great deal of time in the front room, frequently had guests in for candlelight dinners, and would occasionally wave to us across the street, for we too had our most comfortable living space just by the front windows. On the floor above there was a young couple. They were probably still students and still poor, although the young man may have been working at least part time for he was rarely seen, except in the morning and late at night. The woman was obviously pregnant and spent most of her time at home. Except when the sun was bright and warm, they tended to remain away from the front window and never acknowledged anyone outside, for their orientation was decidedly inward. The small top floor, little more than an attic, still had plastic sheeting covering the roof. A single male student lived there and nearly always ate his lunch leaning out the front window alone. His space made one wonder whether the whole building was still a 'squat' for if he was paying a nominal rent, one would have expected the roof to have been fixed, in keeping with the negotiated compromises that have marked what some would call the social absorption of the squatter movement in the 1980s.[3]

This vertical transect through the current status of the squatter movement was matched by an even more dramatic horizontal panorama along the east side of Spuistraat, from Paleisstraat (Palace Street) to the Spui. To the north was an informative sequence of symbolic structures, beginning with a comfortable corner house that was recently rehabilitated with neat squatter rentals (another contradiction in terms?) above; and below, a series of shops also run by the same group of rehabilitated squatter-renters: a well-stocked fruit and vegetable market-grocery selling basic staples at excellent prices, a beer-tasting store stocked with dozens of imported (mainly Belgian) brews and their distinctively matching drinking glasses and mugs, a small bookstore and gift shop specializing in gay and lesbian literature, a used household furnishings shop with dozens of chairs and tables set out on the front sidewalk, and finally a small hand-crafted woman's cloth hat shop.

This remarkably successful example of gentrification by the youthful poor is just a stone's throw away from the Royal Palace on the Dam, the focal point for the most demonstrative peaking of the radical squatter movement that blossomed city-wide in conjunction with the coronation of Queen Beatrix in 1980. A more immediate explanation of origins, however, is found just next door on Spui Straat, where a new office-construction site has replaced former squatter dwellings in an accomplished give and take trade-off with the urban authorities. And just next door to this site, even closer to my window, was still another paradoxical juxtapositioning, one which signalled the continued life of the radical squatter movement in its old 'anarchic colors.'

A privately owned building had been recently occupied by contemporary squatters and its facade was brightly repainted, graffitoed, and festooned with political banners and symbolic bric-a-brac announcing the particular form, function, and focus of the occupation. The absentee owner was caricatured as a fat tourist obviously beached somewhere with sunglasses and tropical drink in hand, while a white-sheet headline banner bridged the road to connect with a similar squat on my side of the street, also bedecked with startling colors and slogans and blaring with music from an established squatter pub. I was told early in my stay that this was the most provocative squatter settlement in the Centrum and was scheduled to be recaptured by the authorities several days after my arrival. When I left, however, the situation was unchanged, at least on the surface.

The view south on Spuistraat presented another urban trajectory dominated by much more traditional forms of gentrification. Some splendid conversion, using fancy wooden shutters, modernized gables (no hook here), and vaulted interior designs was transforming an old structure for its new inhabitants, who were much more likely to visit the boutiques and gourmet restaurants in the vicinity than the shops up the road. The transition quickened in a little restaurant row that ranged from what was reputed to be the best seafood place in Amsterdam and one of the grandest traditional centers of Dutch cuisine (called the Five Flies and fed daily by busloads of mainly Japanese and German package-tourists), to a variety of smaller cafes, Indonesian restaurants (considered part of Dutch cuisine), and fast-food emporia.

By the time you reach the Spui, the street scene is awash again with activity and variety. A large bookstore shares one corner with an international news-center, spilling over onto the sidewalk with newspapers, magazines, and academic journals from around the world. There are hash coffee shops[4] and beer pubs nearby, as well as an American-style cocktail bar and several representatives of the astonishing variety of specialized Amsterdam cafes.[5] One is the best known 'white cafe' (just drinks) but it has been losing its yuppie edge to the stand-up, quick service, 'old-style' cafe next door. Nearly adjacent but stoically distanced is a famous radical cafe, where an older clientele sits and glares at the sipping elites across the way. The dense territorialities here are invisible to the casual visitor and they may be blurring even for the Dutch, as the cosmopolitan mixture of Amsterdam takes over, globalizing the local street scene.

This Spuistraat panorama concentrates the spectrum of forces that have creatively rejuvenated the residential life of the Centrum and preserved its anxiety-inducing *overvloed* (superabundance, literally overflood) of urban riches. At the center of this rejuvenation has been the squatter movement, which has probably etched itself more deeply into the urban built environment of Amsterdam than in any other inner city in the world. To many of its most radical leaders, the movement today seems to be in retreat, deflected if not coopted by an embracing civic tolerance. But it has been this slightly repressive tolerance that has kept open the competitive channels for alternative housing and counter-cultural lifestyles not only for the student population of today but for other age groups as well. It has also shaped, in distinctive ways, the more 'acceptable' gentrification process and helped to make it contribute to the diversity of the Centrum rather than to its homogenization, although this struggle is clearly not yet over.

The contemporary residential rejuvenation of Amsterdam requires some historical and geographical explanation. Decentralization in the 1930s began emptying the inner city of offices and manufacturing employment, and post-war suburbanization continued the process in a heightened flow of residential out-migration not just to the polycentred urban fringe but beyond, to such Christallerian new towns as Almere and Lelystad, planned and plotted on the reclaimed polders of Flevoland. As has happened in every century after the Golden Age, the continued life and liveliness of the Centrum was threatened by exogenous forces of modernization. A turning point, however, was reached in the 1960s, as cities exploded all over the world in often violent announcements that the post-war boom's excesses were no longer tolerable to the underclasses of urban society. A contrapuntal process of urban restructuring was initiated almost everywhere in an effort to control the spreading unrest and to shift economic gears in an attempt to recover the expansionary capitalist momentum. A comparison of the urban restructuring of Amsterdam and Los Angeles over the past twenty-five years becomes appealing at this point, for each has in its own way been paradigmatic. But I do not wish to leave my Spuistraat vantage point too quickly, for it continues to be revealing.

The contemporary residential renaissance of Amsterdam's Centrum, more effectively than any other place I know, illustrates the power of popular control over the social production of urban space. It has been perhaps the most successful enactment of the anarcho-socialist-environmentalist intentions that inspired the urban social movements of the 1960's to recover their 'rights to the city' ('*Le droit à la ville*', as it was termed by Henri Lefebvre). More familiar paths of urban restructuring can be found in Amsterdam, but the Centrum's experience verges on the unique. Uncovering this uniqueness is difficult, however, for it has been blanketed by more conventional wisdoms that see only either a continuation of destructive decentralization emptying the urban core of its economic base (and hence encouraging more drastic forms of urban renewal); or the defeat and cooptation of the most radical urban social movements (leading too easily to a sense of popular despair). Both views can be argued with abundant statistics and effective polemics, but when seen from the outside in a more comparative and global perspective on the past twenty-five years of urban restructuring, Amsterdam looks quite different.

In 1965, while Watts was burning in Los Angeles, a small group of Amsterdammers called the Provo (after their published and pamphleted 'provocations') sparked an urban uprising of radical expectations and demands that continues to be played out on Spui Straat and elsewhere in the 'magic centre' of Amsterdam. Their 'White Bikes Plan' (whereby publicly provided bicycles would be available for free use throughout the city) symbolized the growing resistance to automobile traffic in the Centrum that would far outlive the plan itself. Today, the network of bicycle paths and the density of cyclists is probably the highest in any major industrial or even post-industrial city; urban planners routinely maintain their distaste for automobile traffic while flexibly accommodating its inevitability; and the people continue to take free public transport by simply not paying on the subway, tram, or bus. If the free-riders are caught (by characteristically soft enforcers, usually unemployed youth hired as fare checkers), they make up names, for the Dutch are unique in Europe in having no official identification cards. Driving licenses, the universal stamp and regulator of personal identity in America, are superfluous in the Netherlands and certainly not open to easy inspection.

The Provos concentrated their eventful 'happenings' in both Dam and Spui squares and managed to win a seat on the City Council, indicative of their arousal of wider public sympathies. Their artful challenges to hierarchy and authority lasted only for a few years, but they set in motion a generational revolution of the 'twentysomethings' (my term for the youthful households comprised mainly of students between the ages of 20 and 30 that today make up nearly a quarter of the Centrum's population) that would dominate the renewal of the Centrum over the next two and a half decades. In no other major world city today are young householders, whether students or young professionals, in such command of the city center.

The initial provocations were creatively reinvoked in 1970, when the 'Orange Free State' was declared as an alternative popular government rallying around the last Provo city councillor, a key figure in the Provo movement who was named ambassador to the 'old state' and who today sits again on the Amsterdam City Council as representative of perhaps the most radical anarchist-Green party in Europe. More recently, when it came time to assign a council-member to oversee the current plans to construct a luxury office and upscale housing development in the old Oosterdok waterfront – Amsterdam's antici-pated version of London's Docklands – the same radical anarchist environ-mentalist became the obvious choice. No better symbol can be found of the continuing impact of the twentysomethings: compromised to be sure, far from having any absolute power, but nevertheless aging with significant virtue, commitment, and influence.

The final renewal came with the full-scale squatter or *kraken* movement, beginning in 1976. From its famous 'No Housing No Coronation' campaign in 1980, the movement did not decline so much as become a generalized radical pressure group protesting against all forms of oppression contained within what might be called the specific geography of capitalism, from the local to the global. Squatters, for example, merged into the woman's movement, the anti-nuclear and peace movements, the protests against apartheid (a particularly sensitive issue for the Dutch) and environmental degradation (keeping Amsterdam one of the world's major centers for radical Green politics); as well as against urban speculation, gentrification, factory closures, tourism, and the siting of the Olympic games in Amsterdam. Its greatest local success and ironically the cause of its apparent decline in intensity was to keep the right to accessible and affordable housing at the top of the urban political agenda by 'convincing the local authorities of the urgency of building more housing for young households and of prohibiting the destruction of cheap housing in the central city for economic restructuring, gentrification, or urban renewal.'[6]

The population of Amsterdam peaked around 1965 at over 860,000. Twenty years later the total had dropped to a little over 680,000, but the Centrum had already begun to grow again and after 1985 so has the city as a whole. There are many factors that affected this turnaround, but from a comparative perspective none seem more important than that peculiar blend of democratic spatial planning and regenerative social anarchism that has preserved the Inner City as a magical center for youth of all ages, a stimulating possibilities machine that is turned on by active popular participation in the social construction of urban space.

Off Spuistraat

Anybody who grows up in Amsterdam invariably finds himself (sic) in the area of tension between the imprisonment of the ring of canals and the centrifugal escape via the exit roads of the city. In this area of tension one may not even know major parts of the city and still be an Amsterdammer....

From my very first visit to Los Angeles in the early 1970s, I have had the feeling that the major Dutch cities (with Amsterdam in the lead) deny out of sentimental considerations the fact that they are part of a larger whole (an area as large and diffuse as Los Angeles) and as such completely ignore a dimension of an entirely different order from the one which they traditionally know.

(Dutch architect Rem Koolhaas, in "Amsterdam: An Architectural Lesson," p. 112)

At first glance, a comparison of Los Angeles and Amsterdam seems as impossible as comparing oranges and potatoes. These two extraordinary cities virtually beg to be described as unique, incomparable, and of course to a great extent they are. But they are also linkable as opposite and apposite extremes of contemporary urbanization, informatively positioned antipodes that are almost inversions of one another yet are united in a common urban experience. First I will annotate the more obvious oppositions.

Los Angeles epitomizes the sprawling, decentered, polymorphic, and centrifugal metropolis, a nebulous galaxy of suburbs in search of a city, a place where history is repeatedly spun off and ephemeralized in aggressively contemporary forms. In contrast, Amsterdam may be the most self-consciously centered and historically centripetal city in Europe, carefully preserving every one of its golden ages in a repeatedly modernized Centrum that makes other remnant mercantile capitalist 'Old Towns' pale by comparison. Both have downtowns of roughly comparable area, but only 1 of 100 Angelenos live in the City's center, whereas more than 10% of Amsterdammers are Centrum dwellers.

Many residents of the City of Los Angeles have never been downtown and experience it only vicariously, on television and film. Very few now visit it to shop (except for excursions to the garment district's discount stores and the teeming Latino mercados along Broadway); and surprisingly few tourists take in its local attractions, at least in comparison to more peripheral sites. Amsterdam's Centrum receives nearly 8 million tourists a year and is packed daily with many thousands of shoppers. Amsterdammers may not be aware of the rest of the city, but they certainly know the center.

It has been claimed that nearly three-quarters of the surface space of downtown Los Angeles is devoted to the automobile and to the average Angeleno freedom and freeway are symbolically and often politically inter-twined. Here the opposition to Amsterdam's Centrum, second only to Venice in auto-prohibition, is almost unparalleled. It is not the car but the bicycle that assumes, for the Amsterdammer, a similarly obsessive symbolic and political role, but it is an obsession filled not with individual expression and automaniacal freedom as much as with a collective urban and environmental consciousness and commitment. This makes all the contrasts even more stark.

Amsterdam's center feels like an open public forum, a daily festival of spontaneous political and cultural ideas played at a low key, but all the more effective for its lack of pretense and frenzy. Its often erogenous geography is attuned to many different age groups and civically dedicated to the playful conquest of boredom and despair in ways that most other cities have forgotten or never thought possible. Downtown Los Angeles is almost pure spectacle, of business and commerce, of extreme wealth and poverty, of clashing cultures and rigidly contained ethnicities. Boredom is assuaged by overindulgence and the bombardment of artificial stimulation; while despair is controlled and contained by the omnipresence of authority and spatial surveillance, the substitution of police for *polis*. Young householders are virtually non-existent. In their place are the homeless, who are coming close to being half the central city's resident population despite vigorous attempts at gentrification and dispersal.

In compact Amsterdam, the whole urban fabric, from center to periphery, is clearly readable and explicit. From its prime axis of the Damrak and Rokin (built above the former route of the Amstel River), the city unfolds in layers like a halved cross-section of an onion, first in the 'old side' and 'new side' (with an Old Church and New Church appropriately placed and streets named by their position inside or outside the old city walls), then in the neat crescents of the ringing canals from the inner to the outer Singel girdles, and finally in segments and wedges of inner and outer suburbs, many of which are helpfully named Amsterdam North, East, Southeast, South, and West. This morphological regularity binds Amsterdammers to traditional concepts of urban form and function and encourages its urbanists to be unusually cautious of new theories of urban transformation.

In comparison, Los Angeles seems to break every rule of urban readability and regularity, challenging all traditional models of what is urban and what is not. One of America's classic suburbias, the San Fernando Valley, is almost wholly within the jig-sawed boundaries of the monstro-City of Los Angeles, while many inner city barrios and ghettoes float outside on unincorporated county land. There is a City of Industry, a City of Commerce, and even a Universal City, but these are not cities at all. Their combined populations would be outnumbered by the weekday shoppers on the Kalverstraat. Moreover, in an era of what many have called post-industrial urbanization, with cities being emptied of their manufacturing employment, the Los Angeles region has continued its century-long boom in industrial growth, in both its core and periphery. It is no surprise, then, that Southern California has become a center for innovative and non-traditional urban theory, for there seems little from conventional, established schools of urban analysis that any longer makes sense.

And then there is that most basic of urban functions, housing. One of the most interesting features of the success of the squatter movement in Amsterdam was the absence of a significant housing shortage. Although much of the Centrum is privately owned, the rest of the city is a vast checkerboard of public, or social housing, giving Amsterdam the distinction of having the highest percentage of public housing stock of any major capitalist city, around 80% and still growing I was told. Even what the Dutch planners consider the worst of these projects, such as the huge Bijlmermeer high-rise garden suburb, served effectively to accommodate the thousands of migrants from Surinam and other former colonies during the 1970s in housing that appears embarrassingly substandard primarily to the Dutch.

As noted earlier, the squatter movement was more than just an occupation of abandoned offices, factories, warehouses, and some residences. It was a fight for the rights to the city itself, especially for the young and for the poor. Nowhere has this struggle been more successful than in Amsterdam. Nowhere has it been less successful than in Los Angeles. In the immediate post-war period, Los Angeles was poised to become the largest recipient of public housing investment in the country, with much of this scheduled to be constructed in or around downtown. In no other American city did plans for public housing experience such a resounding defeat by so ferociously anti-socialist campaigners. The explosion of ethnic insurrections in the 1960s and early 70s cruelly accelerated the commercial renewal of downtown at the expense of its poor residential inhabitants. On the central city's 'new side' grew a commercial, financial, governmental, and high cultural fortress, while the 'old side,' beyond the skyscraper walls, was left to be filled with more residual land uses, from the tiny remnants of El Pueblo de Nuestra Senora de Los Angeles (where the city was born over 200 years ago) to the fulsome Skid Row of cardboard tenements and streetscapes of despair, to the Dickensian sweatshops and discount marts of the expansive Garment District.

The core of my oppositional comparison is thus amply clear. But what of the periphery, or the 'larger whole,' as Rem Koolhaas called it? Are there comparative dimensions 'of an entirely different order' that are missed when we focus on the antipodal centralities of Amsterdam and Los Angeles? For the remainder of this interpretive essay, I will set the two cities in a larger, more generalizable context that focuses on contemporary processes of urban restructuring. Here, the cities follow more similar paths than might initially seem possible. These similarities are not meant to contradict or erase the profound differences that have already been described, but to supplement and expand upon their emphatic and extreme particularity.

My own research and writing on the urban restructuring of Los Angeles has identified five intertwined trends that have become increasingly apparent not only in Los Angeles but in most of the world's major urban regions.[7] Each trend takes on different intensities and forms in different cities, reflecting both the normality of geographically uneven development and the social and ecological particularity of place. More important than their individual trajectories, however, is their correlative interconnectedness and the tendency for their collective impact to define an emerging new mode of urbanization, significantly different from the urbanization processes that shaped the industrial capitalist city during the long post-war boom period.

It is appropriate to begin with the *geographical recomposition of urban form*, for this spatial restructuring process deeply affects the way we look at the city and interpret the basic meaning of urbanization. As with the other trends, there is a certain continuity with the past, lending credence to the argument that restructuring is more of an acceleration of existing urban trajectories rather than a complete break and redirection. The current geographical recomposition, for example, is in large part a continuation on a larger scale of the decentralization and polynucleation of the industrial capitalist city that was begun in the last half of the nineteenth century and became periodically accelerated as more and more population segments and economic sectors left the central city.

There are, however, several features of the recent round of polynucleated decentralization that suggest a more profound qualitative shift. First, the size and scale of cities, or more appropriately of *urban regions*, has been reaching unprecedented levels. The older notion of 'megalopolis' seems increasingly inadequate to describe a Mexico City of thirty million inhabitants or a 'Mega-York' of nearly twenty-five, stretching from Connecticut to Pennsylvania. Never before has the focus on the politically-defined 'central' city become so insubstantial and misleading. Complicating the older form still further has been the emergence of 'Outer Cities,' amorphous agglomerations of industrial parks, financial service centers and office buildings, massive new residential developments, giant shopping malls, and spectacular entertainment facilities in what was formerly open farmland or a sprinkling of small dormitory suburbs. Neither city nor suburb, at least in the older senses of the terms, these reconcentrated poles of peripheral urban and (typically 'high-tech') industrial growth have stimulated a new descriptive vocabulary. In addition to Outer City there is also Edge City, Technoburb, Technopolis, Postsuburbia, and my own preferred term, Exopolis.[8]

The growth of Outer Cities is part of the recentralization of the still decentralizing urban region, a paradoxical twist that reflects the ability of certain areas within the regional metropolis (including not only 'greenfield' sites but the inner cities as well) to compete within an increasingly globalized economy. Over the past twenty-five years, the decentralization of manufacturing and related activities from the core of the older industrial capitalist cities broke out from its national containment. Jobs and factories continued to move to suburban sites or non-metropolitan areas within the national economy, but also, much more than ever before, to hitherto non-industrialized regions of the old Third World, creating a new geographical dynamic of growth and decline that not only has been changing the long-established international division of labor but also the spatial division of labor within urban regions.

The geographical recomposition is paradigmatically clear in Greater Los Angeles. Within a radius of 60 miles (100 kilometres) from the booming Central Business District of the misshapen City of Los Angeles there is a radically restructured regional metropolis of nearly 15 million people with an economic output roughly equivalent to that of the Netherlands. At this scale, a comparison with Amsterdam seems totally inappropriate. But if we follow Rem Koolhaas' 'centrifugal escape' via the exit roads of the city, a different picture emerges. A

100-kilometre circle from Amsterdam's Centrum cuts through Zeeland, touches the Belgian border near Tilburg, curves past Eindhoven (where Philips is headquartered) to touch the German border not far from Nijmegen, and then arcs through the heart of Friesland to the North Sea. Most of the nearly 15 million Dutch live within this densely urbanized region and its scale and productivity come close to matching its Southern California counterpart.

The southwest quadrant of this 'Greater Amsterdam' coincides rather neatly with the Randstad, which can, with a little stretching, be seen as a kind of Outer City in itself, but with the defining central core being not an old urban zone but the determinedly preserved rural and agricultural 'Green Heart.'[9] Around the Green Heart are the largest cities of the Netherlands: Amsterdam (700,000), Rotterdam (575,000), The Hague (445,000), and Utrecht (230,000), each experiencing a selective redistribution of economic activities between central city, suburban fringe, and more freestanding peripheral centers. As a whole, the Randstad contains the world's largest port (Los Angeles-Long Beach is now probably second), Europe's fourth largest international financial center (after London, Zurich, and Frankfurt) and fourth largest international airport (Schiphol, surpassed in traffic only by Frankfurt, Paris, and London).

Like Greater Los Angeles, Greater Amsterdam has been experiencing a complex decentralization and recentralization over the past twenty-five years.[10] How useful this larger scale comparison of geographical recomposition might be to a further understanding of urban restructuring I will leave to others to determine. For present purposes, however, it at least forms a useful antidote to 'Centrumitis,' the Amsterdammer version of 'Manhattanitis,' the tendency of urban observers to see the contemporary period of restructuring too narrowly due to an excessive focussing on the dense central city, thereby ignoring a dimension of an entirely different order from the one they traditionally know (quoting Koolhaas, for the last time).

The recomposition of urban form is intricately connected to other sets of restructuring processes. Already alluded to, for example, has been *the increasing internationalization of metropolitan regions*, leading to the formation of a new kind of world city. Amsterdam in its Golden Age was the prototypical model of the world city of mercantile capitalism and it has survived various phases of formation and reformation to remain among the higher ranks of contemporary world cities, whether combined in the Randstad or not. What distinguishes the global cities of today from those of the past is the *scope* of internationalization, in terms of both capital and labor. To the control of world trade (the primary basis of mercantile world cities) and international financial

investment by the national state (the foundation of imperial world cities) has
been added the financial management of industrial production and producer
services, allowing the contemporary world city to function at a global scale
across all circuits of capital. First, Second, and Third World economies have
become increasingly integrated into a global system of production, exchange, and
consumption that is sustained by an information-intensive and 'de-territorialized'
hierarchy of world cities, topped today by the triumvirate of Tokyo, New
York, and London.

Los Angeles and Amsterdam are in the second tier of the restructured world
city hierarchy, but the former is growing much more rapidly and some predict
it will join the top three by the end of the century. Amsterdam is more stable,
maintaining its specialized position in Europe on the basis of its concentration
of Japanese and American banks, the large number of foreign listings on its
Stock Exchange (second in the world to London), the strong and long-established
export-orientation of Dutch companies, and its control over Dutch pension
funds, reputed to be 40% of Europe's total.[11] The banking and financial
services sector remains a key actor in Amsterdam's Centrum, feeding its
upscale gentrification and drawing strength from the information-rich clustering of government offices, university departments, cultural facilities, and
specialized activities in advertising and publishing.

A characteristic feature of increasing internationalization has been an
erosion of local control over the planning process, as the powerful exogenous
demands of world city formation penetrate deeply into local decision-making
processes. Without a significant tradition of progressive urban planning, Los
Angeles has welcomed foreign investment with few constraints. Its downtown
'renaissance' was built on foreign capital to such an extent that today almost
three-quarters of the prime properties in the Central Business District are
foreign-owned or at least partially controlled by overseas firms. The large
number of Japanese firms in particular now routinely contribute to local
political campaigns and fund-raising cultural activities, and have even made
loans to the City government to maintain its pension fund program. The
internationalization of Amsterdam has been more controlled, as one would
expect, but the continued expansion of the city as a global financial management center is likely to pose a major threat to many of the very special qualities
of the Centrum.

The other side of internationalization has been the attraction of large numbers
of foreign workers into almost every segment of the local labor market, but
especially at lower wage and skill levels. Los Angeles today has perhaps the largest
and most culturally diverse immigrant labor force of any major world city, an
enriching resource not only for its corporate entrepreneurs but also for the cultural

life of the urban region. Amsterdam too is fast-approaching becoming a 'majority minority' city, a true cosmopolis of all the world's populations. With its long tradition of effectively absorbing diverse immigrant groups and its contemporary socialist and socializing governance system, Amsterdam appears to have been more successful than Los Angeles in integrating its immigrant populations, socially and spatially, into the urban fabric. One achievement is certain: they are better housed in Amsterdam, for Los Angeles is currently experiencing one of the worst housing crises in the developed world. As many as 600,000 people, predominantly the Latino working poor, now live in seriously overcrowded conditions in delapidated apartments, backyard shacks, tiny hotel rooms, and on the streets.

Intertwined with the geographical recomposition and internationalization of Los Angeles and Amsterdam has been a pervasive *industrial restructuring* that has come to be described as a trend toward a 'Post-Fordist' regime of 'flexible accumulation' in cities and regions throughout the world. A complex mix of both deindustrialization (especially the decline of large-scale, vertically integrated, often assembly-line, mass production industries) and reindustrialization (particularly the rise of small and middle-size firms flexibly specializing in craft-based and/or high technology facilitated production of diverse goods and services), this restructuring of the organization of production and the labor process has been associated with a repatterned urbanization, a new dynamic of geographically uneven development.

A quick picture of the changing Post-Fordist industrial geography would consist of several characteristic spaces: older industrial areas either in severe decline or partially revived through adaptation of more flexible production and management techniques; new science-based industrial districts or techno-poles typically located in metropolitan peripheries; craft-based manufacturing clusters or networks drawing upon both the formal and informal economies; concentrated and communications-rich producer services districts, especially relating to finance and banking but also extending into the entertainment, fashion, and culture industries; and some residual areas, where little has changed. It would be easy to transpose this typology to Greater Los Angeles, for much of the research behind it has been conducted there. Although the Post-Fordist restructuring has not gone nearly as far in Amsterdam, the transposition is also quite revealing.

The Centrum has been almost entirely leached of its older, heavier industries and 25% of its former office stock has been lost, primarily to an impressive array of new subcenters to the southeast, south, and west (e.g., Diemen, Amstelveen, and Sloterdijk) and to the growing airport node at

Schiphol (15 kilometres away), where more than 35,000 people are now employed. One might argue, as many Dutch observers do, that this dispersal represents a sign of major decline in the inner city, due in part to a shift from a concentric to a more grid-like pattern of office and industrial development.[12] Just as convincing, however, is a restructuring hypothesis that identifies the Centrum as a flexibly specialized services district organized around international finance and banking, university education, and diverse aspects of the culture and entertainment industries (fashions, especially for the twenty-somethings, television and film, advertising and publishing, soft drugs and sex, and, of course, tourism, with perhaps the most specialized attractions in the world for the young and the poor traveller). Except for the University of Amsterdam, which is being pressured to reduce his space in the Centrum, each of these other specialty areas has started to reconcentrate in recent years in the information-intensive inner city.

A fourth trend needs to be added, however, before one goes too far in tracing the impact of Post-Fordist industrial restructuring. This is the tendency toward *increasing social and economic polarization* that seems to accompany the new urbanization processes. Recent studies have shown that the economic expansion and restructuring of Los Angeles has dramatically increased poverty levels and hollowed out the middle ranks of the labor market, squeezing job growth upward, to a growing executive-professional-managerial 'technocracy' (stocked by the largest urban concentrations in the world of scientists, engineers, and mathematicians); and downward, in much larger numbers, to an explosive mix of the 'working poor' (primarily Latino and other immigrants, and women, giving rise to what has been called the 'feminization of poverty') and a domestic (white, African-American, and Mexican-American, or Chicano) 'urban underclass' surviving on public welfare, part-time employment, and the often illegal opportunities provided by the growing informal, or underground economy.[13] This vertical and sectoral polarization of the division of labor is reflected in an increasing horizontal and spatial polarization in the residential geography of Los Angeles. Old and new wealth is increasingly concentrated in protected communities with armed guards, walled boundaries, 'neighbor-hood watches,' and explicit signs that announce bluntly: 'Trespassers will be shot'; while the old and new poor either crowd into the expanding immigrant enclaves of the Third World City or remain trapped in murderous landscapes of despair.[14] In this bifurcating urban geography, all the edges and turf boundaries become potentially violent battlefronts in the continuing struggle for the rights to the city.

This dark picture of contemporary Los Angeles can be inverted to describe a brighter side to urban restructuring, but such a flip-flopping description is too simple and would only dilute the need to recognize and respond to the urgent problems facing this still expansive, and still largely unresponsive, urban region. Here again, the Amsterdam comparison is both informative and ambiguously encouraging, for it too has been experiencing a process of social and economic polarization over the past two decades and yet it has managed to keep the multiplying sources of friction under relatively successful social control. The Dutch 'Job Machine,' for example, shows a similar hollowing out of the labor market, with the greatest growth occurring in the low-paid services sector.[15] Official unemployment rates have been much higher than in the U.S., but this difference is made meaningless by the contrasts in welfare systems and methods of calculating the rate itself. Overall job growth, as in almost every other OECD member country, has been much lower than in the U.S. and, except for the producer (i.e., mainly financial) services sector, there has been a decline in high-wage employment, thus limiting the size of the executive-professional-managerial 'bulge.' Increasing flexibility in the labor market, however, is clearly evident in the growth of 'temporary' and 'part-time' employment, with the Netherlands having the largest proportion of part-time workers in the EEC and perhaps the highest rate (more than 50%) in the Western World for women.[16]

Terhorst and Van de Ven have examined the particular forms taken in Amsterdam by the widespread expansion of low-wage, often temporary and/or part-time services jobs.[17] Focussing on the revival of personal services, they gently provide evidence of social and economic polarization in Amsterdam and link this to restructuring processes elsewhere in the world. But again, there is a more human face to this polarization in Amsterdam. Personal services have flourished with expanding immigration, the entry of larger numbers of women into the low-wage workforce, the growth of the informal economy, and the gentrification of the Centrum, but the downside of this process has been ameliorated by, and indeed made to contribute to, the very special nature of the inner city area.

With its exceptional concentration of young, educated, often student households, high official levels of unemployment, still solid social security system, and two distinctive waves of gentrification (one fed by the high-wage financial services sector and the other by multi-job households typically comprised of former students and squatters still committed to maintaining the distinctive quality of life in the Centrum), an unusual synergy has developed around the personal services sector and between various age and income groups. As Terhorst and Van de Ven point out, income polarization has been producing a growing complementarity between the higher and lower income groups with respect to the flexible use of time and place, especially in the specialized provision of such personal services as domestic help and babysitting, late-night shopping, entertainment and catering, household maintenance and repair, educational courses and therapies, fitness centers, bodycare activities, etc.. Such activities in Amsterdam take place primarily in the underground economy and are not captured very well in official statistics. They are also not likely to be a major factor in stimulating rapid recovery from economic stagnation and crisis. But they nonetheless provide a legitimate and socially valuable 'survival strategy' for the poor and unemployed that has worked effectively to constrain the extreme effects of social polarization that one finds in Los Angeles or New York City. Moreover, it is a strategy that draws from the peculiar urban genius of Amsterdam, its long tradition of grass roots communalism, its sensitive adaptation to locality, its continuing commitment to libertarian and participatory social and spatial democracy, and its unusual contemporary attention to the needs of the twentysomething generation.

There is, of course, a dark side to this revival of personal services in Amsterdam's Centrum and the Dutch analysts are always careful to point it out. But here again, the comparative perspective produces a different picture. Viewed comparatively, the restructuring of the Centrum over the past twenty-five years has produced two reconfigurations of the urban political economy that distinguish Amsterdam from other major urban regions. The first arises from what may be the most successful urban implementation of the anarchist, environmentalist, and 'situationist' principles that mobilized the student and other social movements in the 1960s in cities all over the world. That this success is far from complete and continues to be constrained and challenged by both internal and external forces takes nothing away from its distinctive achievement relative to other urban regions. That it can be better understood by rooting it in the deeper historical context of the 'moralizing geography' of Dutch culture and its always paradoxical 'embarrassment of riches' I have discovered after my stay in Amsterdam and have only begun to explore in this essay, thanks mainly to the magnificent spade-work of Simon Schama.

The second distinctive quality of Amsterdam becomes clearer when conjoined with the first and linked to the current literature on flexible specialization and urban-industrial restructuring. Although it would require much more empirical analysis to demonstrate convincingly, there appears to be taking shape in the Centrum of Amsterdam a new kind of specialized agglomeration that is as reflective of current trends in the world economy as the technopoles of California, the craft-based industrial districts of the 'Third Italy,' or the concentrated nodes of global financial management and control in Lower Manhattan and the City of London. It is primarily a services agglomeration, although small scale, technologically advanced, design and information intensive industries remain a significant part of the 'complex.' Producer services, especially in banking and finance, are also very important, for the Centrum remains the focus for a major world city of global capitalism. The most intense and decidedly flexible specialization, however, is locally focussed, extraordinarily innovative, and more advanced in Amsterdam than perhaps anywhere else in the developed world. A large part of its innovativeness lies in the simultaneous preservation and modernization of a unique urban heritage and built environment at a lively human scale. That it has not yet become a Disney-fied theme park for tourists is another achievement rooted both in the power of historical traditions of participatory democracy and socially responsible planning, and in the contemporary influence of several generations of twentysomething activism. This has produced a services complex of remarkable diversity and interpersonal sensitivity, in which basic needs take precedence over market demands to a degree difficult to find in any other world city center. I have no idea what to call this specialized space, but however it might be categorized it is worthy of much greater attention, analysis, and appreciation.

I had originally intended to conclude by addressing *postmodernism and postmodernization* as a fifth restructuring theme and to explore the extent to which this restructuring of the 'cultural logic' of contemporary capitalism can be traced into the comparison of Amsterdam and Los Angeles. In my own recent research and writings, I have argued that a neo-conservative form of postmodernism, in which 'image' replaces reality and simulated and 'spin-doctored' representations assume increasing political and economic power, is significantly reshaping popular ideologies and everyday life all over the world and fast becoming the basis for a new mode of social regulation designed to sustain the development of (and control the resistance to) the new Post-Fordist regimes of 'flexible' and 'global' capitalist accumulation and the accompanying 'new urbanization processes' discussed on the preceding pages. After experiencing Amsterdam, where resistance to the imposition of this neo-conservative postmodernism seems exceptionally strong, it is tempting just to add another polar opposition to the comparison with Los Angeles, where this process is probably more advanced than almost anywhere else on earth. But I will leave the issue open for future research and reflection, and conclude with another example of the 'stimulus of a little confusion' – a suggestion that perhaps the entire text of this paper arises from the political challenges posed in its last paragraph.

Notes

1. The 'miracle' apparently occurred when a sick man, unable to swallow the communion bread, spit it into a fireplace where it remained whole and unburnt.

2. My thanks to Léon Deben, Dick van der Vaart and Jacques van de Ven, for sponsoring my stay in Amsterdam, along with the Department of Social Geography of the University of Amsterdam. Very special thanks also to Pieter Terhorst of the Department of Social Geography, who more than anyone else warmly and informatively shaped my understanding of Amsterdam.

3. I have been told that civic authorities now issue pamphlets on 'How To Be A Squatter' in Amsterdam, still another example of creatively regulated tolerance.

4. For an interesting analysis of the geography of hash coffee shops in Amsterdam, see A.C.M. Jansen, 'Hotelling's Location Game and a Geography of Hashish and Marijuana,' *Geoforum*, vol. 20, 1990. Jansen has written extensively on the retail geography of the Centrum. I wish to thank him here for taking me on a wonderful tour of the inner city.

5. One guidebook lists the following cafe types, each with its own internal variations: white, brown, and neo-brown; cocktail bars, gay bars, beer cafes, student cafes (differentiated by dress codes and academic disciplines), literary cafes, chess cafes, ping-pong cafes, squatters' cafes, theatrical cafes, high tech cafes, 8-2 cafes, discotheques, and night pubs.

6. Virginie Mamadouh, 'Three Urban Social Movements in Amsterdam: Young Households in the Political Arena Between 1965 and 1985,' revised version (September 1989) of a paper presented at the conference on 'The Urban Agglomeration as Political Arena,' Amsterdam, June 1989, p. 15. My thanks to Ms. Mamadouh for giving me a copy of this informative paper and for chatting with me about urban social and spatial movements in Amsterdam.

7. See Edward W. Soja, *Postmodern Geographies: The Reassertion of Space in Critical Social Theory*, Verso (1989).

8. See Edward W. Soja, *Postmodern Geographies: The Reassertion of Space in Critical Social Theory*, Verso (1989).

9. In one of the strangest of ironies, this Green Heart is a primary source of air and water pollution in the Netherlands. The dangerous effluents arise not from factories or automobiles but from the superabundance of livestock.

10. See, for example, Marc de Smidt, 'In Pursuit of Deconcentration: The Evolution of the Dutch Urban System from an Organizational Perspective,' *Geografiska Annaler*, 69B (1987), 133-43; and J. H. T. Kramer, 'The Airport of Schiphol: Economic and Spatial Impact,' *Tijdschrift voor Econ. en Soc. Geografie*, 79 (1988), 297-303.

11. H.W. ter Hart and J. Piersma, 'Direct Representation in International Financial Markets: The Case of Foreign Banks in Amsterdam,' *Tijdschrift voor Econ. en Soc. Geografie*, 81 (1990), 82-92.

12. H.J. Brouwer, The Spatial Restructuring of the Amsterdam Office-Market, The Netherlands Journal of Housing and Environmental Research, Vol.4, no. 3, 1989.

13. See, for example, Paul Ong et al, *The Widening Divide*, a project report by students and faculty of the Urban Planning Program, UCLA, 1989.

14. For a vivid exploration of the dark side of contemporary Los Angeles, see Mike Davis, *City of Quartz*, Verso (1990).

15. Pieter A. Boot and Maarten Veraart, 'The Dutch Labour Market,' *Tijdschrift voor Econ. en Soc. Geografie* 78 (1987), 399-403.

16. The labor market participation rate for women in the Netherlands (34.5% in 1985) is relatively low for Europe and much below the figure for the U.S.. Rates of growth in participation have been very high during the 1980s, however, as large numbers of women entered the labor market for the first time, especially in part-time jobs. See Boot and Veraart, *op.cit.*.

17. Pieter Terhorst and Jacques van de Ven, 'The Revival of Personal Services in Cities: An Expression of Polarization?' *Neth. J. of Housing and environmental Res.*, 1 (1986), 115-138.

Urbanity, tolerance and public space
The creation of cosmopolitans

Lyn H. Lofland

How are people who, when within the privacy of their households or the community of their fellowships, pray to diverging or different gods – how are such people 'to live together in one city'? This, Richard Sennett tells us (1990: 233), is a question that bedeviled classical Greece. It is a question that bedevils us yet today and it is the larger version of the question I am going to try to address here.

Though largely obscured by the chorus of anti-urbanism produced during the last several centuries[1], the rare voices of those who love the city can sometimes be discerned. These voices seek to celebrate the city, especially the 'great city'-places like London or Hong Kong or New York or San Francisco or Amsterdam. Among their rationales for celebration is the assertion that the great city solves the question bedeviling classical Greece. Those who wish to celebrate it argue that the great city is, in and of itself, a settlement form which generates cosmopolitanism among its citizenry; it is a settlement form that produces – by its very nature – a populace that is far more open to and accepting of human variability, far more inclined to civility and less to fanaticism and smug parochialism than are the residents of more homogeneous and intimate settlement forms like tribe, village or small town. In a 1968 review of novelistic images of New York City, the American sociologist, Anselm Strauss, captured this rationale succinctly.

> One classic theme of the urban novel pertains to the diversity of every large city's social worlds and populations. Drawn from the four quarters of the earth (...) the city teems with the people of different races, origins, cultures, and beliefs. Diversity is celebrated for it gives rise to cosmopolitanism. The very multiplicity of populations permits and fosters worldliness – for the city itself and for those of its citizens who 'get around' (1968, p. 6).

Or to quote a perhaps more familiar figure: 'the juxtaposition of divergent personalities and modes of life,' wrote Louis Wirth, 'tends to produce a relativistic perspective and a sense of toleration of differences' (1969: 155, originally published in 1938).

Now at one level, there would seem to be considerable truth to this claim. Our conventional wisdom tells us that as compared with small towns and villages, cities do seem to be 'tolerant' sorts of places. In them, very diverse peoples do live in relative peace. There are, of course, many exceptions, but cities do appear – more than other sorts of places – to allow human variety to be openly expressed. In Robert Parks words:

> Because of the opportunity it offers, particularly to the exceptional and abnormal types of man, a great city tends to spread out and lay bare to the public view in a massive manner all the human characters and traits which are ordinarily obscured and suppressed in smaller communities (1925: 45-46; initial version published in the American Journal of Sociology, 1915).

This passage from his essay 'The City' is probably quoted as frequently as it is because, in fact, it seems to capture what many of us would see as an obvious truth. Nonetheless, anyone who has ever lived in a city or who has ever read a newspaper knows that there is considerable distance between the 'imagery' of the city as the creator of cosmopolitanism and the reality. Cities may generate cosmopolitanism and tolerance, they may create civility in the face of heterogeneity, they may, as Park claimed, provide a stage for ways of being which are 'obscured and suppressed in smaller communities,' but they do not inevitably do so.

So now, the question that concerns me begins to come more clearly into focus. I want to inquire into this matter of how, if cities manage to create civility in the face of heterogeneity, do they do it? To paraphrase Donald Olsen (1988/1990: 9), what do cities 'do' to people to make them urbane? My pursuit of this query is divided into four sections. In the first, I will briefly review some research findings and speculations which address – however obliquely – the question of how cities generate civility. In the second section, I will offer a social psychological – more specifically a symbolic interactionist social psychological – reinterpretation of these findings and speculations. Third, I will attempt to trace the implications of these findings/speculations for the 'ideal' design of urban public space. And in the fourth and final section, I will draw a few conclusions about the meaning of all this for the real, extant world of urban public space.

Before I proceed, however, let me a. mention a rather thorny philosophical and ethical critique that is sometimes made about concerns such as those expressed here and b. define my central terms.

a. It can be argued that ideas like tolerance, cosmopolitanism, civility, and so forth and that serious concern with those ideas have a profoundly conservative character, that they are supportive to the status quo. Thus, to be blase about heterogeneity, for example, is to be blase and unconcerned about the inequities of class and power, about the hegemony of dominant ideologies, about the cruelty of exploitation, about the dangers inherent in some perspectives and groups. (Within the United States uneasiness among some otherwise 'liberal' groups over certain defenses of speech rights made by the American Civil Liberties Union reflects aspects of this critique.) Obviously I cannot here deal seriously with such a charge. Let me just say that I think it contains some kernels of truth. For moral people, there clearly must be limits to tolerance (presumably, for example, an intolerance for intolerance). Perhaps there is need to differentiate among types of tolerance, forms of cosmopolitanism, and so forth. Perhaps these terms themselves are too broad, contain to many diverse images to be especially useful to the social scientist. But I would also argue that the history of the world seems not to suggest any great surfeit of tolerance or cosmopolitanism or civility. At least initially, until we can get to more sophisticated dissections of the phenomena, it seems to me fully justified, both sociologically and ethically, to be concerned with the production of what our philosophical forefathers of the Enlightenment hoped would be a new and better human being. As the historian Gerard De Puymege has noted in his excellent study of the emergence of the concept of fanaticism, 'The need for tolerance, consonant with nature, is a leitmotif of Enlightenment literature (...). Voltaire went furthest on this path. In his view, fanaticism more than despotism, is the principal enemy of liberty, while tolerance for him is the *backbone of a civilized society.*' (1983: 22)

b. I shall, in what follows, be using the related terms tolerance, tolerant, cosmopolitan, cosmopolitanism and civility in their essentially common sense meanings; that is, in their standard dictionary[2] senses. Thus, by *tolerance*, I mean 'a permissive or liberal attitude toward beliefs or practices differing from or conflicting with one's own,' a 'breadth of spirit or of viewpoints.' By *tolerant*, I imply the display of 'understanding or leniency for conduct or ideas differing from or conflicting with one's own.' Or, more delightfully put, to be tolerant is to 'bear contrariety mildly.' The *cosmopolitan* is defined as being 'marked by interest in, familiarity with, or knowledge and appreciation of, many parts of the world.' He or she is 'not provincial, local, limited or restricted by the attitudes, interest, or loyalties of a single section or sphere of activity.' The cosmopolitan is 'marked by sophistication and savoir faire arising from [presumably] urban life and wide travel.' *Cosmopolitanism* is a 'climate of opinion, distinguished by the absence of narrow, national loyalties or parochial prejudices and by a readiness to borrow from other lands or regions in the formation of cultural or artistic patterns.' And, finally, *civility* may be understood simply as 'civil conduct,' in the sense of 'decent behavior and treatment.'

Creating cosmopolitans: research and speculation

To recapitulate: I am pursuing the question of the link between great cities and cosmopolitanism and I propose to begin this pursuit by here reviewing a body of research work which – sometimes directly, sometimes indirectly – seems relevant to my concerns. Two words of caution. First, as I suggested above, while most of this research starts with some empirical materials, it tends quickly to move beyond them into speculation – informed speculation, but speculation nonetheless. I shall have to do the same. Second, also as suggested, I will not provide detailed accounts of the various pieces of research here under review, but will simply summarize the conclusions that can be drawn from them. To learn what each of the researchers was actually doing, the reader will have to return to the original publications.

This work on the relationship between urbanness and urbaneness – as the American sociologist Samuel Wallace[3] has phrased it – provides a considerable range of 'factors' or 'variables' or 'conditions' which are thought to 'contribute to,' 'make possible,' 'account for' urban cosmopolitanism, tolerance and public civility. These conclusions are most easily summarized if we start by drawing a distinction between two 'types' of tolerance: negative and positive. *Negative tolerance* is the capacity to 'put up with' another's difference from self because the different other is simply not perceived and/or because self and other do not intersect. Example: an American male 'tolerates' what he believes to be disgusting changes in the liturgical practices of the Roman Catholic Church because he attends mass only at highly conservative churches. *Positive tolerance*, in contrast, is the capacity to 'put up with' an others *fully recognized* differences from self even under conditions of intersection and, perhaps, sometimes, to do so with a mild appreciation for, or enjoyment of, those differences. A nice example of positive tolerance is found in the responses of some of Léon Deben's informants who, describing the homeless encampment in the Artis Zoo area of Amsterdam, used such words as 'freedom,' 'own identity,' 'interesting,' 'free of shackles' (1990: 16).

Accomplished research and the speculation from that research, then, suggest that *negative tolerance* is generated when:

a. PEOPLE SHARE A LARGER BOUNDED SPACE BUT NOT THE SMALLER PIECES OF IT. Robert Park's contention, which I quoted earlier, that the great city 'tends to spread out and lay bare (...) all the human characters and traits which are ordinarily obscured and suppressed in smaller communities' rested on a view of the city as a 'mosaic' of social worlds which touched but did not interpenetrate' (1925: 40). More recent scholars have continued to echo this theme: the highly specialized space use of the modern city (Lofland, 1985) segregates diversity into homogeneous enclaves, thus making it possible for diverse groups to 'live together' in the same city because they are essentially invisible to one another (see, for example, Hall, 1966; Horowitz, 1987; Hurst, 1975; Karp, Stone & Yoels, 1977, 1991; Lynch, 1960, 1972). Concepts like 'spatial myopia' (Karp, Stone & Yoels, 1977: 145, 1991: 124) have been invented to describe the situation. Ulf Hannerz did not use that term, of course, but he would seem to have been talking about 'spatial myopia' when he wrote that the built environment of Amsterdam is 'dense, unpredictable, unsurveyable, uncontrollable (...) allow[ing] some activities to go unseen, or at least allow[ing] the excuse that they are not seen, whenever one prefers not to see' (1992, p. 19).

b. PEOPLE PHYSICALLY SHARE SMALLER SPACES WITHIN THE LARGER SPACE BUT SEGREGATE THEMSELVES FROM ONE ANOTHER SYMBOLICALLY. Thus, for example, the argument is made by people like Pierre van den Berghe, that in the preindustrial city, given the clear visual signalling of identities and a rigidly controlled system of hierarchy, diverse individuals and groups, despite sharing the same space at the same time, not only did not intersect socially, they often probably did not – in any meaningful sense – 'see' one another (1970; see also, Lofland, 1985). Similarly, many contemporary urban Americans, via the mechanism of non-person treatment (Goffman, 1963: 84), seem able to render the homeless – ubiquitously present on the streets of most urban centers – largely invisible (Anderson, Snow & Cress, forthcoming).

Now 'out of sight, out of mind' – the essence of negative tolerance – is certainly not what city aficionados mean whey they celebrate their preferred settlement form as the mother of cosmopolitanism. No, the central celebrative assertion about the city is that its citizenry is capable of living with human heterogeneity and doing so with civility and at least of modicum of appreciation. How do people come to be like that? Work on the more positive alternative suggests that *positive tolerance* is generated when:

a. DIVERSE PEOPLE ARE NOT SEGREGATED INTO HOMOGENEOUS ENCLAVES AND ARE FORCED TO SETTLE WHATEVER CONFLICTS ARISE AMONG THEM WITHOUT RECOURSE TO CENTRALLY IMPOSED INSTRUMENTS OF ORDER. This, of course is Richard Sennetts argument, one he first promulgated in

Uses of Disorder (1970) and later developed in *The Fall of Public Man* (1977). Under these circumstances, he argues, people learn that they can act together without the necessity to be the same. He adds, however, a crucial proviso. If conflict is not to escalate into violence and thereby undercut the tolerance-producing capacity of the process, the stakes must not be so high that 'winning' is crucial. Whatever conditions ensure that winning will not be crucial (for example, a decent and widely shared level of affluence) must be met.

b. PEOPLE HAVE MASTERED THE COMPLEXITY OF THE URBAN ENVIRON-MENT SUFFICIENTLY TO MOVE THROUGH IT WITH A HIGH DEGREE OF PSYCHIC SAFETY. The argument here is that, since widespread personal knowledge of others is impossible in the city (because of the sheer size and heterogeneity of the population), the mastery of short-hand methods for accurately interpreting who people are and what they are up to allows urbanites to conduct themselves in an appropriate manner under a wide variety of situations and thus allows them to confront the heterogeneity of the city with a minimum of distrust and fear (Anderson, 1990; Lofland, 1985: chapters 5 & 8). A proviso, often mentioned in this regard, is that the environment itself must offer sufficient physical safety to avoid the pro-duction of an urban guerilla or garrison-state mentality, even among the knowledgeable.

c. THE LEVELS OF COMMUNITY CLOSEST TO THE ACTOR (THE HOME, THE IMMEDIATE NEIGHBORHOOD) ARE SECURE AND NON-THREATENING. That is, people can learn to tolerate diverse (and thus potentially threate-ning) others only if they have available to them safe enclaves within which to withdraw (see, for example, Jacobs, 1961; Rieder, 1985; Wallace, 1980.)

d. PEOPLE ARE ABLE TO CONTROL THE CHARACTER AND QUALITY OF THEIR CONTACT WITH DIVERSE OTHERS. The argument is that if close contact is forced, if persons must forego their autonomy over the depth of involve-ment with the different other, tolerance will not be produced (Becker & Horowitz, 1972; Love, 1973; Karp, Stone & Yoels, 1977, 1991).

e. PEOPLE POSSESS CERTAIN DEMOGRAPHIC CHARACTERISTICS, THOSE CHAR-ACTERISTICS THEMSELVES GENERATING A CAPACITY FOR TOLERANCE. Characteristics mentioned in the literature include: highly educated, high status, single, and childless (see, for example, Becker & Horowtiz, 1972; Fischer, 1971; Karp, Stone & Yoels, 1977, 1991). Scholars making this sort of argument also point up the contribution of the contextual effect, that is, as persons are surrounded by others who are more tolerant, they themselves may become more tolerant (Stouffer, 1955; Smith & Peterson, 1980; Wilson,

1985). In this regard, let me just mention that cities or sections of cities that we tend to think of as highly tolerant – the center of Amsterdam, Manhattan, some of the closer-to-the-center neighborhoods of San Francisco – are, in fact, characterized by such population profiles. In the early 1970's, for example, Willem Heinemeijer (1972) was reporting that the inhabitants of the central area of Amsterdam were predominately 20-30 year old, had a high level of educational attainment, and often lived alone.

That then is the bare bones version of the data (and speculations arising from them) on urbanity and tolerance. What I want to do now is to interpret these data and speculations in terms not quite identical to – though, I hope, not in violation of – those used by the authors themselves.

Creating cosmopolitans: a reinterpretation

As I hope I have made clear, the empirical base for these ideas about urban tolerance is considerably less than rock solid. Many of the ideas and speculations arise not out of well-grounded observations of empirical regularities, but out of 'impressions' about what is the case. Even when the indicators of tolerance are empirically grounded, they may not be ones that other scholars – or the researcher, for that matter – find totally satisfactory (verbal expressions rather than behavior, for example) And it is clear that what these various researchers mean by tolerance or cosmopolitanism is not always the same. Nonetheless, despite such drawbacks, there is much to be learned from this work. It gives us a place to start and it points the way toward a more systematic approach to the question of whether and how great cities generate cosmopolitanism. As a small step (and I want to emphasize *small* step) in the direction of that more systematic approach, I intend, as I said I would, to recast this material; to mine it for what it may suggest to us about the link or links between urban living and urbane people; between cities on the one hand and urbanity and tolerance on the other. Before I do so, however, let me locate this rather micro concern within the larger contextual frame also pointed to by this body of work.

The Societal Context for Tolerance. Explicitly and, more frequently, implicitly, most of the work here reviewed tells us that any serious pursuit of questions about cities and cosmopolitanism cannot proceed purely at the social psychological level. We need to ask further about the cultural, economic, historic, political and ideological context within which a tolerance for diversity (of what sorts) may exist and/or flourish. Certainly the linkages are not simple ones, commonsensically given. Urban milieux that might be characterized as cosmopolitan – 18th Century London, Imperial Rome, Berlin in the early

1930's – were themselves extant within societies characterized by great economic inequalities and/or political despotism (a reason, perhaps, for the disease in some quarters about the value of tolerance). And even with the framework of totalitarian religious ideologies, glimmerings of urbaneness may be found (contemporary Teheran, for example). Let me emphasize, then, my recognition of the fact that in talking about urban relationships and urbane people without mention of their highly complex macro-context – as I am about to do – I am omitting what are certainly crucial elements of the story.[4]

Urban Relationships and Urbane People. However differently they may phrase it, the various scholars who have thought about these matters all can be read (or read into) as suggesting that the presence of urbanity, tolerance, civility, cosmopolitanism, in oneself *is linked to a distance in the relationship between self and the relevant other or others. That is, the different other is tolerable, perhaps even worthy of appreciation only if, psychically or physically (that is, symbolically or spatially), he or she is sufficiently distant to pose no threat.*

When negative tolerance is at issue, the link between tolerance and distance is self-evident. By definition, negative tolerance implies psychic and/or physical space between self and other. But distance is a recurring element in discussions of positive tolerance as well. When Sennett suggests that conflicts that can be settled without recourse to centralized authority are those not involving 'crucial' issues, he is implying the necessity for a certain amount of distance between perceived self-interest and the issues/persons with whom one is in conflict. Similarly, to say that short-hand methods of knowing are needed to master the urban environment is to say that persons will have knowledge of one another without being close to one another. The arguments about the necessity for home and neighborhood to be secure and about the utility of controlled contract do not even require translation to be read as saying that the persons and places closest to self must pose no threat and that potentially threatening others must not be allowed to come too close. So too, lines of thought regarding population characteristics and cosmopolitans may be understood as arguing that those persons whose family or other statuses allow them the freedom to 'distance' themselves from unlike others (for example, their children are not required to play together, there is no necessity that they live at close quarters) are most tolerant.

From a social psychological point of view, more specifically, a symbolic interactionist social psychological point of view, this hypothesized link between symbolic and spatial distance on the one hand and tolerance on the other is certainly not surprising. Interactionists take as a given the vulnerability of the self, its need for on-going confirmation, validation, and support. Interactionists would also take as given the fact that the very existence of counter-realities (inherent in most human heterogeneity) poses a potential threat to that self. Further, interactionist understandings about the generation and maintenance of the self lead to a third given: that the most serious psychic assaults on oneself are likely to come from those most significant or closest to one. In short, serious differences between self and other in close or intimate relationships generate not tolerance but cleavage. Obviously, negative tolerance, by definition, is precluded in an intimate relationship. One is not having an intimate relationship with someone who is both 'out of sight and out of mind.' But positive tolerance is precluded as well. That is, if I may shift the language of the argument slightly, urbanity (cosmopolitanism) is generally not possible in the primary group. Intimate voluntary relationships (friendships, modern marriages, links between adult children and their parents), even not-so-intimate kin or community relationships, seem to require for their maintenance a good deal of similarity between or among the parties. As such, while intimate relationships may *preach* positive tolerance, they cannot *teach* it.

In this last assertion, I have, I think, violated our (at least an Americans) common sense understandings of these matters. What better teacher of cosmopolitanism can be imagined than the inter-ethnic or inter-cultural or sub-cultural friendship group? What better demonstrator of the creed of the worth and equality of all humans than the family that takes unto itself, via adoption or marriage, a new member from a different religion, class, life style, race? Yet the point I wish to make – more accurately: the hypothesis I wish to put forth – is that what is being taught in such groupings has nothing to do with urbanity, tolerance or cosmopolitanism. The lesson learned – both by participants and observers – from such 'fusions of heterogeneity' is that some kinds of differences are unnecessary barriers to closeness. Put simply, the lesson is: others may say that characteristic Y makes A very different from B, but experience teaches that A and B are very much alike and that Y is irrelevant. Translated into highly sexist but familiar language: this is the 'brotherhood of man under the fatherhood of god' kind of idea. Were all human beings under the skin. The differences between and among us are superficial and should not get in the way of appreciating our mutual membership in the human family.

This is a very appealing notion, of course. And in some contexts it is a very useful one. But tolerance, cosmopolitanism, urbanity, have nothing to do with such a notion. *Much to the contrary, tolerance, cosmopolitanism, urbanity are about the fact that humans differ significantly along important lines and that these differences matter to them. Tolerance, urbanity, and cosmopolitanism have to do with living civilly with such a reality*.

The idea of relational 'distance' pointed to so consistently, if not always explicitly, by those sociologists who have thought about the link between the urban and the urbane, between city living and urbanity, then, may be phrased in another way. The learning of tolerance, the creation of cosmopolitanism may require the existence of and repeated experience with 'non-intimate' 'non communal' relationships. *Limited, segmental, episodic, distanced links between self and other, may constitute the social situations that both allow and teach civility and urbanity in the face of significant differences.* And this assertion brings us to the matter of public space.

Urbanity, tolerance, and ideal public space

The urban public spaces of cities are among the very few settings which, on a recurring basis, *can* provide (they may not and, often, do not do so) the opportunity for individuals to experience limited, segmental, episodic, distanced links between self and other. Such spaces are, in fact, probably the locus for a significant portion of all non-communal, non-intimate relationships which humans form with one another (Lofland, 1994). When negotiating a crowded intersection, when managing civil disattention (Goffman, 1963) on a crowded tram or subway, when watching the human comedy play itself out on a plaza, when giving or receiving minor assistance (what Carol Brooks Gardner [1986] calls 'public aid'), when purchasing a drink or a meal, in these and myriad other ways, it seems to me, persons in the public space of cities can truly learn the lesson that 'one can act together [more accurately, one can *interact*] without the necessity to be the same' (Sennett, 1970, 1977).

I have just said that urban public spaces *may* provide the settings for this important lesson but that they do not inevitably do so. What, then, does my argument imply about what public space ought, ideally, to be like? Let me offer for your consideration four characteristics.

1. The city should be small and compact – a pedestrian or mass transit-oriented city. This allows people, naturally, as a part of their daily lives, to be in public space just as a consequence of getting from point A to point B.

2. If the city spatially segregates persons and functions (and almost all contemporary cities do this to some degree), the segregation should be quite small-scale. This allows people, naturally, as a part of their daily lives, to encounter diverse others.

3. The difference between and among the citizens must be viewed by them as 'meaningful' differences. That is, they must, in the normal course of their everyday lives, rub shoulders with – accomplish uneventful interactions with – persons of whom they disapprove, with whom they disagree, toward

whom they feel at least mild antipathy or who evoke in them at least mild fear. That means that any city that is capable of teaching urbanity and tolerance must have a hard edge. Cleaned-up, tidy, purified, disney-land cities (or sections of cities) where nothing shocks, nothing disgusts, nothing is even slightly feared may be pleasant sites for family outings or corporate gatherings, but their public places will not help to create cosmopolitans.

4. I have just said that a city must have a hard edge; its public space must – at least occasionally – generate mild fear. But the crucial fourth and final characteristic is that a city's public space must not be viewed by its citizenry as 'too' dangerous. Beyond some minimal level of fear, they will not venture forth and then, of course, no lessons can be learned.[5]

In sum and put somewhat differently: To teach tolerance – to create cosmopolitans – a city must show a substantial amount of 'anarchy.' But if the anarchy is not to overwhelm and negate the lesson, it must be regulated. A city characterized by a 'highly regulated urban anarchism,' to use Soja's (1991: 11) description of Amsterdam, will be a tolerant, a cosmopolitan city.

Urbanity, tolerance, and the 'real world' of public space

In this final section, I want to explore four implications of the above argument not for an ideal public space but for urban public space as it is currently constituted or as planners and others hope it will be constituted.

First, if there is any validity at all to this argument, then it is clear that some of the expectations that planners, urbanists, politicians, and academicians hold for public space, some of the 'functions' they expect it to serve are not very realistic.

Jan Oosterman (1992) has argued that planners and architects and city government officials often have very high – and in his view, unrealistic – expectations of what will happen in public space, especially in plazas. These locales, they anticipate, will serve as democratic centers for political and cultural exchanges, centers where people will manage to breach whatever barriers of difference separate them and come together in some kind of community. His own study (1993) of a highly sociable plaza-type area in Utrecht suggests that people are doing nothing of the sort. While the people he observed were certainly tolerant of surrounding others who were unlike themselves, their fellowship groupings, their sociability clusters, were remarkably homogeneous. Of course, if, as I have argued, serious diversity is impossible in intimate relationships, then this is hardly surprising. And Oosterman's conclusion that urban public space is extremely unlikely to create any great amount of 'community' among diverse others seems absolutely 'on target.'

Similarly, Richard Sennetts hope, expressed in his most recent book, *The Conscience of the Eye* (1990), that somehow if we just design cities correctly, their public spaces will allow individuals to find their balance, to eschew a desire for wholeness and completeness and thus come to terms with themselves as individuals-in-process, in sum, to become 'centered,' seems, again, highly unrealistic. Certainly for some persons, encounters with diversity, as Thaddeus Mullers research on the 'warm city' (1992) suggests, do seem to have the transformative potential that Sennett predicts. But given the self-threatening character inherent in human diversity, I dont think we ought to count on such transformations for the multitudes.

A second implication is, that if we are willing to forego positive tolerance, if we are content to live only with negative tolerance, then cities in many parts of the world, most especially cities in the richest countries of the world, can just go on playing out the logic of the large-scale spatial segregation and architectural features that have marked their growth patterns for the last several hundred years. In fact, one might sardonically suggest that many contemporary cities (most particularly in the United States where urban devotion to automobile-generated spatial organization is religious in character) were deliberately designed to avoid even the possibility of positive tolerance. Such cities can, of course, ensure tolerance for their diverse citizenry only as long as everyone agrees to stay tidily in their respective homogeneous enclaves. But any failure to stay 'in place' may have serious, sometimes fatal, consequences. Los Angeles seems to be such a city, as does Brasilia. Mike Davis (1992, see also 1990) has written that the spatial organization of Los Angeles is best described by an 'ecology of fear' composed of a variety of mutually fearful large-tract and internally-homogeneous 'social control districts': abatement districts, enhancement districts, containment districts, exclusion districts. And Marshall Bermans description of Brasilia, echoed in every study of that city with which I am familiar, captures a corollary feature. '[O]ne's overall feeling (...) is of immense empty spaces in which the individual feels lost, as alone as a man on the moon. There is a deliberate absence of public space in which people can meet and talk, or simply look at each other and hang around' (1988, p. 7). In some U.S. cities, where the 'hard edge' has not been contained within a large-scale district, homogeneous enclaves have been achieved architecturally. Enclosed suburban shopping malls, security-conscious galleries of the central cities, and second or third story level sky-way systems that link fortress-like parking garages with offices and retail establishments all ensure that persons of diverse class, ethnic, or other status groups can, relative to one another, remain 'out of sight and out of mind.' To enter Chicago's Michigan Avenue galleria, for example – which is presumptively a shopping center open to everyone

– is to leave behind on the cold streets anyone who fails to pass the scrutiny of the security guards – and that will include the homeless, the poor, the inebriated, the non-respectable young, the political activist. Or, to enter Spokane, Washington's, Cincinnati, Ohio's or Atlanta Georgia's skyway systems is to enter an almost exclusively middle-class world where women who clean toilets for a living and men who work from the backs of garbage trucks can only be glimpsed when one is on the 'bridges' between the buildings and then only if one deliberately looks down, onto the street, some one or two stories below.

A third implication is that the fear of urban crime among urban residents – which many sociologists tend to dismiss as unrealistic – must be taken very seriously. Relative to Amsterdam, for example, an American visitor, especially, might be forgiven for viewing expressed concerns with 'rising crime rates' as merely alarmist. Yet Lodewijk Brunt (1992) has certainly found high levels of fear among residents of certain areas of the city – levels of fear which, in fact, do see to lead persons to avoid some public spaces. Again, if the argument I have been developing here has any validity, anyone who values and hopes to preserve Amsterdam's world-famous urbanity, tolerance and cosmopolitanism cannot afford to dismiss Brunt's findings. We are forced to concede that the young muggers being studied by Gert Vogel (1992) are far more dangerous than either their numbers or the volume of their crimes would signify.

Finally, the fourth implication of what I have been saying is that the efforts of those few cities whose public spaces are currently conducive to the generation of urbanity and tolerance (Amsterdam, for example) to become 'fun cities,' disneylands for visiting corporate executives and visitors on bus tours, should give us pause. What the citizens of Amsterdam, by simply living their lives in a compact, minimally segregated city with a hard edge and a reasonable level of safety, have learned to tolerate, the executive from Chicago and the family from Spokane are likely to find unendurable. To make the world safe for such visitors is to risk destroying the precious environment of their hosts.[6]

Notes

1. Largely produced by American and British intellectuals. See, for example, Schorske, 1968; White & White, 1962.

2. *Webster's Third New International Dictionary (Unabridged), 1971).*

3. Wallace, 1980.

4. See, for example, the Becker & Horowitz case study of *Culture and Civility in San Francisco* (1972), in which they argue quite persuasively that the city's vaunted cosmopolitanism is, in part, a product of particular historical circumstances (e.g., the Barbary

Coast tradition and a strong liberal working class presence). On the cultural, historical, economic and ideological context of Dutch tolerance, see Goudsblom, 1967; Schama, 1988.

5.   Some cities noted for their tolerance do, in fact, seem – on the surface at least – to meet these ideal criteria. San Francisco and Amsterdam, for example, are both relatively compact settlements characterized by small-scale spatial segregation. In fact, both cities may be considered historical anomalies due to the rather late expansion of their boundaries. While many 19th c. European and American cities were galloping into their surrounding countrysides, citizens of San Francisco and Amsterdam continued to live in compact settlements which were densely packed by many small scale specialized areas. Also, both cities were historically and are now viewed by their surrounding societies as deviant and/or 'sinful' (i.e., both have a hard edge), yet in neither city is the level of fear sufficient to keep people off the streets. A careful comparative study of these two settlements might yield much information about the conditions for urbanity and tolerance.

6.   I am enormously grateful to all the people who shared with me their knowledge and love of Amsterdam and who helped me to feel at home in this wonderfully cosmopolitan and tolerant city. Particular thanks are due to Lodewijk Brunt, Leon Deben, Willem Heinemeijer, Thaddeus Muller and Gert Vogel. Thanks also to Heleen Ronden for her generous assistance in transcribing and thus clarifying a portion of the question and answer section of my lecture.

References

Anderson, Elijah
    1990   *StreetWise: Race, Class, and Change in an Urban Community*. Chicago: The University of Chicago Press.

Anderson, Leon, David S. Snow, and Dan Cress
    forthc.   'Negotiating the Public Realm: Stigma Management and Collective coming Action Among the Homeless.' In Spencer E. Cahill & Lyn H. Lofland (eds.), *The Community of the Streets*. Greenwich, Connecticut: JAI Press.

Becker, Howard and Irving Louis Horowitz
    1972   *Culture and Civility in San Francisco*. New Brunswick, New Jersey: Transaction Books.

Berghe, Pierre van den
    1970   'Distance Mechanisms of Stratification,' In: *Race and Ethnicity: Essays in Comparative Sociology*. New York: Basic Books.

Berman, Marshall
    1988   *All That is Solid Melts Into Air: The Experience of Modernity*. New York: Penguin Books. (Originally published by Simon & Schuster, 1982.)

Brunt, Lodewijk
    1992   'Coping With Urban Danger.' Amsterdam: University of Amsterdam Working Papers in Sociology.

Davis, Mike
    1990   *City of Quartz: Excavating the Future in Los Angeles*. New York: Vintage Books.

1992 *Beyond BladeRunner: Urban Control, The Ecology of Fear.* Westfield, New Jersey: Open Magazine Pamphlet Series.

Deben, Leon
1990 'Urban Landsquatting: Another Way of Living in Amsterdam.' Amsterdam: University of Amsterdam Working Papers in Sociology.

De Puymege, Gerard
1983 'From Priest to Philosopher: The Origins of the Concept.' In: Andre Haynal, Miklos Molnar and Gerard De Puymege, *Franaticism: A Historical and Psychoanalytical Study.* New York: Schocken Books.

Fischer, Claude
1971 'A Research Note on Urbanism and Tolerance.' *American Journal of Sociology*, 76: 847-856 (March).

Gardner, Carol Brooks
1986 'Public Aid.' *Urban Life*, 1:37-69 (April).

Goffman, Erving
1963 *Behavior in Public Places.* New York: The Free Press.

Goudsblom, Johan
1967 Dutch Society. New York: Random House.

Hall, Edward
1966 *The Hidden Dimension.* Garden City, New York: Doubleday

Hannerz, Ulf
1992 *Culture, Cities and the World.* Amsterdam: Centrum voor Grootstedelijk Onderzoek.

Heinemeijer, W.F. and R. van Engelsdorp Gastelaars
1972 'Conflicts in Land Use in Amsterdam.' *Tijdschrift voor Economische en Sociale Geografie*, Mei/Juni: 190-199.

Horowitz, Ruth
1987 'Community Tolerance of Gang Violence.' *Social Problems*, 34: 437-450 (December)

Hurst, Michael
1975 *I Came to the City.* Boston: Houghton, Mifflin.

Jacobs, Jane
1961 *The Death and Life of Great American Cities.* New York: Vintage Books.

Karp, David A., Gregory P. Stone and William C. Yoels
1977 *Being Urban: A Social Psychological View of City Life.* Lexington, Massachusetts: D.C. Heath & Company.
1991 *Being Urban: A Sociology of City Life*, Second Edition. New York: Praeger.

Lofland, Lyn H.
1985 *A World of Strangers: Order and Action in Urban Public Space.* Prospect Heights, Illinois: Waveland Press. (Originally published by Basic Books, 1973.)

1994   'Social Interaction: Continuities and Complexities in the Study of Non-Intimate Sociality.' In: Karen Cook, Gary Alan Fine & James House (editors), *Sociological Perspectives on Social Psychology*. New York: Allyn & Bacon.

Love, Ruth Leeds
1973   'The Fountains of Urban Life.' *Urban Life and Culture* (now *Journal of Contemporary Ethnography*), 2:161-209 (July).

Lynch, Kevin
1960   *The Image of the City*. Cambridge, Massachusetts: MIT Press.
1972   *What Time is This Place?* New York: Harcourt, Brace.

Muller, Thaddeus
1992   'Amsterdam Inner-City Life: Intimate Aspects of Social Interactions in the Public Domain.' Presented to the conference on European Cities: Growth and Decline, The Hague, April 13-16, 1992.

Olson, Donald J.
1988/1990 *Time and the City & Urbanity, Modernity and Liberty: Two Essays on Urban History and Amsterdam*. Amsterdam: Centrum voor Grootstedelijk Onderzoek.

Oosterman, Jan
1992   'Welcome to the Pleasure Dome. Play and Entertainment in Urban Public Space: The Example of the Sidewalk Cafe.' Paper presented to the conference on European Cities: Growth and Decline, The Hague, April 13-16, 1992.
1993   *Parade der passanten: de stad, het vertier en de terrassen*. Utrecht: Uitgeverij Jan van Arkel.

Park, Robert
1925   'The City: Suggestions for the Investigation of Human Behavior in the Urban Environment.' In: Robert E. Park, Ernest W. Burgess and Roderick D. McKenzie, *The City*. Chicago: The University of Chicago Press.

Rieder, Jonathan
1985   *Canarsie: The Jews and Italitans of Brooklyn Aginst Liberalism*. Cambridge, Massachusetts: Harvard University Press.

Schama, Simon
1988   *The Embarrassment of Riches: An Interpretation of Dutch Culture in the Golden Age*. Berkeley: University of California Press.

Schorske, C.E.
1968   'The Idea of the City in European Thought: Voltaire to Spengler.' In: Sylvia Fava (ed.), *Urbanism in World Perspective*. New York: Thomas Y. Crowell.

Sennett, Richard
1970   *The Uses of Disorder: Personal Identity and City Life*. New York: Vintage Books.
1977   *The Fall of Public Man*. New York: Alfred A. Knopf.
1990   *The Conscience of the Eye: The Design and Social Life of Cities*. New York: Alfred A. Knopf.

Smith, Leslie Witener and Karen K. Peterson
1980   'Rural-Urban Differences in Tolerance: Stouffer's 'Culture Shock' Hypothesis Revisited.' *Rural Sociology*, 45: 256-271 (Summer).

Soja, Edward W.
  1991   *The Stimulus of a Little Confusion: A Contemporary Comparison of Amsterdam
           and Los Angeles.* Amsterdam: Centrum voorGrootstedelijk Onderzoek.

Stouffer, Samuel
  1955   *Communism, Conformity and Civil Liberties.* Garden City, New York: Doubleday.

Strauss, Anselm
  1968   'Urban Perspectives: New York City.' In: Anselm Strauss (ed.), *The American City:
           A Sourcebook of Urban Imagery.* Chicago: Aldine Publishing Co.

Vogel, Gert
  1992   'Reversal of the Tourist Gaze? Mugging in Amsterdam.' Department of Sociology,
           University of Amsterdam. Unpublished paper.

Wallace, Samuel E.
  1980   'The Urbanite.' Knoxville, Tennessee: Slide Tape Research Systems.

White, Morton & Lucia White
  1962   *The Intellectual Versus the City: From Thomas Jefferson to Frank Lloyd Wright.*
           Cambridge, Massachusetts: Harvard University Press.

Wilson, Thomas C.
  1985   'Urbanism and Tolerance: A Test of Some Hypotheses Drawn from Wirth and
           Stouffer.' *American Sociological Review*, 50: 117-123 (February).

Wirth, Louis
  1969   'Urbanism as a Way of Life,' In: Richard Sennett (ed.), *Classic Essays on The Culture
           of Cities.* Englewood Cliffs, New Jersey: Prentice-Hall.

The cultural dimension in restructuring metropolises
The Amsterdam example

Paul Claval

Impressions of Amsterdam

There are two ways for a foreigner to discover Amsterdam. First impressions are completely different if one comes by train (I) than if one arrives by car or plane (II).

Amsterdam I

Arriving at the Central Station, the visitor is immediately immersed in a city of the Baroque Age (Figure 1). Wonderful tall and narrow brick mansions with picturesque gables mirror in scores of canals. The streets are bustling with pedestrians and cyclists, many of them of exotic descent. Much of the traffic is by streetcar. The only metropolis in the Western world where such an extensive old city centre has been preserved is Venice – partly for the same reason, the canals, and for a long time the fact that it was so difficult to build houses higher than four storeys. The centre of Amsterdam is very much alive, with a large residential population and tens of thousands of commuters employed in banking and a wide variety of professions, or headed for the thriving shopping streets such as Kalverstraat or Leidsestraat. Tourism is one of the major industries, and the city has more to offer than its great museums. The night life around Rembrandtplein or Leidseplein attracts numerous foreigners, as do the Red Light and drug district of the core area.

In the former working-class neighbourhood the Jordaan, as in other parts of the old city, fascinating social and cultural metamorphoses have taken place. Until the 1970s, the aging of the residential population resembled similar processes virtually throughout the core areas of Western cities. It has recently been replaced by a rejuvenation process. Many of the young residents are students, as is the case in Groningen, the Netherlands, in Cork, Ireland, in Santiago de Compostela, Spain, and in Poitiers or Aix-en-Provence, France, but these cities are much smaller than Amsterdam. The new residents include many well-educated young couples, but few of the yuppies elsewhere associated with the gentrification process. As emphasized by Edward Soja,[1] the creativity of contemporary Amsterdam is certainly best exemplified by this evolution.

The fascinating *Provo*, *Kabouter* and squatters' movements[2] of the 1960s and 1970s aroused the curiosity of urban specialists. The utopian radical atmosphere of the 1960s and 1970s waned in Amsterdam, as it did all across the globe, but its impact was less ephemeral than most observers anticipated. Whenever social experiments such as 'communes' developed in rural environments, they faded without leaving any permanent imprint. The fate of urban movements was generally similar, but there were a few exceptions: San Francisco in America and Amsterdam in Western Europe. Both cases were associated with drug use and sexual permissiveness, the allure of which has since been reduced by AIDS and changing attitudes. In Amsterdam, the drug culture is still in evidence. Cheap and virtually legal hashish is certainly one reason why so many young people from Europe, America or elsewhere visit the city, but what they enjoy goes deeper, and is based on different aspects of the social experiments.

The success of the Jordaan is intriguing. Traditionally a lower-class area, its architecture is less impressive than in other parts of the city centre, and competition for housing was consequently not very fierce in the 1960s. Industrial use of the premises there decreased, and residential use took its place. These factors explained the concentration of young bachelors or couples, all looking for housing they could afford. There were, however, also more significant reasons for the area's popularity. They had to do with its physical characteristics: low houses and narrow streets allow for high density, and convey a feeling of conviviality which is important to the young generation of urban dwellers. The small informal-looking houses are more reminiscent of village life than the impressive aristocratic mansions or dignified apartment houses of most eighteenth or nineteenth century neighbourhoods. The population concentration is high enough for a wide variety of commercial and personal services to be available close by. A new urban way of life developed. Part of its charm is the wide variety of social relations it easily provides, as is only feasible in urban areas where public transportation is good. One of the severe constraints it implies is: no cars. Its attraction thus only works for social groups who can accept the idea of reduced mobility in exchange for specific forms of social relations.

For foreign visitors, the older part of town is generally the only one worth exploring. Many of the Dutch people who are there in the daytime and at night

Figure 1. Amsterdam I, II and III.

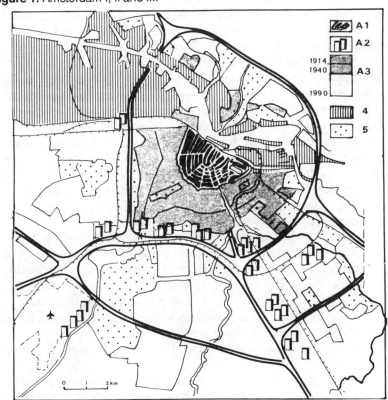

Legend:
1. Amsterdam I: the Medieval and Baroque city
2. Amsterdam II: developments of the 1980s
3. Amsterdam III: the city of the Industrial Revolution and the Socialist Era
4. The harbour district
5. Parks and wooded areas

commute from the outer ring and suburbs, but there is also a substantial number of permanent residents. They have little reason to leave the downtown district and often ignore the other parts of the metropolitan area.

Amsterdam II

Foreign businessmen who come for a quick meeting with their Dutch counterparts get quite a different impression of Amsterdam (Figure 1). They land at Schiphol Airport, and head directly for one of the new office districts.[3] Most of the office buildings have been built along the major motorway, railway and mass transit corridors: the main axis from Schiphol to the city, and the ringway from Teleport to the west to Amsterdam-Zuid through the World Trade Centre and RAI. Almost all the huge office buildings and exhibition centres along these axes date from the past fifteen years. The architecture of many of them has a distinctive post-modern flavour. Amsterdam II is a city of lawns, hedges, and steel, concrete and glass buildings. Silver or blue metallized glass dominate.

Some of the major Amsterdam hotels are located along the ringway near the main office concentrations. Businessmen who come to talk shop have no reason to go to downtown Amsterdam. They have excellent accommodations with all the services they need close to the sites where their meetings are scheduled. If they do have any time at all to visit Amsterdam I, it is often for a drink at one of the spots near Rembrandtplein or Leidseplein, or for a boat trip along the canals. They ignore the real life of this part of the city.

Amsterdam II has the urban ecology (an expression coined by Reinhart Barnham to refer to Los Angeles) of the no-place metropolises of our global time.[4] It was conceived to provide maximum interaction opportunities with business partners. Even if post-modernism has introduced some fancy features into the built environment, the whole setting is an outstanding example of functional planning for a transient population with no reason to go to Amsterdam except to encounter other transient people.

Amsterdam I and Amsterdam II are in close proximity, but many visitors are only acquainted with either one or the other. To a certain extent, this is also true of Amsterdamites, at any rate those of them who virtually never leave the central part of the city, or the businessmen, professionals, executives and managers who rarely go downtown, most of whom live outside Amsterdam I and II in Amsterdam III, which is largely ignored by visitors.

Amsterdam III

Most of the metropolitan area escapes the attention of tourists and foreign businessmen (Figure 1). It consists of three ecologies: the outer ring of the city, the huge developments to the west, south, southeast and north of the city,[5] and the low density suburbs Gooi and Kennemerland. Most of the people who work in Amsterdam live in these areas.

Expansions of the seventeenth-century fortifications began to be constructed when the growth of the city resumed at the beginning of Industrial Revolution in the Netherlands in the 1870s.[6] The 1877 Kalff Plan was still based on the concentric street lay-out that had characterized the development of the city from 1612 onward. The Plan Zuid, drawn up by Berlage in 1917, did not change this. The neighbourhoods conceived according to Berlage's plan and built by the architects of the Amsterdam School differed from the late nineteenth-century ones in their social dimension. Amsterdam III is to a large extent a socialist city. No other metropolitan area in the Western world has been so profoundly influenced by Social Democratic ideals (except perhaps Stockholm, and up to a point Tel Aviv; the experience in Frankfurt was a short-lived one). Urban expansion was planned for a dignified middle class, in which blue collar and white collar workers were to merge. Everyone was to have good housing and an excellent network of public services: schools, libraries, athletic facilities, and an efficient transport system based on tramways. The quality of architecture was excellent, but the uniformity could sometimes be a bit oppressive.

In the 1920s and 1930s, it became clear that the expansion of Amsterdam could not go on indefinitely on the traditional concentric street patterns. Cars were invading in the city. The decision was made in 1935 to initiate a new type of urban structure. For the first time, the growth of a major city was planned according to revolutionary principles. Instead of the concentric or radio-concentric patterns which resulted elsewhere from market economies, Amsterdam was to stop the expansion of the massive concentric structure, leave a small zone of empty land, and organize the new developments along radial corridors of transport, with green zones in between. The ideas developed by urban planners in Amsterdam were soon emulated all over the World. In keeping with the specifics of the city, planning solutions were sought in radial expansion along a few axes, the development of new towns, or the creation of a parallel city able to compete with the old one. Everywhere the idea of inventing progressive city forms prevailed.

The overall urban design changed in 1935, but the Social Democratic orientation remained dominant. With the use of reinforced concrete, it was possible to build higher. Amsterdam urban developers anticipated or adhered to many of the ideas of the International Congresses of Modern Architecture, as formulated in the Charter of Athens. As a result, just before World War Two, Sloten was conceived as a garden city, and the new areas of Bijlmermeer, Buitenveldert and Amsterdam-Noord, launched in the late 1950s, were designed in the prevalent international style. No more bricks, streets and canals, but green spaces and huge lakes in the central areas of the new neighbourhoods. The desire to create an egalitarian socialist city was as clear as in the outer ring of the period between the two world wars.

Tramways and railways made long-range commuting feasible in the 1880s and 1890s. Men of substance liked to live in handsome houses in the wooded sandbelts to the west (Kennemerland) and east (Gooi) of the city. With

Amsterdam's growing tendency toward socialism, the contrast between suburbs and areas controlled by the city became stronger. Amsterdam III is an interesting case of segregation between a majority of lower and middle-class people in the central part of an urban area, and a wealthier elite in municipalities run according to different social and political principles.

From Amsterdam II to Amsterdam III

There is ostensibly no continuity between Amsterdam II and Amsterdam III. The recent transformations of Amsterdam were only partly the responsibility of the municipality. Planners participated in an expansion they did not conceive or control. Even if the national government does consult the municipalities, it is responsible for the plans that are central to restructuring the agglomeration. It cooperates with Amsterdam as regards the exploitation and expansion of Schiphol. It plans new motorways and railways.

Because of the decisions made in 1935, an empty zone was left between the densely built central part of the city and the new expansions. The ringway was drawn according to the potentials thus provided. It is – or will be – combined with railways and subways, good connections to Schiphol and the whole Randstad.

Amsterdam II is more the result of national government decisions than the outcome of a careful plan drawn up by the municipality.[7] This is only logical in a way, since in order to compete in the new global economy, the Netherlands relies heavily on the performance of Schiphol, the Amsterdam urban area and the whole central part of the Netherlands. Even if the levels of interaction among the various cities in the Randstad are lower than their proximity suggests,[8] they all benefit from the global connections at Schiphol.

Amsterdam III is a reflection of the growing importance of metropolization in a global economy, and its relations to Amsterdam I and II are a local illustration of the conflicts associated with the ensuing spatial restructuring.

Globalization and metropolization as interrelated processes

Traditional organization of international economic relations

From the beginning of the nineteenth century to the 1950s or 1960s, the main trends in the evolution of the world economy did not change much. Concentrated forms of energy, coal and later oil, and the use of steam and later internal combustion engines and electric turbines made it feasible to develop large-scale manufacturing. The improved productivity of land and labour allowed for a better food supply, and fewer people were employed in the farming sector. Steam ships and later motor ships and railways reduced transport costs, thus opening world markets to new raw materials, food products and manufactured goods. The newly emerging large-scale international economies favoured central locations – hence the dynamic tension between cities' centres and their peripheries, and the concentration of manufacturing and service activities in areas with the best accessibility to markets and more complex productive structures.

The transfer and processing of information remained costly. As a result, world markets had to be surveyed by way of fragmented chains of information. If national production was too low to meet local demands, wholesale traders relied on importers who had relations with foreign exporters and ordered from them. Export firms bought the required products from the national manufacturers they worked with. This structure was efficient for trade in raw materials, energy, food produce and manufactured goods. It did not work for parts and industrial semi-products. Hence the tendency to have national companies for industrial production. International trade occurred before or after industrial processes. The world system could function because there were certain sites, generally ports, where the fragmented chains of information were connected, and because there were interface structures.[9]

Telecommunication, computer revolutions and air transport

The transition from the industrial to the post-industrial age was made possible by the vast progress in data processing and information transfer. The advances in these fields began before World War Two, but the transformation they induced did not become significant until the late 1950s or early 1960s. The generalization of feed-back controls made machines increasingly easy to operate, simplifying a great deal of industrial labour, and making it easier to transfer technologies to developing countries. Western countries and Japan lost the monopoly they had had in the field of manufacturing for about a century.

With information transfer now easier and cheaper, the necessity to fragment information chains disappeared. For the first time, industrial companies could work efficiently with plants spread over wide areas. As a result, the share of company branches dramatically increased in international trade, and the number of multinational or transnational corporations rapidly grew. In a way, economic globalization started at the time of the discoveries in the late fifteenth and sixteenth centuries. If people only recently became aware of this evolution, it is because problems were not perceived on the global scale when information chains were fragmented. This awareness is easier today, since so many firms operate on a global scale.

Before the communication revolution of the past thirty years, the division of labour among firms was mainly geographic. They operated within limited territories, and were connected at the intersections where interface functions accumulated. A new division of labour has now appeared. For a first group of firms, expertise is increasingly based on the capacity to conceive and organize the production and distribution of specific goods or services on a global scale. Their functions are essentially concentrated in the sector of market innovation and logistics, i.e. communication and information processing. A second group of enterprises is mainly organized to efficiently manage machines, lorries, planes or ships. They focus on technical problems. They try to keep costs as low as possible by optimally utilizing production capacities. In this way, the flexibility of the whole economic system is greatly improved.[10]

Metropolises as control points of new global economy

Instead of places where interconnections between geographically limited systems occurred, we now have a global system in which the main contact is between hierarchically structured firms – logistic ones versus productive ones. Telecommunications are unable to solve all the problems of this new global economy. When important decisions are made, executives have to meet their business partners, for it is difficult to evaluate some of their capabilities and skills without face-to-face contact.

Without the development of air transport and to a lesser extent high speed trains, economic globalization would have been far more difficult. In order to reduce air fares, networks of air lines had to be structured at important hubs, thus making it possible to achieve high seat occupancy on long distance flights. Hence the advantage for cities that are large or specialized enough in indirect service activities to have a major airport.

The nexuses of the world system of communication are increasingly concentrated in metropolises, and this helps explain their dynamism. Thirty years ago, people thought the main consequence of the communication revolution would be counter-urbanization. It did indeed occur, as was illustrated by the results of censuses in the 1970s, but more recently, the tendency towards metropolization has been more conspicuous.[11]

The new centres of the world system differ from the interface ones of the industrial age in various respects. They now house global logistics enterprises specialized in banking and finance, transport, travel, tourism, and the design and distribution of equipment or consumer goods, and facilitate the interaction between logistics and productive firms.

A major geographic aspect of economic globalization has been the shift of communication functions from large seaports, the main interface points in the economies of yore, to the most important cities or economic decision centres – from Le Havre, Marseille or Bordeaux to Paris in France, from Genoa, Trieste and Venice to Rome and Milan in Italy, from Hamburg or Bremen to Frankfurt and increasingly to Berlin in Germany, and from Montreal to Toronto in Canada. In some cases, new metropolitan functions remained in the traditional interface centres. This occurred if the port cities were large enough or specialized enough in international service activities to become major hubs of air networks, as was the case with London, New York, and Amsterdam.

The decision to locate the airport at Schiphol played an essential role in the conversion of Amsterdam. It was made as early as 1926, which demonstrates the quality of the municipal authorities at the time. The significance of the choice was evident to the director of KLM, where the word Randstad was coined to show that the role of Schiphol would not be limited to Amsterdam, but was to be regional.

From capitals to metropolises

Many of the control points of today's world economy are capitals. It is as true of major inland cities like Paris in the developed world and Mexico City or Delhi in the developing one, as it is of large seaports like London, Amsterdam or New York, though neither of the latter two ever served major political functions.

A capital city is not necessarily the seat of a national government and the site of the central administration associated with it. Its superiority lies in its capacity to innovate in the field of culture and provide the entire population of a country – and perhaps elsewhere as well – with models for social and cultural life.[12] A capital sets standards for language use, attracts leading intellectuals and artists, houses publishers, and nowadays, movie and television companies.

The intellectual functions of capital cities can be partly explained by the early concentration of collective memories, the huge libraries or museums located there. These facilities have often enabled them to play a role in higher education and in the arts and music. Wealthy patrons and their artistic and literary interests and taste tended to make capitals even more attractive. A wealthy and educated elite was often instrumental in establishing a tradition of social and cultural creativity in the early phases of capitals, and later in organizing art markets. Artists and authors had to develop close ties with connoisseurs and amateurs, or with the art galleries and critics who played a central role in their functioning. They took advantage of the wide range of social conditions so characteristic of large cities. In Edo as well as Paris, new tastes evolved out of the close relations between local aristocratic or bourgeois elites and working-class neighbourhoods.[13] The social fabric of capital cities was conducive to the development of new attitudes and the rise of counter-cultures.

Because of the accumulated art collections and the quality of the historic architecture, capital cities are generally very attractive to tourists. Vienna, Prague, London, Paris, Amsterdam, Rome, and former capitals like Florence or Venice are swamped by visitors. Their downtown area is often one gigantic open air museum – the part of a country where it is possible to discover what is most specific in its culture.

A past as a capital city is a valuable asset for a modern metropolis. The businessmen who visit it and the highly skilled managerial, professional and executive classes essential to its functioning are quick to appreciate all the aspects linked to a long and rich artistic or literary tradition. They are only too happy to attend concerts, plays and opera performances, and stroll through museums. If they have children, they know they can benefit from a wide gamut of educational facilities from elementary schools to universities. At the same time, however, the transition from traditional capital functions to new metropolitan ones can jeopardize some of the most attractive aspects of their cultural life. Social changes have important implications for artistic and literary life: creativity is sometimes impaired if the variety and blending of statuses is reduced.

Amsterdam was never a classic capital, since its role was not based on political power or the presence of a court. The city is rich in beautiful houses dating back to the seventeenth or eighteenth centuries, but has few public monuments of that era – churches being the main exception, and of course the Royal Palace, the former City Hall. The influence of the leading Dutch city came from the enlightened elites who ruled over it since the Reformation, and from their artistic tastes and commitment to intellectual life.[14]

Restructuring metropolitan areas

The forces at work in restructuring metropolitan areas are in many ways similar to those in all contemporary cities. With the generalized use of private cars for commuting, urbanized and suburbanized areas have greatly expanded. Severe congestion has consequently overrun the downtown districts. As a result, many commercial or service activities had to leave and relocate at major intersections of the motorway systems, especially those that are close to the main crossings between radial and concentric thoroughfares or perpendicular axes of supergrids.

Metropolitan restructuring[15] differs in some respects from the transformations that can be observed in other cities. Until forty years ago, people entered major urban areas through their central train stations, which were close to the downtown districts. Today, railways are mainly used by daily commuters. High speed trains still have only a limited impact on urban structure. They only improve accessibility for medium-range distances. They were conceived for reaching the traditional central stations, but suburban stations are appearing, particularly to insure good connections with major airports. Everything is thus indicative of the overwhelming influence of airports in the restructuring process. The whole organization of metropolitan areas is now geared to them.

In most large agglomerations, restructuring is an expensive and time-consuming process. The new infrastructures of transport, whether airports, motorways or railways, have to be drawn through already urbanized areas. Since the first generation of outlying commercial and business centres developed at a time when air transport was still insignificant, their relation with airports is not always an easy one. This is the case with *La Défense* in Paris.

Amsterdam was fortunate to be able to capitalize on very early good planning decisions. Since ample room was reserved for the corridors of highways and railways, the adaptation of the metropolitan area to the new conditions was quick and efficient. Hence the spectacular growth of Amsterdam II in the past few years.

At the beginning of the 1960s, a choice between two types of basic transport infrastructures seemed possible in major urban areas: growth could be achieved either by mass transit systems or by efficient motorway networks. Thirty years later, it is increasingly evident that both systems have to be used, and that they are complementary. Mass transit systems are mainly efficient in preserving accessibility to downtown districts. Motorways provide easy connections when flows are multidirectional. In the major metropolitan areas, it is clear that even a dual system can not prevent congestion. Hence the significance of techniques that substitute information transfers for physical mobility.

Amsterdam is in many ways a major metropolitan area, since it is the control centre of an urban area that houses more than six million people. Its traditional polycentric structure makes its traffic problems easier to address than in more concentrated urban areas. Urban planners always stressed mass transit systems, but did not ignore the need for efficient motorways. As a result, the Amsterdam metropolitan area has some of the best conditions for work and daily life in the contemporary world.

Economic and social transformations of metropolises

Restructuring economic activities

In a global economy, the location of activities does not follow the same pattern as fifty years ago. Major metropolises of industrialized countries have changed in two important ways.[16] Firstly, they have lost or are losing jobs in many of their traditional sectors, just like countries themselves, because of more profitable conditions in the industrializing parts of the world. Manpower industries have been the most severely hit. Secondly, due to the high price of land and strict environmental regulations, a process of filtering down has developed within national economies. Smaller cities are more attractive for industries that need a great deal of space.

The process of transformation has positive aspects. The losses in heavy or traditional industries are balanced in part by gains in service activities associated with the growing role of control functions.[17] Some manufactures are able to pay high land prices and can often use relatively cheap migrant manpower, since they take advantage of the proximity of control structures and the wide range of contact possibilities.

Modern metropolises thrive because they offer the best conditions for innovation in some fields. At a time when scientific and technical research needs the most recent information, face to face contacts are more significant in research laboratories than a generation ago. Research centres generally avoid the downtown districts of metropolitan areas, where land is expensive and the atmosphere sometimes too crowded and noisy for reflection, but many of them have settled within a radius of an hour's travel from a major airport. Research has to be backed by development policies. It is in this field that metropolitan regions offer the best conditions. The availability of numerous specialized service firms is important if new products are to be tested and their commercial viability evaluated. High-tech industries, especially in the computer sector, have often settled in metropolitan areas, as was demonstrated by Allan Scott and Edward Soja in Los Angeles.[18]

Some activities depend on the processing of ever new information. This is particularly true of cultural industries like publishing, advertising, radio and television. In a similar vein, fashion is at home in large cities, where there is access to the best designers, the external economics linked to the accumulation of competing firms, and sometimes relatively cheap migrant labour.

Evolving social fabric of modern metropolises

Social change is linked with the restructuring of urban space and transformations in employment. Due to the dramatic decrease in skilled blue collar work, unemployment is high in this sector and there is an accumulation of older workers. Younger workers often migrate to regions where industrial activities have better withstood international competition, or manage to develop new abilities. Since the new industrial labour force is less skilled and more mobile than a generation ago, it is weakly unionized.

The rise in the service sector often counterbalances losses in industrial employment. A substantial portion of the new jobs are linked to control activities. This means there are more executives, managers and professionals than ever.[19] The situation for less qualified office workers is different. They generally increased in number up until the beginning of the 1980s, but their ranks have been reduced in the past fifteen years, ever since the new generation of computers greatly improved the efficiency of data processing. The new machines caused a rapid rise in the floor space required for office jobs. As a result, offices have fewer positions in metropolitan areas than they used to: the work is done more efficiently, and some of it has been transferred to locations where land is cheaper.

Firms look for buildings more adapted to the new conditions than their former premises in the downtown areas of many of the large cities. Depending on the local conditions, this either means a redevelopment of the central part of the city is going on or the growth of the new outlying business centres has been accelerated.[20]

Impact of greater mobility

The changes affecting metropolitan areas are not only linked to their occupational structure. They have also resulted from the increased mobility of the labour force. Traditionally, two segments of the metropolitan populations were rather stable: the skilled blue collar and the lower qualified, often female, white collar workers. Both are now declining in number. The developing industrial firms employ either engineers and skilled technicians or unskilled workers. The first group comes from the universities and technical colleges and is recruited all over the country. The new blue collar workers are often of foreign descent and willing to accept underpaid jobs.

In the indirect service sector, the situation is similar to the one in the high tech sector, but with a higher proportion of foreigners brought in by multinational or transnational corporations. The mobility is also highlighted by the transient population of businessmen, young executives, managers or engineers who come to attend meetings. Tourists, who are numerous, since metropolitan areas are generally extremely attractive, add to this transient population.

Mobility has always been characteristic of capital cities and seaports – the major interface points of yesterday's societies. The demographic turnover in postmodern metropolitan areas is however higher. In a way, post-modern metropolises have ceased to be real cities in the sociological sense of the word. They are just stages, where skilled workers live for a few weeks or years before moving on to other metropolises, or to one of the other sites where the companies that employ them have chosen to locate their factories, research centres or branch offices.

Industrialized countries have developed efficient welfare policies since the beginning of this century or the 1930s. Their metropolises have launched and financed additional initiatives by providing housing, education and health services. For people in the developing world, the living conditions in these large cities are much better than in the rural or urban areas of their own country, even if there are no jobs there for them. Hence the high rate of immigration, and the fact that it is so hard to restrict. Their family structures keep many foreigners moving back and forth between their native country and their new one, which only serves to increase the transient character of metropolitan populations.

Reactions of metropolitan groups to new occupational structures

Mobility is widely valued by young people who like to experience new places and benefit from the career opportunities that grow from the capacities they develop this way. This is not the case with other segments of the population. Many older people are dissatisfied with the restructuring process that ousted them from their old neighbourhoods or transformed the environment in such a way that they ceased to feel at home in the city where they were born. There are also young people who are more attracted by a pleasant, be it more modest life in a friendly environment than by the supposed advantages of mobility. They choose to stick to the parts of the city they like, even if there are no jobs available; they are often dependent on National Assistance.

Some of the people attracted by metropolitan areas are more interested in the life style, cultural facilities and atmosphere than the job opportunities there. In many metropolitan areas, the income of some groups has ceased to be based on productive activities. They are content with petty domestic services. These groups often withstand the economic forces working to adapt the urban scene to the new metropolitan functions.

Specifics of Amsterdam

Amsterdam has been greatly affected by the occupational restructuring associated with its new metropolitan functions. It was never a major manufacturing centre. The decline of employment in the blue collar sector was nonetheless significant. The professional, executive and managerial classes had always been an important component of the active population of the metropolitan area, and from the start the affluent suburbs of Gooi and Kennemerland attracted them.

In many respects, the reorientation of metropolitan economies is more qualitative than quantitative. The English language, for instance, is increasingly used by transnational corporations. The language skills of the Dutch have made this easier to accept than in many other non-English speaking countries. The higher categories of transient skilled foreign specialists often have problems adapting to Dutch life, but they generally settle easily in the Netherlands. One can make oneself understood without necessarily speaking Dutch. The Dutch educational system offers numerous options to the children of foreigners.

Because of the heavy commitment of the Netherlands and Amsterdam to welfare policies, the proportion of urban dwellers who have decided to live in Amsterdam because of its atmosphere, freedom, and the high quality of its social and cultural facilities, and not for economic reasons, is particularly high. This is one reason why Amsterdam, a relatively small metropolis, has experienced acute socio-cultural tension over the past thirty years.[21]

Third World immigrants came partly from the former Dutch colonies, a feature Amsterdam shares with old imperial cities like London, Brussels or Paris. There are two other significant groups, Moroccans and Turks, and in their case the situation is closer to the Central European one. The influx of Third World migrants started in the 1950s, but reached a peak in the 1970s. It occurred during the early stages of contemporary metropolitan restructuring.

In some of the metropolises of today, the foreign labour force has played a significant role in the development of new industries, whether high tech (many Asiatic immigrants work in the Duke and Orange County factories in the Los Angeles metropolitan area) or the garment industry. Since social regulations are more strictly enforced in Amsterdam than in Paris, Los Angeles, Milan or Barcelona, immigrants have fewer job opportunities and their unemployment rate is high. The presence of this foreign population is often more of a liability for urban or national communities than an advantage.

Cultural dimensions of metropolitan restructuring

Economic globalization and the resulting counter-urbanization and metro-polization trends mainly proceeded from the communication revolution of the past thirty years. Cultural transmission has been greatly affected by this transformation, and although changes have been felt all over, their impact is more conspicuous in large cities. Contemporary metropolises have cultural traditions linked to their former functions as capital cities or interface centres between economic systems. They have been altered by the occupational shifts and higher mobility that are correlates of the economic restructuring.

Traditional forms of cultural transmission

Until a generation ago, cultural transmission occurred by way of: a. oral communication and visual imitation, and b. reading. Oral communication and visual imitation were essential during the early years of life. They were how babies learned the language of their parents and the behaviour patterns and attitudes of daily life. Cultural transfer from one generation to the next was consequently a close-range process. The role of reading and the school system based on it came in at a later stage, and did not concern as wide a range of cultural elements as oral and direct visual transmission.

The role of oral transmission was always paramount, but the written word widened the spatial range of some aspects of cultures: moral principles, ethics, religion, and scientific knowledge. It prevented the local differentiation of languages by maintaining relations over longer spans of space and time. Since the role of oral transmission and reading differed from class to class, traditional cultures had two complementary versions. Oral and direct visual transfers were central to popular or folk cultures. They explained their geographic *distinctiveness* and their deep local roots. They pertained to skills necessary for daily life and productive activities. High or elite cultures relied more on reading and writing, and were less place-related. For centuries, they mainly focused on religious, ethical and political issues, which explained their early role in unifying extensive areas.

The transmission of the folk components of cultures is a time-consuming process, but since it results from the kind of interaction that takes place naturally within families or small neighbourhoods, no one has to pay for it. It involves age structures in which older and younger people remain in close contact. A facet of folk cultures is also transmitted through age class interaction.

The acquisition of an elite culture is more time-consuming, since reading and writing abilities require years of work at school. For centuries, only the upper social classes had access to it. It gave them a mastery of the values and social techniques needed to build control structures over wide areas, and imbued them with the ideologies central to the social and political world they dominated. Political organization and class division thus had cultural correlates. It was partly because high culture was difficult to acquire that it was linked to the hierarchical structure of societies. Before the development of modern science, it mainly centred on ideological or religious beliefs, and consequently supported the existing class structure and power division. The sense of superiority high cultures gave people was also rooted in their artistic and literary dimensions.

The boundary between folk and high cultures has never been a fixed one. Many fashions, attitudes or techniques (as soon as scientific progress provided elite cultures with possibilities for innovation in this field) moved down the social scale by way of a filtering process. Young lower-class adults employed by aristocratic or bourgeois families adopted some of their attitudes and tastes.

In Western countries, a process of modernization started in the late Middle Ages. It first sprang from an egalitarian interpretation of Christian faith. Everyone deserved the right to become acquainted with the Scriptures and be admitted into Paradise. As a result, the democratization of learning was central to Western societies. It was achieved relatively early, at least at an elementary level, in Protestant societies, but the process was also present in Counter-Reformation Catholicism. The democratization of the ability to read and write was certainly instrumental in the diffusion of the Industrial Revolution, and the resulting higher incomes allowed for the generalization of school, and later of longer school attendance. The aim of modernization policies in the cultural field was to upgrade popular cultures and progressively align them with elite ones. Hence the stress on the diffusion of higher forms of literature, theatre, music and art down the social pyramid.

High cultures were not static ones. Since they stressed the aesthetic and ethical dimensions of life, they were open to innovation. Capital cities served as the major centres for the development of new beliefs, attitudes, fashions and aesthetic forms.[22]

Impact of telecommunication on cultural transmission: mass culture versus specialized learnt cultures

The first stages of cultural transmission were not changed by the mass media. Young children are still dependent on their parents and the neighbourhood where they live in the first years of their development. Thanks to television, however, oral and visual transfers of knowledge have ceased to be only short-range processes. By the age of two or three, children know how to switch on the family television set to receive messages from far away. They soon become more familiar with the broadcasted songs, than with the traditional folk lore of their group.

The results of this change are manifold. The uniformization of cultures, particularly of their folk component, which started long ago with the increasing role of schools has been greatly accelerated. Reading and writing are less valued than in the past, since they have ceased to be the only route to escape daily life realities. In some developed countries, the percentage of illiterate adults is increasing.

Mass cultures also differ from traditional folk ones in their emphasis on consumption and entertainment. What young girls used to learn from their mothers or grandmothers was how to cook, do the laundry, iron clothes, sew, and keep house. Young boys were trained to work in the stables, harness oxen or horses, till and sow. They were soon able to help their fathers repair roofs, maintain machines, and go hunting or fishing. Thanks to the mass media, nowadays young people learn the fashionable rhythms and songs. They develop a taste for dancing and entertainment. Productive skills are practically non-existent in the television programmes or video clips that are central in the new culture.

Inter-generational communication has been greatly reduced by the mass media. School attendance initiated this process, but for most of the time, young people worked under the supervision of teachers. The new society consists of age classes that develop different musical tastes, hold different views about what is important in their lives, and gather in different places.

The process of massification resulting from the mass media is going on everywhere, but its impact is strongest in large cities. With higher densities, it is easier to organize age classes there. Since families are often disrupted by the prevailing conditions of urban life, the older generation has ceased to provide young people with models to follow. Modern forms of urbanism often prevent the emergence of local communities. The mixture of ethnic groups in the same areas also contributes to these developments.

As a result urban societies, particularly metropolitan ones, are characterized by a disrupted transmission of the folk components of culture. The moral references of the younger generations differ a great deal from those of their parents. They do not master as wide a range of productive techniques. This situation favours the development of many forms of delinquency, and the rise of marginal social structures such as gangs. Immigrant populations are particularly affected by these transformations.

The new conditions and techniques for the transmission of knowledge also have a wide variety of consequences in the realm of high culture. Access to higher education has ceased to be the privilege of a minority. In many fields, it has become easier to learn outside the educational system by way of films, cassettes or video discs. It is now quite feasible to learn a foreign language in the comfort of one's home. It is possible to acquire specialized techniques, know-how or scientific knowledge at any time, and the role of adult education is growing.

Traditionally, the main content of high culture was religious or ideological. Today people are not mainly seeking an overall integrative intellectual structure when they decide to acquire advanced knowledge. They are looking for efficient techniques, and in a completely different domain, for esoteric ideologies. If mass cultures are more consumption-oriented than traditional folk ones, the specialized cultures that have replaced the high ones of yore have an important productive dimension. It is partly for professional reasons that people work hard to master new fields of knowledge. However, today's specialized cultures also have other characteristics. Since people have more leisure time, hobbies have become more important. Many of the efforts to acquire specialized skills are motivated by the desire for more fruitful leisure activities. Some people explore traditional crafts such as weaving. Others like to learn all about horses. Amateur sailors are often better navigators than fishermen.

In the societies of the past, folk cultures were spatially differentiated, and it was the high cultures that provided the unifying principles. With the end of history, as described by Francis Fukuyama,[23] or more precisely the end of the philosophies of history that have been central to most Western high cultures for two centuries, our world is confronted with totally new cultural patterns. Mass cultures are conducive to a growing standardization of behaviour patterns and styles of daily life. Specialized cultures are responsible for the fragmentation of ideological orientations. Their diversification reflects the increased division of labour in more diversified economic systems. It also expresses the desire to escape the trivial environment of daily life and explore other avenues and possibilities. The new learnt cultures revive old ideological or religious traditions or develop new ones. Past societies were unified by a shared conception of progress. Modern-day ones are characterized by an explosion of counter-cultures.

Capital cities and cultures

In the past, capital cities played a major role in the realm of culture, since they at least partly shaped the high culture upon which the social structure and political organization of the State were founded. In medieval France, Paris was one of the main centres of Roman Catholic theology, thus enabling the King of France to vie with Rome or the Emperor and contest their right to dominate the Church and the world. Moreover, its University enabled Paris to play a decisive role in the development of late medieval philosophy.

The Renaissance and Reformation modified the nature of high cultures. Revelation was always essential for people seeking Truth, but its significance differed from one country to the next. In Lutheran societies and England, the new interpretation reinforced official power structures and limited the need for new ideological support for political systems. In Calvinist areas, the ethical dimension of social organization was stressed. In Roman Catholic countries, the influence of Rome was reinforced. The religious diversity in many parts of Europe eroded the religious basis of authority.

The rediscovery of Antiquity presented a new source of intellectual and political legitimacy. The Italian princes of the time were in a more difficult situation than the kings of Spain, England or France. According to the prevailing medieval political philosophies, the only legitimate authority in northern and central Italy was the Emperor. In Florence, Venice, Genoa or Milan, political leaders were looking for new principles to support their power. In the fifteenth century, they discovered the advantages to be drawn from literature modeled after classical Roman works, inspired by the redis-covered Greek philosophers, and backed by a new conception of the arts. In Florence, Cosmo the Elder started to patronize humanists and artists, and was rewarded by strong support from the new intellectual and artistic circles. His policy was continued and reinforced by Lorenzo the Magnificent, and became one of the main characteristics of the Medicis' conception of power when they became Dukes of Tuscany. The early Renaissance popes patronized artists and clearly understood the prestige it gave them; doing so became central to Counter-Reformation policy and changed Rome from the time of Pope Sixtus V in the 1580s.

In other countries, the support to be gained from new forms of high culture was clearly understood by sovereigns like Francis I in France and Henry VIII in England. They patronized artists, invited Italian, Flemish and German painters or sculptors to settle in their countries, and invented a new style of power relations. In France, the influence of the Italian cultural policy and the use of the capital city as a show place became more evident with the Medici queens, Catherine from the 1550s to the 1580s, and Mary in the early seventeenth century.

A capital city in Classical or Baroque Europe always owed its influence and role in part to its prestige and cultural prominence, but the Italian and later French models, with their emphasis on the ideological unity of society and reliance on royal patronage, were not the only ones. In Calvinist countries, the cultural significance of capitals was linked to the rise of a more conscious and organized civil society. Amsterdam was the best example of this new type of city.[24] Compared with Paris, London, Stockholm or Berlin, it had fewer huge monuments. Artistic development was supported by successful businessmen or corporations. As a result, painting was more central to artistic achievements than architecture.

In Amsterdam, the option to develop a pluralist conception of high culture was implemented for the first time. The foremost actors in the city were members of the Reformed Church, but some of them were from families of recent exiles from Flanders or France. Many interpretations of the Scriptures had gained supporters, and there were no convincing reasons to select one and exclude the others. Roman Catholics had no civil rights, but were not excluded from civil society. Sephardic Jews from Spain and Portugal rapidly gained influence in the city, and Rembrandt was only too glad to be patronized by De Pinto.

In the eighteenth century, the Amsterdam model of a capital city began to be emulated. London at the time of the Hanover kings owed more to wealthy Whig patrons than to royal initiatives. In France, Versailles had only been the hub of artistic life for a short period, and the intellectual supremacy of Paris had never been challenged. In the eighteenth century, with the increasing role of bankers, traders and businessmen as patrons, the situation began to resemble the one in Amsterdam, the major difference being the central role of tax collectors in the new elite. Ever since the United States became independent, the major Atlantic seaports competed for primacy in the new nation. Philadelphia had the influence of a capital in the period when Benjamin Franklin was living there and the First Congress met, but Boston always retained a leading role in the intellectual field, and in the early nineteenth century New York began to emerge as the main centre of economic control and cultural supremacy. Because of its cultural diversity, lack of political significance and emphasis on business, from the start it presented many analogies with Amsterdam.

The success of operas was the best sign of the growing influence of civil society. Royal patronage was important in the diffusion process that gave this Italian innovation a European dimension by the beginning of the eighteenth century. Lulli, an Italian musician invited to the Court of Louis XIV, was instrumental in introducing the new genre to Paris, Versailles and France. As of the early eighteenth century, the presence of a wealthy and educated high society appeared to be more significant than royal support. Mozart started in Salzburg, where he was patronized by the Prince Bishop, but the chances he had in Vienna gave him access to an audience he could never have had in Salzburg. The Vienna operas gave him an opportunity to add a prophetic and in a way revolutionary dimension to his music.

The French Revolution and industrialization introduced new motifs in the field of cultural evolution. The high cultures produced in capital cities ceased to have as their main function the legitimation of existing social and political structures. Their role was increasingly to further alternative sets of values: it was a period when counter-cultures began to flourish. Since the values aesthetics and ethics were based upon had ceased to be considered purely rational ones, change and modernity began to be viewed as valuable replacements. Hence the rise of new aspects in the cultural role of major urban centres. Capital cities like Paris were often associated with revolutionary movements. Their creativity was increasingly linked to their social diversity and the opportunities they offered for contact between folk and high cultures. It was also an expression of the transient population who frequented them, provided artists with patrons, and gave rise to new demands. Immigrant populations were already numerous, but at a time when the dominating ideologies agreed on the idea of progress, the integration of newcomers into the national society was generally achieved efficiently. It was the period when major American cities served as melting pots, Vienna absorbed hundreds of thousands of Slavs and Hungarians, and Paris attracted an increasing number of Belgian, Swiss, or Italian workers, and Yiddish-speaking Jews from Central or Eastern Europe.

Compared with the eighteenth-century situation, Paris at the end of the nineteenth century illustrated the reinforced role of civil society, the reduced influence of State patronage, and the growing significance of foreigners in artistic and literary life. The attraction and influence of capital cities were however still largely the outcome of institutions founded in the sixteenth century and modernized in the early nineteenth century, the museums, art academies, conservatories and libraries. In some ways, the situation in the major Far Eastern capitals was not very different from what could be observed in Western cities at the time. Everyone agrees on the role of the Edo merchants and popular classes in the transformation of Japanese culture, the rise of new forms of theatre and painting and a modernization process which in many ways predated the opening to Western influences. The Beijing opera resulted, in the late nineteenth and early twentieth century, from the blending of the various regional traditions of the new elites living there. The declining Manchu dynasty had nothing to do with this development.

The local geography of cultural creativity expressed these new social conditions. In a city like Paris, artistic and literary life ceased to gravitate around the focal point of the city, the Louvre Royal Palace, which was still essential in the eighteenth century: *Salons* were organized there. They were instrumental in creating the Parisian artistic market and insured the transition from royal or aristocratic patronage to a bourgeois organization. As of the mid-nineteenth century and because of the high price of housing in the central part of the city, young artists had to move to more peripheral locations. As a consequence of haussmanization, Paris was then experiencing increasing spatial segregation between the lower and higher segments of its population: wealthy people moved to the west, blue collar workers to the east. Artistic life settled along the north-south line between the two halves of Paris, oscillating from Montmartre to the north to Montparnasse to the south.

There were no major transformations in the patterns of cultural creativity in the 1920s and 1930s. The main focus was still on high culture, and major capital cities competed more eagerly than ever for world prominence – Vienna against Berlin, Berlin against Paris, Paris against London and increasingly New York. After World War Two, New York was to eventually head the painting and sculpture market. The quality of its museums and the wealth of its patrons made it increasingly important in the international world of culture. The shift of cultural creativity from Europe to North America had, however, other correlates. In Europe, institutional customers gained influence, but private purchasers always played a significant role. In the United States, private art collectors relied more heavily than their European counterparts on experts and critics. Since companies were increasingly active on the art markets, this trend was reinforced. It was influential in the development of forms of art so esoteric that their appeal to most people was greatly reduced. In a way, Western high cultures were in a deadlock.

Cultural creativity and modern metropolises

The modern structure of cultures is completely different from the traditional one. The enthusiasm for many of the traditional expressions of high culture has not disappeared. Never did as many people go to museums, operas or even foreign cities to see the original settings where civilization thrived. However, the meaning attributed to the traditional forms of high culture has changed. What people want is a sophisticated form of recreation and entertainment, rather than the pursuit of a personal achievement. In a consumer society, the consumption of cultural goods is important, but has been dissociated from the traditional dimensions of high culture. The eclecticism so characteristic of post-modern times is an expression of this transformation.

We have to look to other aspects of either mass or specialized learnt cultures to understand the world of today. Cultural creativity is significant in three fields:

1. themes that structure mass culture and are broadcasted on modern media,

2. specialized forms of knowledge that have displaced high culture and are essential to the productive side of modern societies, and

3. specialized ideologies developed by specific groups in an effort to give meaning to a divided society.

Ad 1.

Many Europeans complain of the Americanization of their culture. They do not realize that the American culture they criticize differs in its very foundations from its European counterparts. As of the late nineteenth century, cultural creativity in the United States has been more geared to the wishes, tastes and aspirations of 'ordinary people' than in Europe. In his excellent study on the Virgin Lands, Henry Nash Smith demonstrated a generation ago how the Western myth and Western 'reality' were created to conform with a popular American fantasy. Instead of being based on historical events, the Western saga was a repetitive one with a few standardized characters, the cowboy, the farmer, the Indian. It did not involve any prior knowledge of a complex history. At the same time, jazz and country music began to offer parallel forms of escape and entertainment.

The commercial exploitation of art forms adapted to popular fantasies did not develop in the major cities on the east coast, where plays, operas and other forms of high culture were the main focus of cultural promoters. Los Angeles, which was not organized as a traditional city but as a loosely structured suburban area, became the first centre to use modern media – first movies and then television – to diffuse themes adapted to the mass sensibility. Mass music had its roots in the culture of folk music recorded in New Orleans or Nashville, although it soon developed independently. Its main centres of inspiration have often changed in the course of the last generation. Western American metropolises played a role, as did Puerto Rican or black neighbourhoods in New York or other eastern cities. In Europe, the already declining lower-class areas of Liverpool were the first to enter the cycle of contemporary mass creation.

There is an inherent contradiction in modern mass culture. Its roots lay in lower-class folk cultures. The evolution of modern cities, and more specifically of major metropolises, is such that their traditional lower-class groups have been either ravaged by the ongoing occupational restructuring or displaced and fragmented by the spatial reorganization. The rootlessness of much of the metropolitan population prevents the formation of stable sub-cultures, and the impact of mass media promotes standardized tastes.

As a consequence, modern metropolises do not emerge as the sites where today's mass cultures are created. Instead, their role is to provide the expertise needed to transform cultural raw materials into the elaborate and streamlined products marketed by the mass media. In this way, cultural customers get the goods they want. Because of their sizeable immigrant populations, large metropolises offer channels to tap popular cultures that are still alive elsewhere. They thus provide rhythms and themes people are unable to invent locally. Metropolises have become more active in adapting cultural products than in creating them.

A city like Amsterdam has prime conditions for these activities. The multifarious ethnic origins of its population are a positive factor. Since industrial traditions were less significant there than in other metropolitan areas, the preservation of some Dutch folk traditions would not have been possible without the social movements of the 1960s and 1970s.

Ad 2.

Many of the factors that contributed to high culture creativity in metropolitan areas have disappeared. It is always easy to build a *Musée Imaginaire,* as André Malraux noted a generation ago, thanks to the high-quality photographs available today. Good artistic and musical educational facilities have been developed in smaller cities. Telecommunication has made it increasingly easy to gain access to the books in the huge libraries of major metropolitan institutions.

The high mobility of metropolitan populations has other consequences: people are less concerned with local problems and do not support local initiatives in the same way. Metropolitan areas still have significant advantages. They provide intellectuals with the diverse and easy contacts that are essential at some stages of the creative process. The major exchange points of global communication systems are active innovation centres, but the institutions where research and development take place have a tendency to be located on their outer fringe, where accessibility is still good, land is cheaper, and the stress of congested areas is absent. Fundamental research is often conducted in metropolitan areas, but its main contribution to modern forms of scientific culture lies elsewhere. Metropolitan areas are mainly successful in research and development. What they provide best is expertise in evaluating the commercial potential of new products, deciding how to advertise them and organizing the best combinations to produce and distribute them.

A medium-sized metropolitan area like Amsterdam is more likely to attract research centres than a larger one. Amsterdam also has trading traditions that account in part for the quality of its multifarious professional services. Its emphasis on inexpensive and high quality communication facilities as exemplified at Teleport is also important to firms that need good contact between their research departments and distant factories. The impressive growth of these sectors of metropolitan activities in the past fifteen years and the prominent position they occupy in the townscape of Amsterdam II are evidence of the location advantages of the metropolitan area.

Ad 3.

Specialized facets of contemporary culture also focus on daily life and leisure. Metropolitan areas pioneered transformations in these fields. Their sheer size and the variety of their social, ethnic and professional groups served to open any number of avenues. In the United States, San Francisco was the major arena for innovation in modern-day life styles, and in the 1960s and 1970s Amsterdam exhibited many similarities to the Golden Gate City. It is obvious that something of the dynamics at work at the time has since been lost. Central Amsterdam is undergoing a museumification process similar to those in many former capital cities or huge metropolitan areas. Tourists are curious to see Amsterdam's picturesque Golden Age setting and its present-day residents. In a way, Amsterdam is a kind of reservation, where a fascinating and almost extinct population of social innovators can be observed.

The replacement of former squatters by yuppies is another sign of the recent transformation. The mobile high-income segment of the metropolitan population enjoys the atmosphere reminiscent of the social turbulence of the past three decades, though it does little to promote its further development.

Cultural tension and problems in metropolitan areas

Cultural creativity is still part and parcel of modern metropolises, but they do not make the same contributions today as they did in the past. Exchange functions are far more essential in the control points of our global systems than innovation. Their main share in the elaboration of new know-how, knowledge or forms and styles mainly lies in their ability to shape new logistic combinations, explore new development pathways and launch new economic ventures. They thus shape an important dimension of the social and cultural life of today. What is lacking is the overall unifying function that major capital cities traditionally played.

In Amsterdam, the egalitarian ideologies prevailing in the municipality and among urban planners throughout most of the twentieth century have contributed to equalizing social hierarchies. Compared with other cities of the same size, the income range is smaller in Amsterdam, which is a predominantly middle-class city. The desire not to differ too sharply from one's neighbours is expressed in the deliberate choice of plain quality clothes. Originality is sought in bright colours rather than in high quality. In many ways, the egalitarian ideologies prevailing in Amsterdam paved the way for the massification of its culture, which was easier and occurred earlier than in many other places. The Dutch, especially in Amsterdam, are more Americanized than elsewhere in Europe. The down-grading of central city shops is another example of this evolution. It certainly does much to reduce the commercial appeal of this part of the metropolitan area. Downtown is not a small island of high culture in a massified society. It offers an original way to interpret the themes of mass culture and combine them with the variety introduced by the flourishing of many new specialized conceptions of social life.

Because of the complexity of their professional and ethnic composition, the high mobility of a significant segment of their population, and the impact of visitors, whether tourists or members of the executive, managerial and professional classes, metropolitan areas have accumulated more than their share of social problems and tension. In the global inflation of the 1980s, they experienced sharp rises in land prices and housing costs. As a result, social segregation has generally become harsher and more conspicuous.

High population instability has combined with unemployment to threaten local blue collar neighbourhoods and the familial and community structures of immigrant groups, resulting in rising delinquency rates. Mass culture is most conspicuous where traditional structures have been most impaired by contemporary evolution. In many cases, the urban environments developed in keeping with the doctrines of the International Congresses of Modern Architecture intensified the effects of social disintegration.

Amsterdam has its share of the ills plaguing many modern cities, but the structure of its housing market has maintained low rents for most of the residential population. Their early involvement in the modern architecture movement enabled Amsterdam planners to devise a metropolitan organization that favoured the modernization of the city and its restructuring, but fostered the type of social housing neighbourhoods where social control is difficult. Residents' movements of the 1960s and 1970s thus bore testimony to the reactions of 'ordinary people' confronted with problematic environments. The ensuing shift from systematic urban renewal to renovation and restoration allowed for the preservation of the most fascinating part of the old city, its modernization and the solution of some of its traffic problems.

Amsterdam confronts the same social and cultural problems as other modern metropolises, but the pioneering experiences launched two generations ago and the social movements of the 1960s and 1970s produced an efficient urban system preserving many of the conditions required for cultural innovation, and the well-being of today's residents.

Notes

* Editing by Sheila Gogol

1.   Soja, Edward, 1991, *The Stimulus of a Little Confusion. A Contemporary Comparison of Amsterdam and Los Angeles*, Amsterdam, CGO.

2.   Mamadouh, Virginie, 1992, *De stad in eigen hand. Provo's, kabouters en krakers als stedelijke sociale beweging*, Amsterdam, SUA.

3.   On the new locations of offices in Amsterdam:
     Brouwer, H.J., 1989, 'The Spatial Restructuring of the Amsterdam Office Market', *The Netherlands Journal of Housing and Environmental Research*, vol. 4, pp. 257-174.
     On Schiphol Airport:
     Kramer, J.H.T., 1988, 'The Airport of Schiphol. Economic and Spatial Impact', *Tijdschrift voor Econ. en Soc. Geografie*, vol. 79, pp. 297-303.

4.   Castells, Manuel, 1989, *The Informational City. Information Technology, Economic Restructuring and the Urban Regional Process*, Oxford, Blackwell.
     Friedmann, John, Goetz Wolff, 1982, *World City Formation*, Los Angeles, U.C.L.A., Comparative Urbanization Studies.
     Sassen, Saskia, 1991, *The Global City*, Princeton, Princeton University Press.

5.   On the stages in the development of Amsterdam, a good summary can be found in:
     Architectuurkaart / Architectural Map, Amsterdam, Arcam/Stadsuitgeverij, 1991.

6.   Wagenaar, Michiel, 1990, 'Amsterdam 1876-1914', Amsterdam, *Amsterdamse Historische Reeks* 16.

7.   It is as true of Amsterdam III as of Amsterdam II, but for different reasons: welfare policies rather than transport policies (cf. Faludi).

8.   Numerous studies have been devoted to the evolution of the contemporary Randstad, the level of interaction among its urban centres, and the rapid growth of employment in service activities, with the highest dynamism for the ring around Amsterdam and Schiphol.

Atzema, O.A., Marc de Smidt, 1992, 'Selection and Duality in the Employment Structure of Randstad', *Tijdschrift voor Econ. en Soc. Geografie*, vol. 83, pp. 289-305.

Cortie, Cees, Martin Dijst, Wim Ostendorf, 1992, 'The Randstad as Metropolis', *Tijdschrift voor Econ. en Soc. Geografie*, vol. 83, pp. 278-288.

Dieleman, F.M., S. Musterd, 1992, *The Randstad: A Research and Policy Laboratory*, Dordrecht, Kluwer.

Hooimeijer, P, S. Musterd, P. Schröder (eds.), 1991, *De Randstad: balans van winst en verlies, 1*, Utrecht, Stedelijke Netwerken.

Knol, H., W. Manshanden, 1990, 'Functionele samenhang in de noordvleugel van de Randstad', Amsterdam/Utrecht, *Nederlandsche Geografische Studies*, 109.

Konings, Rob, Erik Louw, Piet Rietveld, 1992, 'Transport and Infrastructure in the Randstad: An International Perspective', *Tijdschrift voor Econ. en Soc. Geografie*, 83, p. 269-277.

Korteweg, Piet, Robert Lie, 1992, 'Prime Office Locations in the Netherlands', *Tijdschrift voor Econ. en Soc. Geografie*, 83, pp. 250-262.

Laan L. van der, 1991, *Spatial Labour Markets in the Netherlands*, Delft, Eburon.

Lambooy, J.G., 1990, 'De configuratie van diensten, kennis en technologie; de noordelijke Randstadvleugel als K-Regio', in: Stam, W.J. (ed.), *De internationale concurrentie-positie van de Randstad*, Delft, Delftse Universitaire Pers.

Smidt, M. de, 1990, *De Randstad in internationaal perspectief*, Utrecht, Stedelijke Netwerken Werkstukken 21.

The best statement on the Randstad policy is in:

Kreukels, A., 'The Restructuring and Growth of the Randstad Cities: Current Policies Issues', in: Dieleman F., S. Musterd (eds.), 1992), *The Randstad: a Research and Policy Laboratory*, Dordrecht, Kluwer, pp. 237-262.

9.   On these problems, cf. the works of André Vigarié on European Atlantic seaports.

10.   It is mainly this aspect that studies on metropolitan restructuring stress:
       Castells, Manuel, 1989, *The Informational City. Information Technology, Economic Restructuring and the Urban Regional Process*, op. cit.
       Robins Kevin , Andrew Gillepsie, 1992, 'Communication, Organization and Territory', in: Kevin Robins (ed.), *Understanding Information. Business, Technology and Geography*, London, Bellhaven Press, pp. 147-164.

11.   Claval Paul, 1990, 'L'avenir de la métropolisation', *Annales de Géographie*, vol. 99.
       Smidt, Marc de, E. Wever, 1991, *Complexes, Formations and Networks*, Utrecht, Royal Dutch Geographical Society.

12.   On this point, the main reflection is based on the distinction proposed by Redfield and Singer between folk and high cultures (see for instance Cortie). Capital cities and their contemporary evolution have been recently studied by Dutch authors:
       Cortie, Cees, 1993, *European Capital Cities: A league of their own?* forthcoming.
       Dijkink, G., 1993, *Windows to the World: the Political Future of European Capitals*, forthcoming.
       Lambooy, J.G., 1991, 'Europese hoofdsteden - rivaliteit en suprematie', *Geografisch Tijdschrift*, pp. 434-441.
       Vries J. de, 'Power and the Capital City', in: Deben, L., W.F. Heinemeijer, D. van der Vaart (eds), *Capital Cities as Achievements*, Amsterdam, CGO, pp. 31-36.

13.   Claval, Paul, 1993, *La géographie au temps de la chute des murs*, Paris, L'Harmattan.

14.   On the problem of the preeminence of Amsterdam:
       Cortie, Cees, 1993, *European Capital Cities: A league of their own?* op. cit.

Vries J. de, *Power and the Capital City*, op. cit.
Wagenaar, Michiel, 1993, *Monumental Metropolis, Airy Suburbs. Two Spatial Strategies to Solve European's Urban Crisis, 1850-1914*, forthcoming.

15. On the role of airports in the restructuring of Paris:
    Claval, Paul, 1992, 'Planning the Parisian Region', in: Herman van der Wusten (ed.), *The Urban Political Arena*, Amsterdam, Netherlands Geographical Studies, pp. 138-150.

16. Most of the publications on metropolitan restructuring are centred on economic activities. See for instance:
    Castells, Manuel, 1989, *The Informational City*, op. cit.

17. In Amsterdam, the overall employment balance is a positive one:
    Atzema, O.A.L.C., C.A. Bargeman, E. Lensinck, 1991, 'Winst en verlies of de randstedelijke arbeidsmarkt', in S. Musterd, P. Hooimeijer (eds.), *De Randstad: balans van winst en verlies*, Utrecht, Stedelijke Netwerken, pp. 45-66. See Fig. 5-1, p. 47 ('Groei van de werkgelegenheid in de Randstad, 1984-1988).
    Hessels, M., 'Zakelijke diensten: winnende en verliezende deelmilieus in de Randstad', in: Musterd, S., P. Hooimejer (eds.), *De Randstad: balans van winst en verlies* 2, op. cit., pp. 67-79. See Fig. 6-2, p. 70 ('Zakelijke diensten in de Randstad, 1981-1988').

18. Scott, Allan, 1986, 'High Technology, Industry and Territorial Development. The Rise of the Orange County Complex', 1955-1984, *Urban Geography*, 7, pp. 1-43.
    Soja Edward, 1986, Taking Los Angeles Apart: Some Fragments of a Critical Human Geography, *Environment and Planning D*, Space and Society, 4, pp. 255-273.
    Soja, Edward, Rebecca Morales, Goetz Wolff, 'Urban Restructuring: An Analysis of Social and Spatial Change in Los Angeles', *Economic Geography*, 59, pp. 195-230.

19. Azema, O.A.L.C., C.A. Bargeman, E. Lensinck, 1991, *Winst en verlies of de randstedelijke arbeidsmarkt*, op. cit. See Table 5-1, pp. 47.

20. The presence of preserved areas in the central part of a city often prevents the local adaptation of the redevelopment of its office buildings. This explains part of the difference between Amsterdam and Rotterdam.

21. Soja, Edward, 1991, *The Stimulus of a Little Confusion*, op. cit.

22. Claval, Paul, 1993, *La géographie au temps de la chute des murs*, op. cit.
    Cortie, Cees, 1993, *European Capital Cities: A league of their own?* op. cit.

23. Fukuyama, Francis, 1992, *The End of History and the Last Man*, Toronto, Free Press.

24. Olsen Donald J., 1990, '*Time and the City*' and '*Urbanity, Modernity and Liberty*'. Two Essays on Urban History and Amsterdam, Amsterdam, C.G.O.
    Schama Simon, 1987, *The Embarrassment of Riches. An Interpretation of the Dutch Culture in the Golden Age*, New York, Fontana Press.

Thinking about culture in cities

Ulf Hannerz

'The locus of study is not the object of study,' Clifford Geertz, one of the most influential anthropologists of recent times, has pointed out, in what is in turn probably his most influential book, *The Interpretation of Cultures* (1973: 22). 'Anthropologists don't study villages (tribes, towns, neighborhoods...); they study *in* villages. You can study different things in different places, and some things (...) you can best study in confined localities. But that doesn't make the place what it is you are studying.'

That is a useful point. But what kinds of 'confined localities' are good for the study of what kinds of things, and since anthropologists have obviously had a soft spot for villages as vantage points, what are cities good for? No doubt there are many possible answers to this question, but the one I will try to argue for here is that at this point in time, not least, they are useful in thinking about culture, that key idea of my discipline. At the same time, however, I must note that not all ways of doing anthropology in the city make equal use of what may be the peculiar potential of cities in this regard.

The urbanization of anthropology

Urban ethnography, as a systematic, mostly qualitative study of ways of living in cities, began, it may be argued, with the sociologists of the Chicago School in the 1920s and 1930s, and their portrayals of neighborhoods, minority groups, street gangs, deviant occupations, and offbeat institutions.[1] As a part of social and cultural anthropology, urban studies had their most significant beginnings in the 1950s and 1960s, in research for example in the mining towns of Central Africa or in the hillside squatter settlements of Latin America. In the 1960s, too, mainstream America rediscovered poverty and ethnic differences in its own back yard, and this would soon considerably increase the number of anthropologists with urban research experience. Yet it was only then, and in the years which followed – let us say especially since the 1970s – that urban anthropology emerged as a somewhat distinct specialty, and not least as an incipient community of researchers and academic teachers with their own associations, conferences, journals, textbooks and courses.

A couple of decades have passed since this institutionalization of urban anthropology, which should certainly be enough to allow us to ask questions about its accomplishments. Such questions, however, can be of different kinds. Some would be about more down-to-earth accomplishments – what anthropologists at work in cities may actually have been able to tell practitioners and policy makers about the everyday functioning of health care, educational or judicial institutions, for example, and about possible improvements which might make them more efficient, or more equitable. Much of the effort has obviously gone into such matters, and I think it has often been valued even when it is understood that the complexities of life are such that problems cannot always find perfect solutions.

The kind of question I am more concerned with here, however, is what difference urban anthropology has made, or alternatively, can make, to more general anthropological habits of thought. How do the latter fare in the city, and if new light is indeed cast on them, have other anthropologists paid much attention?

It has often been asserted that anthropology in recent decades has become increasingly fragmented. The development of an urban anthropology can be seen as only one of many examples of this. Yet alongside this fragmentation, this balkanization, there has always been an anthropological 'mainstream,' an intellectual space where the debate has proceeded among more general theoretical tendencies, over more overarching intellectual issues, and also over somewhat arbitrarily chosen 'classical' problems. This space even the inhabitants of the various specialisms can apparently ill afford to ignore; on the other hand, the structure of attention is asymmetrical, as those who situate themselves more fully in the mainstream often pay little attention to whatever may be the current excitements of the peripheral specialisms.

Some years ago now, the American anthropologist Sherry Ortner (1984) published her review of theoretical developments in anthropology from the 1960s to the early 1980s – the period, that is, which saw the beginnings of urban anthropology. In passing, while discussing issues of theory, Ortner also offered an occasional glimpse of the ethnographic materials which helped anthropologists fashion central theory during the period: New Guinea pig slaughters, South American myths about jaguars, Balinese concepts of time, the arrival of Captain Cook in Hawaii. On the whole, not things you find in your street. The early crop of urban ethnographies had obviously had rather little discernible impact on main currents in the discipline as a whole. This impression is confirmed by Roger Sanjek (1990: 151), in his recent overview of urban anthropology. At least as things stood a decade ago, Sanjek suggests, urban anthropology was 'arguably the narrowest and theoretically least influential' of all the new anthropological specialties of recent times.

Culture as contested concept

It is against this background that I want to use the opportunity here to express some opinions about cities and city lives as food for thought for anthropologists when they continue to engage in theorizing about culture. Again in the last few decades, there has been in some quarters of anthropology, at least, an intense intellectual involvement with the idea of culture; with the notion that individuals of the human species are born quite incompletely programmed (to draw on a computer metaphor), and that consequently they must be understood as cultural beings; as users of meanings and meaningful forms acquired through social life, with all the variation and arbitrariness this might imply. Yet in the same period, culture has also been a contested concept, and critics have used epithets such as 'culturalism' or 'culturology' (largely synonymous, I believe) to draw attention to what they see as the recurrent biases and errors of cultural analyses.[2]

In considerable part, this has been a materialist critique of what has been seen as idealist thinking; I will not go much into that aspect of the debate. Culturalism is also said to construe human beings more as products than as producers of culture. In other words, it is weak on agency. Knowledge, beliefs, norms and values seem just to be there, or doing things on their own, or 'through' people. It is also taken to be weak on history: its culture concept is seen as static, referring to some timeless essence.

At least some of the anthropologists who continue as committed to cultural studies as ever are now certainly distancing themselves from what might have been culturalist errors. But where could the weak senses of agency and history have come from, so naturally perhaps that it has taken some struggle to identify and repudiate them? While any single answer to this question would surely be too simple, I suspect that some of the assumptions of culturalism grew in the village rather than in the city.

In Washington, D.C.

This, at least, is what my own experience suggests to me; for during these recent years when so much effort has been spent on dissecting the uses and misuses of the culture concept, I have often been a little impatient with it all. And I am sure this is in no small part because some twenty-five years ago, I happened to become an anthropologist in a rather complicated urban context where any attempt to make sense of what was going on in cultural terms promised to be controversial, and where it was thus a major challenge to figure out what speaking of culture could and could not be allowed to imply.

This was in Washington, D.C., in the late 1960s, where I did field work for two years in a Black American low-income neighborhood.[3] It was a time when public debate in the United States was more than usually occupied with issues of poverty. The 'war on poverty' was on, the notion of a 'culture of poverty' was hotly debated. It was also a period when Afro-Americans were reformulating their ethnic identity. The interest in Africa was revitalized, soul music and soul food were symbolically charged, the Black Power movement was in the streets, and (rather more, actually) on the campuses and in the news. The complicatedness of the situation, then, had something to do with a certain ideological crossfire. Looking at poverty in terms of a cultural tradition could distract attention from the need to change wider economic and social structures; yet to deny that Black people had their own cultural heritage was equally inappropriate.

Anthropologists may be inclined to test the patience of their audiences by lingering nostalgically on the topic of their first field experiences. These are of course often periods when our perspectives are enduringly shaped. I will try not to do so here any longer than necessary. What I learned from the everyday life of my neighborhood in Washington, anyway, was to look at culture as an ongoing practical, intellectual and affective adaptation to circumstances, carried out through interactions and communications, within the community as well as across its boundaries, between generations as well as among age mates. People would find solutions to problems modeled by their neighbors (perhaps not always good solutions), and would quite likely also hear comments on those solutions from other neighbors; they would develop expectations about life based on observing what went on around them, debate alternatives with friends and family members, and organize them into meaningful patterns through evenings of streetcorner mythmaking.

It was easy to develop a sense of agency here. These were individuals grappling with the diversity of the world of meaning surrounding them, trying to make practical and moral choices for the long or the short term but facing the sometimes harsh constraints built into the situation, arguing sometimes furiously among themselves and not necessarily coming to the same conclusions.

Neither could I, in Washington, possibly separate culture from history. Black Americans have been through dramatic changes, from the villages of West Africa by way of a traumatic sea passage to plantation slavery, from there to rural poverty in the South, from there again on to the cities of the North, continuously discarding some experiences and habits, while accumulating others as parts of an enduring heritage. It could only be an error to disregard all this and see the contemporary life of the low-income neighborhood as nothing but a forced adaptation to present socio-economic conditions, however important these also are.

And at the same time, the equation involved more than the internal cultural processes, and the external material constraints. There was also, for one thing, the powerful influence of the general American cultural apparatus, beaming its messages at Americans whether black or white through schools, courts, welfare institutions or media; ensuring that no minority would be left alone developing its culture to fit its own situation.

Frameworks of cultural process

Cities and city people are not all alike. My Washington field experience need not be typical. Yet I think urban life is often good to think with, if one wants to develop an understanding of culture without culturalism. Let me try to give this claim some more general conceptual underpinnings.[4]

Culture is meaning and meaningful form developed and acquired through social life, and it follows from this that a major part of cultural process consists of the ongoing social organization of meaning. Anthropologists, however, have not over the years given too much systematic attention to the varied forms of such process, and the current troubles with cultural theory have much to do with this. We have been content to assume that culture somehow makes its way through the structure of social relationships effectively enough, and have then concentrated attention on the meanings and the symbolic forms as such.

Much of this disinclination to give more orderly thought to cultural process may have to do with the traditional focus of anthropology on small-scale societies, on village communities. Here more or less the entire flow of culture can occur through a free, reciprocal, continuous and at the same time almost imperceptible exchange of ideas and their expressions between people in what we may see as an ecology of everyday life. Ideas are closely tied to personal experiences and practical conditions of life, and your neighbors and fellow human beings whom you observe and listen to are mostly engaged in the same routines as you are. At least over time, in their life cycles, then, people are more or less equals in the give and take of the cultural process: specialist roles in the production and dissemination of culture are weakly developed.

Culture passes here, that is, without anybody having to take too much notice about this fact in itself. The purposes of the activities which move culture through the social relationships are quite different: people make a living, exercise or defer to power, eat and drink, pray to higher beings. The fact that the activities at the same time *communicate* about livelihood, power or higher beings is a by-product, in large part taken for granted and thus disregarded by natives as well as anthropologists.

Such an unspecialized cultural flow, embedded in daily life, obviously occurs in all societies, including ours. As that eminent investigator of the economics of knowledge, Fritz Machlup (1980: 179-180), once put it: 'every person alive (and not in a coma) has at his disposal an almost continuous flow of free knowledge.' Yet it is in the situation where almost everybody can unqualifiedly recognize himself in his neighbor, and where personal experience and the flow of meaning from others merge without much surplus forming on either side, that it can be most readily taken for granted that culture will keep circulating so unproblematically. The redundancy of everyday communications will tend to distribute culture fairly uniformly within that population whose members are in frequent and broadly defined face-to-face contact with one another, and the social organization of collective consciousness approximates closely the ideal formula, 'I know, and I know that you know, and I know that you know that I know.'

Now not least as inhabitants of contemporary cities we know for one thing that this kind of 'keeping culture flowing without really trying' does not necessarily involve such a uniform experience, and for another that other forces are also involved in shaping our worlds of meaning. My suggestion here is that we can at least get a great deal closer to a more complete accounting for the entire cultural flow in our kind of society by identifying four major organizational frameworks for cultural process which have different, partly contradictory tendencies, yet occur intertwined in our lives. The four frameworks are easily recognized.

I call one of them the *form of life* framework, and this is the one I have really already been describing, that mostly unplanned flow of culture which, as Machlup had it, we get for free simply by not being in a coma; what we learn and simultaneously help produce merely by dealing with the largely practical issues of the daily round and, in the same contexts, by observing one another and communicating with one another.

In the small-scale local community I sketched before this framework may perhaps be altogether dominant. Elsewhere, as with us, it continues to contain a very large portion of the entire cultural flow. On the one hand, however, it partly changes characteristics internally, and on the other hand it coexists with other organizational frames. Internally, that free and largely unplanned flow of culture passes more, relatively speaking, between people of different characteristics, and less between people who are basically of the same sort; and precisely what is sameness and what is difference may actually turn out to be problematic. When society is at its most heterogeneous, and every individual is like some other people in some way and like no other people in others, the distinction tends to be dissolved.

But again, if the form of life framework has a part in organizing cultural process everywhere, it is nowadays hardly ever alone. Two other organizational frameworks, those of *state* and *market*, seem also to be engaged in the production and distribution in most places where human beings are found, and often – and certainly not least in the last few decades in the West – we also have to take into account a fourth framework, that of *movements*.

In all their varieties, these frameworks are culturally constructed, yet at the same time they organize cultural flow in their own ways. (It is specifically the management of meaning and meaningful form I am concerned with here; not so directly what other things that for example state and market do.) If within the form of life framework culture passes simply between fellow human beings, it moves within the state framework between the apparatus of the state and its subjects, in the market between sellers and buyers, in the movement framework between those converted and those not converted.

And it follows from this that the cultural process within each framework also get its own set of characteristic features; recurrent tendencies and recurrent problems in the handling of what may otherwise be quite varied ideas and modes of expression. Thus the state, market and movement frameworks all tend to entail a more deliberate, planned flow of culture than that we have seen to be largely characteristic of the form of life framework. The state and the market, with specialists engaged in the production and dissemination of ideas and meaningful forms, must finance this activity, and therefore integrate cultural flow more directly into the material economy than the form of life framework does, and often that of movements as well. They also centralize the sources of cultural flow a great deal more, it becomes an asymmetrical flow from the comparatively few to the many. The organizational frameworks may also have their particular means of regulating the passage of culture: through censorship in the state framework, for instance, or through copyrights in the market.

Not least do the frameworks relate differently to time and space. As far as spatial organization is concerned, it is obvious that the form of life framework often contains a primarily local, face-to-face cultural process. However, decentralized media such as writing and telephones, as well as the increasing physical mobility of the people themselves also make this kind of improvised, everyday flow of culture less place-bound. Movements are also often rather local, but in recent times we have seen several which have spread at least through the western world: the women's movement, the environmental movement. About the market it is often said that it has little respect for boundaries. When that scenario of a cultural homogenization of the world is suggested, the global spread of cultural commodities from center to periphery is held to be the prime mover. The involvement of the state in the flow of culture, in contrast, tends naturally enough to be more spatially restricted, as the state itself is territorially defined. Insofar as the state strives to be a nation it seeks its legitimation as a guardian of culture rooted in the form of life framework within its boundaries, and may attempt to constrain the influx of culture from the outside. Yet in other ways, not least when it comes to securing certain kinds of knowledge skills, the state may be a leading importer of culture.

With regard to the time dimension it is clear that while movements may engage large numbers of people in an intense cultural process, it is in their nature to be relatively unstable. The market flow of culture also has its tendencies toward instability, since the market strives toward innovation and expansion even when the commodities are meanings and symbolic forms. In the form of life framework, on the other hand, stability is more likely normal, as daily routines may not be altered unless circumstances change – which they do, of course, often enough. At least a part of state organized cultural flow also has a bias toward stability. When the state defines itself as a nation, it usually tries to find historical support for its community of culture. But simultaneously, as the state promotes a modern knowledge society, it may also have a part in cultural change and expansion.

I would not insist that the conceptual boundaries between the four frameworks I have proposed are altogether sharply drawn, nor that taken together, they will be absolutely certain to encompass all there is of contemporary cultural process. But I do not think they leave out a great deal. Questions of cultural process today, that is to say, often involve the ways in which meanings and meaningful forms are produced and disseminated in relatively systematic ways partly within, partly between the four frameworks; and not least how they are influenced – how they are transformed, amplified, or suppressed, or how they change speed – in the interfaces and passageways between the frameworks.

City, village, nation

Now I get back to what thinking about cities and city people can do to develop and enrich our understandings of culture. To repeat, it is predominantly with the help of observations made in small-scale communities, around the village square, that anthropologists have engaged, more or less self-consciously, in cultural theorizing.

Such observations need not lead to culturalism, and culturalism is not necessarily the culture theory appropriate to studies in, or of, villages. But the prototypical village community of the anthropological research tradition may offer rather limited resistance to culturalist simplifications. In the homogeneity and redundancy of its cultural flow, more or less contained within the form of life framework, it appears as if 'everybody shares the same culture'; and then the individual can be anonymous, a nobody. And they often have an appearance of time standing still; again, in the form of life framework, culture is in large part practical routine, not changed unless it is necessary.

But again, I am not arguing that culturalism is simply a product of the anthropological village experience. Such culturalist predilections as anthropologists may show also have their historical ties to nineteenth century European nationalism, with its celebration of the purity and integrity of culture, defended toward the outside, shared and continuous through time within.[5] In this current of thought, the images of the village and the nation more or less coincide as, to paraphrase Benedict Anderson (1983), the nation likes to imagine itself as a community.

The anthropologist has thus often come, equipped with a kind of understanding of culture propagated especially, we have seen, in the state framework, to the village variety of a form of life organization of culture; and there is an elective affinity between the two. What cities and their people can do in anthropology now is, for one thing, to offer some useful, consciousness-raising resistance to that union of ideas. They can point the way to more encompassing conceptions of culture and cultural process.

Not that urban ethnography has always lived up to that challenge. Much of the time, this is no doubt because its practitioners have identified some more limited focus of interest in a largely common sense manner – family life, say, or some public institution. Yet there has also been the tendency to bring in theoretical assumptions, or prototheoretical guiding metaphors, which rather lead the ethnographers away from an intellectual engagement with more overarching conceptions. I would not really want to blame Herbert Gans, who with his study of the Italian-Americans of Boston some thirty years ago (1962) probably coined the term 'urban village,' for the point he was making was that a low-income neighborhood could have its own pattern of informal, small-scale organization, rather than the disorganization people often expect in a 'slum.' But the willingness to excise some small part of the larger urban entity and proceed to examine it as if the people involved had very little to do with the rest seems to bring the habits of village anthropology into contexts where they can only be partially useful.

'Social life,' Oscar Lewis (1965: 497) argued in a critique of Louis Wirth's classic statement on urbanism as a way of life, 'occurs for the most part in small groups, within the family, within households, within neighborhoods, within the church, formal and informal groups, and so on. Any generalizations about the nature of social life in the city must be based on careful studies of these smaller universes...' Yes, the point is valid to a degree, but then describing these units as 'universes' somehow sounds a little odd. The early Chicago sociologists often had a similar conceptual bias, with their rhetoric of 'social worlds.' It was a way of emphasizing diversity, but also separateness. And the overall view we get is then that of a mosaic, a metaphor which is in some ways quite unfortunate. For it shows a pattern of pieces of more or less the same kind and size, each of a single colour, and not least importantly, hard-edged; distinctly bounded toward one another.

Beyond the mosaic metaphor

Working out the cultural currents of city life in terms of the four organizational frameworks suggested before, and not least looking at the various ways they can mingle in the experience of individuals as well as groups, we get a very different view.

We realize, to begin with, that the form of life framework, that where we continuously but often diffusely and distractedly observe our fellow humans, only partly offers us that village-like quality of looking, mirror-like, at others like ourselves, in the same fairly set, taken-for-granted routines. For it is typical of cities that they also contain people not like us. They bring these people in from the outside world, from places with other traditions, thus importing diversity; but they also generate diversity inside, partly through the division of labour elaborated for example into occupational and class cultures, partly by containing, in a kind of segmentary demography of culture, sufficient critical masses for the development and amplification of many subcultures. The experience of such diversity within the form of life framework can no doubt be recognized in Georg Simmel's (1964: 410) characterization, somewhat extreme as it may be, of the mental life of the metropolis: 'the rapid crowding of changing images, the sharp discontinuity in the grasp of a single glance, and the unexpectedness of onrushing impressions...'

In Washington, such diversity was to a degree even part of the neighborhood scene, as people lived under somewhat different circumstances, and had rather different outlooks on life. But the wider experience of difference involved the city beyond the neighborhood, other people in the streets, other people at places of work; and in particular the experience of mainstream, middle-class white Washington, from the working-class or lower-class black perspective. This view was constantly intertwined with the closeup view of neighbors, friends, and kinspeople, and thus contributed to a flow of meaning in no small part characterized by ambiguity, contradiction, and debate.

The flow of meaning in the state framework can in itself be expected to be less varied, and less marked by the distinctiveness of urban life. Views of certified knowledge and appropriate conduct as communicated with some authority by agencies of the state, to make citizens and keep them in line, may in principle be the same everywhere within its territory. Yet some of the state-organized culture – museums, parades – may end up largely as ingredients of the local culture of the state capital. Moreover, as in the case of the people of the Washington ghetto, the uniform meanings propagated by the state, through schools, courts or welfare agencies, can again be confronted with the diversity of those of the form of life framework in a problematic way.

This is no less true of the cultural commodities circulating in the market framework. It is widely understood that products made for a mass market will in their own way contribute to homogenization. To a degree one is exposed to their meanings and symbolic forms whether one wants to or not. On the other hand there is also the possibility of exercising some choice within the mass market – the men and women in that Washington neighborhood tended to switch to those soap operas, crime movies and sports events on network television which in one way or other showed some fit with their everyday concerns. And what is not least important in the urban context is the likelihood of a greater segmentation of the cultural market place.

Just as the city may provide the demographic base for more subcultures, it may allow more cultural entrepreneurs to develop their own niches by finding their particular sets of consumers, and this is obviously a question of interplay between the market and the diversity within the form of life framework. We can see also that the commoditization of culture can have its own role in making the overall social organization of meaning and symbolic form more fluid, less mosaic-like, as culture packaged for sale can cross boundaries which in the form of life framework tend to be more sharply drawn. Black radio stations of the Washington inner city could have many listeners among white suburban teenagers; as home cooking is transformed into ethnic restaurant cuisine, cosmopolitans and locals may compete for tables.

We might look at movements, to say something about them as well, as shifts out of the form of life framework which occur as something happens to routines. The latter are threatened, and people stand up in defense; or people begin to think more reflectively about the way things are, and get together to do something, and make others think in the same new way (the Black Power movement would be my Washington example). There seems to be hardly anything peculiarly urban about this. Yet it seems that cities have a large share when it comes to generating movements and making them spread. In part, this goes simply with having a fund of diversity in the form of life framework from which to generate movements. Perhaps if cities are more volatile – keep having more history – their routines also more often come under threat. Confronting diversity, people may more readily see alternatives for themselves, not only as individuals but in terms of collectivities to be mobilized. And there is the fact that the meanings and expressive forms of movements can also be commoditized; with cities offering the most promising markets.

Diversity and agency

I have tried to sketch a way of looking at cultural processes more or less generally, and to suggest a few reasons why cities are special. With this view, then, goes a certain sense of why cities are interesting and useful sites for thinking about culture.

The critics of culturalism in anthropology sometimes reach the extreme conclusion that we should dispense with the culture concept altogether. This has always seemed to me like throwing out the baby with the bath water, and hardly realistic anyway; if anthropologists, after so many years of propagating the idea of culture, were suddenly to try and abolish it, or pretend that it is not theirs, they would probably be neither credible nor successful. But I sympathize with Johannes Fabian's (1978: 329) proposal for 'a liquidation, literally speaking, of the concept of culture'; for Fabian plays on words here, and wants culture 'liquefied,' to emphasize 'how perceptions, experiences and problems are being 'worked out' in an open, never-ending process.' This view of culture is something Fabian himself 'worked out' in that same way, I believe, in studying urban popular culture in Zaire, and it seems directly parallel to the understandings which I reached in Washington.

What, then, are the somewhat peculiar circumstances of this 'working out' in an urban context? Like villages, obviously, cities are limited spaces with concentrations of people, even if there is rather more space, and many more people. But these concentrations tend to be made up rather differently. To borrow an illuminating contrast from Anthony Wallace (1961), if the anthropologist's archetypical village has involved a 'replication of uniformity,' the city in cultural terms is often an 'organization of diversity.' The frameworks of cultural process typically bring more varied culture to the city than to other places.

To be a city dweller is typically to find oneself again and again entangled with other people's culture; not only the meanings which one actively and continuously deals with oneself and the overt shapes one gives them, but also the meanings and meaningful forms which are to one degree or other accessible to one's senses and mind, yet more directly attributable to others. As city people we may have our own routines that we might not think much about, but we may be provoked by what other people in our habitat do, even when, some of the time, the cause of provocation is only these people's own everyday practices. And at times, these will also cast new light on what we took to be common sense.

'Working out' culture – which is to say, the relationship between culture and agency – as far as urbanites are concerned is in no small part a matter of dealing with the overall cultural flow in one's surroundings, and taking some kind of stand, reflectively or not, on what is relevant to one's own thought and action; what might be appropriated (wholly or selectively), what should be resisted, what should in some other way be reacted to, what can safely be ignored. In part, this is a question of dealing with quite specific meanings and meaningful forms in equally specific contexts. Yet perhaps we also see broader, more enduring and encompassing strategies emerging, what we can describe as metacultural frames for handling actual and possible diversity.

One aspect of this may be identified as involving the relationship between practice and imagination. Arjun Appadurai (1991: 198), one of those anthropologists now engaged in rethinking culture in other-than-village settings, has recently suggested that in the past, available traditions provided a relatively finite set of 'possible' lives, really to be enacted, while imagination and fantasy were residual; confined to special persons, moments and places. Now, in contrast, Appadurai points out, the media – cinema, television, VCR technology – offer the materials for imaginary alternatives on a much wider scale, and if one can still only live one life, or at least not very many, this is a reality seen through the prism of other lives readily available to be thought about. The balance has shifted, that is to say, between what is done and what can be thought.

No doubt the media are important here, but the city would seem to work in a similar way. The urbanite can hardly allow his practical line of action to be influenced by all the possibilities and alternatives modeled around him, but they can be present in his imagination.[6] It is one question, of course, how one deals with this in ethnography. Fiction writers have so far dealt with this more fully, and more successfully, than the urban anthropologists, and undoubtedly it is in some part because the latter have been so preoccupied with describing the more tangible facts of ordinary living and its commitments that city people sometimes seem to be not so different from villagers.

Whether translated into observable action or mostly making the mind a livelier place, the management of meaning in the context of urban diversity is at one level small-scale cultural process, where individuals and face-to-face groups develop and reproduce their shares of the wider culture. As an analytical point, I think it may well be useful to give more thought to variations in cultural organization even here. Among anthropologists, culture is almost always taken to be a sociocentric concept; it refers to a property of a collectivity, be that collectivity large or quite small. But even as we accept that culture is socially organized meaning and meaningful form, it would appear that not least in cities, people can place themselves quite idiosyncratically at different crossroads of personal experiences and cultural currents. And they can handle these positions also in different ways, synthesizing or compartmentalizing, integrating or segregating within their personal cultural repertoires.

At another level, however, the complexity of cultural organization in the city should also make it a privileged site for considering how the varied logics of the management of meaning in different organizational frameworks are aggregated into broader patterns, combining for example the symmetries of the form of life frame with the asymmetries of state and market, processes of limited reach and processes reaching very far. Here, it is true, cities as 'confined localities' are not in the end sufficient as units of analysis; yet as the world is now organized, city people will still be prominent actors on those even larger arenas we may identify. I will come back to this in the next installment.

In Amsterdam

This has been an argument mostly in quite general terms for thinking about culture in an urban context. But one of the sources of error in theorizing about the city, it is sometimes pointed out, is that it tends to be about The City, everywhere; not about particular cities, or about varieties of cities. This is true, and I have hardly taken the problem into sufficient account here. Not least for that reason, it seems appropriate to add a few notes on one particular city, Amsterdam – not because I know it well, which I do not, but because it has offered me the context of drawing these thoughts together.

One of the first things that strike any visitor to Amsterdam – any foreign visitor, I should perhaps say, as an indigenous Netherlander will be less surprised – is the windows. A very large proportion of the facade of just about any building in the city seems to be taken up by windows, from the lowest floor to the highest. There may be good practical reasons for this. Houses are often deep, and want to draw in all the daylight they can get. Yet in terms which have more to do with what has been said above, they offer the sensation of great openness: culture flows through these windows, as it were, from private to public spaces and vice versa. It may be a conspicuous claim that 'I have something to trade,' made by a scantily dressed young woman in a window framed by red neon lights; or, simply and piously, that 'we have nothing to hide,' in the instance of the elderly couple glimpsed through the next window, with their backs turned, lace curtains not drawn. Through the window the market displays its goods, and forms of life other than one's own can be inspected, at least surreptitiously, in passing. And this is a two-way flow, for windows also allow you to keep an eye on the street scene. By the way, there has been some interest among anthropologists in the meaning of mirrors; what you see when you see yourself.[7] And I have suggested, metaphorically, above that in the village, your neighbors may be like mirrors – they more or less resemble you. In Amsterdam, there seem to be more than in any other big city of those little mirrors where you do not see yourself, but which, placed sideways from the facade, serve as window amplifiers, and again allow you to look at other people.

It is also obvious that Amsterdam has a great deal of 'other people,' not only of the same kind, but of many kinds. It has drawn them from the outside for centuries, and whether people have come from far away or not, they have been there in sufficient numbers to maintain a great many viable subcultures. Diversity within the form of life framework, then. But the market also seems to offer a noteworthy variety of cultural commodities. This probably has something to do with the scale of the built environment. Some cities have been built, at least as far as their central business districts are concerned, to give preferential accommodation to large enterprises, and car traffic. In Amsterdam it seems as if there is a hole in the wall, with a window in front, for just about every business idea, with easy access for anyone who happens to pass by, on foot or bicycle. Nonetheless, I am surprised by some of these ideas. Amsterdam is known throughout the world, of course, for some of its museums, and museums are great devices for importing diversity from the outside, or for maintaining it by preserving the past. What I had not really expected, however, was a cannabis museum, or a museum of torture.

The street scene itself, of course, can also be a spectacle, a place for scanning diversity, a source for the life of imagination. In Amsterdam, as certainly in many cities, people seem noticeably aware of this. It can be seen in the variety of entertainers – musicians, dancers, jugglers or whatever – who seek out places almost any day on the Dam, in the Kalverstraat or in front of the Centraal Station. Also, I have been told, the number of sidewalk cafés is increasing. This is hardly just because of the drink and food they offer, or because of fresh air and sunlight, but not least because they are street observatories. If the view of human traffic usually makes up much of the cultural flow in what I have called the form of life framework, here we note that in choice locations, it can be commoditized.

Diversity, again, can be handled in different ways in different cities. Some are very heterogeneous as wholes, but make the least of it in their parts, by constructing something rather more like a spatial mosaic of more or less homogeneous, segregated entities. Amsterdam has some of this as well. Yet partly due to the nature of the built environment, and partly to the way the powers that be have handled this resource, much of Amsterdam also exhibits unusual diversity at the micro level of street and neighborhood.[8] This may result in both excitement and unease, but it probably enhances the complexities of cultural process I have dwelt on here.

With regard to matters of metaculture, I am reminded of a little book on San Francisco, where Howard Becker and Irving Louis Horowitz (1971) describe its 'culture of civility.' San Francisco, they say, has long had a tolerance of deviance, even a readiness to take difference to be a civic asset. Its history as a seaport, its tradition of radical unions, the fact that it has in large part been a city of single people or couples rather than families has contributed to such a climate. It would seem that very similar things can be said about Amsterdam, and given yet greater historical depth. This, of course, is one of its attractions to many natives; but also, as I will note again, to many strangers.

Notes

1. I have reviewed these studies in a chapter in Hannerz (1980), but this is of course only one contribution to a large and continuously growing body of commentary on the Chicago School.

2. For some examples of such critiques, see Fox (1985), Kahn (1989) and Abu-Lughod (1991).

3. This study is most fully reported in Hannerz (1969).

4. The point of view which I sketch here is developed at greater length in Hannerz (1992).

5. See Handler's (1985) comments on the relationship between anthropological thought and nationalist ideology.

6. As Victor Turner (e.g. 1977: 71) might have put it, in 'the subjunctive mood'; an aspect of liminality.

7. See e.g. Fernandez (1980) and Hannerz (1983).

8. See e.g. Anderiesen and Reijndorp (1990), and the comments by Soja (1991: 16 ff.)

For references see next chapter

Cities as windows on the world

Ulf Hannerz

In Bijlmermeer

Take a seat by the window in a café on one of the squares in the Amsterdamse Poort shopping center on a Saturday afternoon, enjoy the pancake of your choice; and as you watch the everchanging scene outside, you may marvel at the way the public spaces of larger cities in western Europe and North America have become transnational commons, where white, black, brown and yellow people mingle. And this mingling continues in the Shopperhal block next door. Much of its merchandise is of the kind you can get anywhere in Amsterdam. But at the more distant, I believe northern, end of the Shopperhal, the scene begins to become a little different. One of the stalls sells beauty aids for non-European women, and across the aisle from it a food stall carries tropical specialties; there are *Surinaamse bollen* as well as *Berliner bollen*. You continue past the Razaq Islamic butchery and leave the Shopperhal through a nearby exit.[1]

And then, in the square outside, and in the housing area beyond it, you see almost only black people. This is Bijlmermeer, sometimes described as the second largest city of Surinam, nestling inside the largest city of the Netherlands. In the landscaped grounds between the rather rundown ten-story apartment buildings, some boys are throwing fire crackers, which echo loudly between the walls; from an open window high up in one building you hear an old Bob Marley tune. A little further up in the air, a large jet plane is just coming in from the east to land at Schiphol airport. On your way back, you come upon a smaller, modest shopping area where the most prominent establishment is the Hi-Lo Supermarkt. Here you can get frozen fish straight from Surinam, frozen cassava, also dried fish, fresh okra from Kenya, plantains, and printed-in-Bombay greeting cards with a picture of Ganesh, the elephant god, on the cover and the text 'We wish you that festive Deepawali bring you and your family all round prosperity' inside. A small stall next to the Hi-Lo sells the same kinds of printed cloths which have always tempted me in the market places of West Africa, and exhibits a male mannequin in a flowing, richly embroidered gown. The record and cassette store across the hall has Indian and Caribbean music, next to it a stall sells roti, and a few steps away the Pacific Travel Centre announces that it is the agent for Surinam Airways, while the Chez Polly hairdressing salon proclaims its expertise in handling Afro, Euro and Asiatic hair.

Back in the main area of the Amsterdamse Poort again, you may rest in a reasonably credible likeness of a brown café, fringed lamp shades, carpeted tables, pool tables and all. Here again you see almost only white people, and only men. But a little darkskinned girl in bright clothes dashes in through the door, looks among those standing at the bar, and leaves with her burly, blond father.

In Amsterdam, a city of windows, the notion comes readily to one's mind that cities can be seen as windows on the world. In Bijlmermeer, and its Hi-Lo Supermarkt, you encounter the Caribbean: sights, sounds, smells, tastes. In Kalverstraat, Europe goes shopping, while a block or so away, you can browse in newspapers and magazines from almost everywhere in the Athenaeum Nieuws Centrum. The Jewish History Museum tells the story of people who came to the Netherlands and to Amsterdam, lived there for generations and had a part in shaping it, and then were taken away from there. At the Tropenmuseum, formerly a colonial museum, you get a sense of where the Dutch went in earlier years, and what they found there.

If cities are windows on the world, you see different things through different windows. As a short-term visitor, I can only hope here to catch a glimpse through the window that is Amsterdam. Yet I will try at the same time to fit whatever impressionistic and superficial understandings I may thus have gained into my more general sense of what contribution urban studies can make to a macro-anthropology of contemporary culture.[2]

The global ecumene

The point of departure here is that we can identify two major ways of thinking about the organization of culture in the world. According to one of them, that which I believe has long been dominant, cultures belong to territories, and are rather clearly bounded. We may see it as the idea of the global mosaic (and remember the criticism of the mosaic metaphor I had in the first lecture). It is of course grounded in the fact that through most of history, the great majority of people have been more or less sedentary, and the flow of meaning and meaningful form has passed mostly within the face-to-face relationships among them. Cultural process thus tends to be localized. But at least for a couple of centuries now, the idea of the global mosaic has also drawn ideological support from being the understanding of culture preferred by the nation state, a political unit defined by bounded territory and seeking cultural legitimacy matching that definition; I commented on that in the preceding lecture.

The other view is more emergent, resulting from a certain pressure to reconsider the culture concept against the background of changes in the world which are hardly altogether new but which have grown more and more conspicuous. It may as yet be more fuzzy, more intellectually disorderly, as developing clusters of understandings tend to be, but it begins with the very fundamental assumption that as a collective system of meaning, culture belongs primarily to social relationships, and to complexes of such relationships; and only indirectly and without logical necessity to territories.

The point here, of course, is that culture now exists under conditions which makes it less place-bound than ever before. Whether labor migrants, refugees or tourists, jet set or brain drain, people in the twentieth century move about readily, quickly and over great distances, aided by transport technology. And when they thus move about, they bring at least some of their culture with them. Moreover, even when people stay put, culture also moves through media and by way of other material objects, not least those produced by industries oriented toward mass consumption. Clearly not everybody has become equally footloose, nor have face-to-face contacts lost their importance in the world as it is now. But there is a more complicated mixture of local and long-distance relationships, and thus the coincidence of territorial and cultural boundaries cannot be taken for granted. Instead of a global cultural mosaic, there is a global ecumene, a single field of persistent interaction and exchange between cultures.[3] Less often do we face unsurmountable barriers; more often open, ramifying networks. Rather than living in perhaps blissful ignorance of all but a small portion of the combined cultural inventory of the world, each one of us comes into some, if only fleeting, contact with a larger part of it. And the idea of cultures in the plural itself becomes more problematic, insofar as the demarcation of lesser units within the overall organization of diversity becomes fairly arbitrary, a matter of rhetoric or of analytical convenience.

Because of the ways in which they tend to combine intricate local cultural processes with a great variety of links covering greater distances, cities are strategic sites for observing the cultural organization of this global ecumene. Insofar as it has followed a dominant tradition of ethnographic research in concentrating on the local, the face-to-face in society and culture, urban anthropology as practiced in the last few decades has somewhat lost sight of this fact. Mostly, that is, it has taken an inside view; a grassroots view, if that metaphor is not too inappropriate for the urban context. But we must not forget that cities are usually centers. They influence the surrounding space politically, economically, socially, and also culturally. And the facts about the internal life of the city are often connected to such external capacities. To see what cities do in the global ecumene, consequently, we might well try to combine the local with the long-distance, the inside view with the overview.

But, to repeat, you see different things through different windows. All cities do not operate over the same distances, nor do they do the same things in organizing culture and social relationships. Each of them fits into the various frameworks which organize cultural process in its own way, has its own place in a partly hierarchically ordered, partly competitive network of urban places, and is a product of its own evolving history. Certain of them seem somehow to resonate better than others with the idea of a global ecumene. Where, in such terms, is Amsterdam?

The past in the present

While I am primarily concerned with the present, I think in this case there is no way of ignoring the past. Despite perhaps unpromising beginnings as a fishing village, threatened by the destructive powers of wind and water, Amsterdam in time grew quickly in size as well as importance, and did so on the basis of the long-distance relationships reaching out from its port. And thus in cultural terms, it took on the characteristics of one of what has been seen as two basic types of cities in human history. I am referring here to Robert Redfield's and Milton Singer's classic article on 'The Cultural Role of Cities' (1954), where they contrast orthogenetic and heterogenetic cities.

The orthogenetic cities, Redfield and Singer suggested, are cities as sacred centers, engaging with the modest, simple, mostly homogeneous folk tradition of the countryside around them, refining it into a high culture and using the authority of the latter as an instrument of rule. The heterogenetic cities, in contrast, tend to be characterized by administrative and commercial rationality, and by the diverse cultural origins of their inhabitants; and it more or less follows from this that their influence cuts across whatever may be the boundaries of traditions.

Amsterdam, by these criteria, soon evolved into a heterogenetic city. And it seems that the ethos it established as a heterogenetic city shows remarkable continuity and distinctiveness. I have been intrigued in this connection by some comments of one of my predecessors in the city council's generous scheme for the education of instant Amsterdamologists, Donald Olsen (1990: 20). First of all, there is his characterization of the city in its seventeenth century golden age – 'capitalistic, individualistic, tolerant, republican, cosmopolitan, pragmatic, rationalistic, and scientific.' Many of these terms seem equally true of the city three hundred years later. Yet Olsen goes on to note that even if Amsterdam in its golden age seems to anticipate the twentieth century, it was really rather 'the last great medieval city,' a successor to city states like Venice and Florence. As the nation states of Europe came into being, such independent cities were brought into submission.

And so, something perhaps reminiscent of what Redfield and Singer called orthogenetic cities became a dominant urban model. It was the earliest cities of human history which probably best exemplified orthogenetic cities, and in their pure form such cities are hardly around any more.[4] Yet the urban centers to which the nation states gave shape seem to have borrowed something from them. These states are not really, or only partly, theater states, but their capital cities may be conspicuously engaged in defining, refining and celebrating national culture, and somewhat jealously watching the integrity of its own bounded domain.[5] And in that sense, there is a greater affinity between them and what I have called the mosaic model of world culture.

Again, Amsterdam seems to show little of this; continuing, it seems, proudly heterogenetic, carrying that heritage of medieval urbanism and at the same time becoming very much a city of the contemporary global ecumene. If this is in any way enigmatic, the explanation for it may of course be found to some extent in the division of labor between Amsterdam and the Hague, and also, I suppose, in the somewhat peculiar nature of the Dutch nation state, historically itself so much a creation by its cities, for its cities.[6]

And now, the time for something resembling the medieval city may be here once more. The cities which in the late twentieth century we call world cities are beginning to lead lives rather distinct from those of their territorial states again, and entities such as Singapore and Hong Kong may even suggest that city states can at least in some ways be viable social forms.

Commerce, migrants, tourists, media

But does then Amsterdam at this point count as a world city? This is apparently something one can hold different opinions about. Various lists of such cities are in circulation. New York, London and Paris are no doubt on all of them, but Amsterdam, alone or as part of a Randstad conglomerate, is on some and not on others.

Of course, it is not a very big city. New York is the Big Apple; Amsterdam, arranged by the canals into layer upon layer until you get to the core around the Dam, is more like a medium-sized onion. To get back to the metaphor of cities as windows on the world again, perhaps you expect to see more through big windows. That may be true to a degree, but what matters more is certainly how the window is placed relative to what is to be seen.

In other words, I think it is more important to consider what number and variety of linkages that a city has beyond the boundaries of its nation. I will want to say something here summarily about Amsterdam and transnational commerce, about migrants to Amsterdam from other continents, about Amsterdam and tourists, and about media and Amsterdam. These, I think, have much to do with giving Amsterdam its place in the global ecumene; a place with some features shared with other more or less central places, and others quite distinctively its own.

What are nowadays mostly thought of as world cities are, above all, nerve centers of the global economy.[7] They are cities of managers and entrepreneurs, and of all the people managers and entrepreneurs need in their offices; they need not, on the other hand, be much involved in manufacturing. 'The way such men use the city,' Melvin Webber (1968: 1096) points out in an article already a couple of decades old, 'reveals its essential character most clearly, for to them the city is essentially a massive communications switchboard through which human interaction takes place.' Cities, that is, are rich in information, and in world cities you can get information from practically anywhere.

I am reminded again of Amsterdam in its golden age. In *The Embarrassment of Riches* (1987: 347), Simon Schama describes the conduct of business in the city of that time:

> 'News was of the utmost importance in these floating transactions, and the regular publication of the courants supplied political and military intelligence to help investors make informed decisions. Strategically placed relatives or correspondents in ports across the globe helped pass on relevant information, but professional punters on the bourse regularly used couriers, eavesdroppers and spies in the coffeehouses of the Kalverstraat to glean tidbits about an enterprise's prospects, or indeed to propagate optimism or pessimism as their stance required.'

In this period, it seems, Amsterdam was indeed a world city with respect to global business. It has not descended so very far from the heights of that business now either. If the port is no longer so important for communications, one can see Schiphol as its heir, not the world's largest airport but often said to be its finest (as I heard again and again some years ago in Singapore, whose Changi airport tended to come in second place and thus had to try harder). Yet in business terms, by now, Amsterdam is not at the level of New York, London, or Tokyo, and also has alternatives like Frankfurt, Zürich and Brussels to compete with.[8]

'Transnational elites are the dominant class in the world city, and the city is arranged to cater to their life styles and occupational necessities,' write John Friedmann and Goetz Wolff (1982: 322) in a brief but important analysis of such centers, and this statement can be used to bridge the gap between global managers and global retail business. As windows on the world, for the rich and for those of modest means, for natives and visitors, cities are not least shop windows.

It is one of the theoretical tenets of the globalization of the market place that a superior product finds its niche, its segment of the local market, anywhere in the world (cf. Levitt 1983). To modify this a little, I would suggest rather that the market segments for some commodities are now just about everywhere, some are recurrent in a great many places, and others again are highly local. And as far as consumer goods are concerned, they are represented to the extent that they match locally represented forms of life, with their characteristic resource bases, values and everyday practices.[9]

It is of course often those commodities which are everywhere, and those which are recurrent, that provide much of the support for the notion that globalization equals a global homogenization of culture.[10] As there is a branch of Sotheby's on Rokin, we can assume that Amsterdam's elite is not doing too badly, and has tastes not altogether dissimilar from elites in at least a handful of other cities; yet P.C. Hooftstraat, sophisticated as it may be, is not really the last word in opulence. With regard to commodities at various points further down-market, Amsterdam also has Benetton, Marks & Spencer, IKEA, Kentucky Fried Chicken, and MacDonalds, all of which may or may not also be found in Singapore. In a way, of course, all these transnational retail enterprises serve to make Amsterdam a window on the world, not least for the Dutch.

Nonetheless, commerce in Amsterdam also makes it a cultural crossroads by way of things found in few other places; sometimes perhaps nowhere else. No visitor walking through Amsterdam can fail to notice its unusual mixture of fast foods, junk foods, 'out-of-the-wall foods'; it is not all McDonalds, and not all herring, eels, *poffertjes* or croquettes either, but also *loempia* and *saté*. In other words, Amsterdam's market place also offers the traditions of immigrants from far away in readily accessible commodity form. And immigrants have for centuries contributed to the heterogenetic qualities of Amsterdam, in the form of life framework as well as in the market.

This has been an unusually open city, to Sephardic Jews departing in the seventeenth century from Spain and Portugal, and to Ashkenazic Jews coming later from the east; to Huguenots from France in the eighteenth century, and to a great many others arriving at one time or other through the port or the Centraal Station, in recent years not least to Turks and Moroccans in search of a livelihood. But the walk through Bijlmermeer, and the *loempia* in the street stand and the *saté* sticks in a brown café, remind us that not least, it has been an openness to a lingering empire.

One can perhaps more readily take the Pakistanis and the Jamaicans in London and the Senegalese in Paris for granted, since London and Paris are undisputedly world cities of the first rank. But the Surinamers and the Javanese in Amsterdam, whether first, second or third generation, are more like the Angolans and the Goans in Lisbon in demonstrating that the global ecumene, however its coherence may have increased in later years, is still a creation of history, and derives some of its enduring polycentricity from this fact. Colonial and postcolonial memories are not always (probably never) unambiguously happy, on one side or the other, but in different ways old metropoles, even in what have become small countries, remain centers to which scholars, tourists and sometimes exiles from old dependencies continue to be drawn. Sometimes these are merely brief visits. In the Dutch case, however, decolonization has also entailed some noteworthy waves of permanent migration. That of the mid-1970s, when one third of the population of Surinam chose to move to the Netherlands, is the last but perhaps most striking example.

As far as foreign tourists in Amsterdam are concerned (and the first thing to observe here is that Amsterdam is both energetic and successful in presenting itself as a tourist city), they may not mind the MacDonalds restaurants and the Benetton stores so much; in a paradoxical way, in the global ecumene it may be such sights that in an alien environment remind them comfortably of home.[11] What positively attracts them more, presumably, is whatever is not everywhere, for tourism must always feed on difference (if only a managed, balanced difference).[12] These things, in Amsterdam, are partly things typically Dutch, for from the tourist perspective, these also make Amsterdam a window on the world: the houses and the canals, the museums, the brown cafés. Yet the tourists, taking in Amsterdam with all their senses, are also likely to be struck by the particular diversity of origins of people and things, in Kalverstraat, or in the Albert Cuypstraat street market, or – if they ever get there – in Amsterdamse Poort. And the official tourist brochures are certain to make a point of recommending the exotic *Rijsttafel*, even as they are mostly silent about the native pea soup.

One more thing, it seems to me, which makes cities special places in the global ecumene, and some cities more so than others, is the media situation. I have already mentioned the Athenaeum Nieuws Centrum, with all its varied Dutch and foreign periodicals. It may appear as an odd idea to point to media as urban phenomena, for in a way they could be anti-urban, facilitating other than face-to-face communication, making concentrations of people in space less necessary. But this is not the way it works, for it is still in the market places of the city that the widest range of media and media products are available. And it is here that the meanings and meaningful forms from everywhere tend to make claims on your attention: through the newspaper headlines on the street corner, the pop music from the record store, the large assortment of cable television channels. In a city like Amsterdam, it is all on your doorstep, or even already inside it, simultaneously present. (Did I get it right, as I was only half listening to the weather forecast on CNN? 'The weekend begins with rain in many parts of the world...').

Making culture from diversity

What, then, do people make of it all? The city in the global ecumene, I have said, is characteristically a combination of the variety of outside links with a web of local processes. What do Amsterdammers do with the diversity of their city as they manage meaning and meaningful form in their daily lives?

The overarching metacultural stance which the people of Amsterdam have evolved toward diversity, it is frequently said, is one of tolerance, of cultural *laissez-faire*; I touched on this in the preceding lecture. Perhaps this came early, as the Dutch passed through, and learned from, their own historical crises and clashes over differences in belief and practice; it was already on the list of traits which Donald Olsen enumerated with regard to the golden age. Just how it has been shiftingly influenced over the years by a range of quite different experiences – 'pillarization,' *verzuiling*, and its crumbling; the cultural upheavals of the late 1960s and early 1970s, with their testing of established assumptions (commemorated at the Nieuwmarkt underground station); the rowdiness normally to be expected in a port city where sailors seek release from the harsh constraints of life on board; the influx of groups of aliens – would be difficult for anybody to work out, and impossibly so for me as a visitor.[13]

Anyway, one may suspect that as far as newcomer groups are concerned, it has probably helped Amsterdammers take a rather relaxed view of their incorporation into the social fabric that these have in several instances not shown very high-profile differences. The Sephardim did not seem so unlike other prosperous burghers. The people from the East Indies, and the Surinamers, have been through an anticipatory socialization for Dutch life by growing up in Dutch colonies. Possibly there is now a little more worry about the Moroccans and the Turks, who do not necessarily fit in quite so readily.[14]

Diversity and tolerance of it, however, do not only pertain to matters of ethnicity and religion. Amsterdam also has its reputation for allowing, in its easy-going manner, various other kinds of conduct, and the commerce catering to them, for which greater obstacles tend to be created in many other cities: of such phenomena the red-light district has obviously been around the longest, depending in history no doubt on the demands of a major port. Such acceptance is necessarily in some part a fact of local life, at the levels of official and unofficial native reactions. At the same time, at present, it also has its part in the attractiveness of Amsterdam to what one may term international subcultural tourism. Jansen (1991), in his study of the geography of cannabis in Amsterdam, notes that many of the visitors to the coffee houses of the central city are young foreigners who know little of the city except the names of some famous outlets for soft drugs. Perhaps Jansen's English-language monograph itself attracts readers as a guide to such facilities.[15]

Generally, I suppose, in Amsterdam or anywhere else, tolerance is very often more of a passive and distracted rather than an active stance. As people go about their own affairs, others can conduct theirs in their own way, as long as they cause no significant disruption. What plays some part in Amsterdam is presumably the fact that a large proportion of the residents of the inner city are now single people, or double-career couples, rather than families with children.[16] Even if they do not think of the moral diversity of their neighbor-hoods as something providing interesting local colour, they are at least not easily bothered. Tolerance as an accomplished fact may likewise have some-thing to do with the micro-ecology of the Amsterdam built environment. Dense, unpredictable, unsurveillable, uncontrollable, it allows some activities to go on unseen, or at least allows the excuse that they are not seen, whenever one prefers not to see. It is a part of the history of the city that for minorities during times of difficulty or persecution, this environment has provided at least temporary sanctuaries: a Catholic church in an attic in the seventeenth century, a Jewish family behind a hidden door in the 1940s.

Tolerance, however, is not all that has come out of the Amsterdam experience of diversity. Its handling in cultural process has also included the passage of cultural forms between groups and contexts, along with reinterpretation and innovation. This is surely also something which make cities like Amsterdam intriguing observation posts in the global ecumene. There are the Yiddish loan words characteristic of the Amsterdam dialect, and the somewhat bland *nasi goreng* served for lunch in a Dutch old people's home.[17] Interesting chains of ethnic and cultural shifts seem to go on here. The cuisine of the East Indies was no doubt introduced to the Netherlands by immigrants from there, and by returning colonialists; then as it was gaining popularity, I have been told, the resulting niche for small restaurants was taken over and expanded by Chinese seamen on Dutch ships, coming ashore in a period of economic depression. Thus almost every small town in the Netherlands seems with time to have been colonized in its turn by that special culinary institution which is part Chinese, part Southeast Asian, and certainly part Dutch. And as a late twist, but not necessarily the last, the Amsterdam street trade in *loempia* rolls now provides an opening for the Vietnamese.

The cultural careers of young black Surinamers, settled in Bijlmermeer or elsewhere, can be no less interesting. Here again I rely on the research of local colleagues.[18] The Surinamers who came to the Netherlands in large numbers especially in the 1970s were mostly people of fairly limited education and not very much cosmopolitan sophistication. As they encountered the faster pace and rather bewildering heterogeneity and strangeness of Amsterdam and other cities, some found it a bit threatening, and turned inward to their kin and friendship networks and to the Moravian church they had brought from home. The younger people, as usual, were quicker to explore the new habitat. Boys, predictably, tended to be in the streets and other public places, and at least some of them made contacts with their Dutch counterparts there. Surinamese and Dutch girls likewise sometimes became friends, but more often they went to each other's homes. Thus it was the Surinamese girls who often became more familiar with the domestic aspects of Dutch life.

When the young Surinamese came to Amsterdam, however, they also found transnational youth culture waiting for them, among their peers and in the market place. Some became 'disco freaks,' with whatever this implied in terms of clothing fashions and musical taste. In their case, as elsewhere in Europe, it turned out that in one particular context at least, being black was no handicap; among the devotees of popular culture inspired from the United States and the Caribbean, belonging to an ethnic minority was rather a social asset, and Surinamers could find themselves as stylistic leaders on the dance floor. If there was a disadvantage to this, it might rather be that they were tempted to devote the larger part of their energies to the night shift.

On the other hand, there were the Rastas. There had been no Rastafarianism in Paramaribo, or anywhere else in their old homeland. In Amsterdam this movement, or style, was apparently largely unknown until Bob Marley and his Wailers came for a concert in 1976, but then it caught on. Groups of the new Surinamer Rastas from Amsterdam might go over to London, European capital of Rastafarianism, and trade Dutch marihuana for Rasta hats, badges and records. They could find inspiration, as well, in movies playing in a couple of ethnic-oriented theaters in Amsterdam. Like Rastas elsewhere, they looked for purity in their African roots, only with the special Surinamese twist that to the consternation or even horror of their elders, they began to identify with the Bush Negroes of the Surinamese hinterland, treated in Paramaribo rather as exemplars of the idiocy of rural life. Yet Amsterdam Rastafarianism was also a cultural *mélange* of varied ingredients. From elsewhere in the countercultural landscape of Amsterdam, it drew on the romantic environmentalism of 'being in touch with nature.' Meanwhile, if in a manner and to a degree Amsterdam Rastas thus became Greens, when Amsterdam coffee shops could no longer be quite so straightforward about being cannabis outlets, they adopted the red, yellow and green emblematic colors of Rastafarianism, and the national flag of Jamaica, to advertise their merchandise in a slightly more roundabout way.

And so cultural mingling and recombination goes on and on, weaving its way between contexts and organizational frameworks, in Amsterdam and others of those cities which are central places of the global ecumene. Ideas and symbols make their passage from Kingston, Jamaica, to Amsterdam by way of London, and inspire a wistful look back to the bush beyond Paramaribo; not quite the shortest route from one Caribbean place to another. But then that is the way center-periphery relationships work, and it means that the centers are often centers not because they are the origins of all things, but rather because they are places of exchange, the switchboards of culture.

This, obviously, is also a strong reason why those of us who are anthropologists should be in such centers, not only looking at what goes on in them as limited spaces, 'confined localities,' but also looking out through them, at the world which they are engaged in organizing. It is a world where for people, 'tumbled as they are into endless connection, it is increasingly difficult to get out of one another's way'; the words are Clifford Geertz' (1988: 147), in his most recent book. If, as Geertz also suggests, it is this world which anthropologists must now try to come to grips with, and preferably also help these people themselves to understand, we have a long way to go. But perhaps we can begin by hanging around in the places where such 'endless connection' most conspicuously goes on, in Kalverstraat, at Schiphol, or in Bijlmermeer, at the Hi-Lo Markt.

Notes

1. I realize that I will return again and again to exemplifying the cultural diversity of Amsterdam by way of its foods; not only, I suppose, because they are among the cultural forms of which a temporary visitor like myself most readily becomes aware, but also because food has a significant place in the definition of ethnic identities and cultural changes.

2. I have discussed aspects of the role of cities in transnational cultural processes in two other papers (Hannerz forthcoming a and b), and various other aspects of the globalization of culture elsewhere (e.g. Hannerz 1989 and 1992, especially chapter 7).

3. For a similar point of view see de Swaan (1991).

4. Wheatley (1971) offers a major analysis of such cities.

5. They are prominent sites, that is, for the cultural flow of the state framework, as identified in the preceding lecture.

6. See de Vries (1988: 35): 'the Revolt of the Netherlands could be described as the creation of a state controlled by the cities, to avoid their being subjugated by a territorial state.'

7. For an extensive recent treatment see King (1990).

8. Note here the discussion by Lambooy (1988) of the world economic system, the rivalry of global cities within it, and the position of Amsterdam in such rivalry, as well as the related comments by Soja (1991: 27 ff.).

9. I refer here, obviously, to my discussion of form of life and market as organizing frameworks for cultural process, and of interrelations of such frameworks, in the first lecture.

10. For a critique of the scenario of global homogenization see Hannerz (1991).

11. I am reminded here of Anne Tyler's novel *The Accidental Tourist* (1985), where the hero (or rather anti-hero) is an author of guidebooks for travelers who want to encapsulate themselves in the familiar.

12. Tourism has a somewhat complex relationship to two of the organizational frameworks of cultural process identified in the first lecture, those of market and form of life. At one level, entire territories such as cities are packaged as commodities; you can go into a travel agency somewhere in the world and buy Amsterdam as one whole package of experience. Once you arrive, of course, much of that experience is again in the form of life framework, available for free as you walk about, sit around, observe and eavesdrop. Yet travel to another place also means access to particular local markets and their commodities; that particular access, then, is a part of the more generalized commodity of place.

13. For a brief statement on *verzuiling* see Goudsblom (1967: 120 ff.)

14. One gets some sense of this in Brunt's (1989) study of Turks and Moroccans in Utrecht.

15. There is also in the bookstores a specialized guidebook for gay visitors to Amsterdam.

16. Becker and Horowitz (1971) point to a similar background to tolerance in San Francisco.

17. On the relationship of the Dutch to exotic cuisines, see van Otterloo (1987).

18. See van Wetering (1987), van Niekerk and Vermeulen (1989) and especially the unpublished work of Livio Sansone (1991a, 1991b).

References

Abu-Lughod, Lila
    1991   Writing against Culture. In *Recapturing Anthropology*. Richard G. Fox, ed. Santa Fe, NM: School of American Research Press.

Anderiesen, Gerard, and Arnold Reijndorp
  1990   The Stabilization of Heterogeneity - urban renewal areas in Amsterdam and
            Rotterdam. In *Residential Differentiation*. Léon Deben, Willem Heinemeijer and
            Dick van der Vaart, eds. Amsterdam: Centrum voor Grootstedelijk Onderzoek.

Anderson, Benedict
  1983   *Imagined Communities*. London: Verso.

Appadurai, Arjun
  1991   Global Ethnoscapes: Notes and Queries for a Transnational Anthropology. In:
            Recapturing Anthropology. Richard G. Fox, ed. Santa Fe, NM: School of American
            Research Press.

Becker, Howard S., and Irving Louis Horowitz
  1971   The Culture of Civility. In: *Culture and Civility in San Francisco*. Howard S.
            Becker, ed. Chicago: Transaction/Aldine.

Brunt, Lodewijk
  1989   Foreigners in the Neighbourhood: Ethnic Groups and Institutions in Utrecht. In:
            Dutch Dilemmas. Jeremy Boissevain and Jojada Verrips, eds. Assen/Maastricht:
            Van Gorcum.

Fabian, Johannes
  1978   Popular Culture in Africa: Findings and Conjectures. *Africa*, 48: 315-334.

Fernandez, James
  1980   Reflections on Looking into Mirrors. *Semiotica*, 30: 27-39.

Fox, Richard
  1985   *Lions of the Punjab*. Berkeley: University of California Press.

Friedmann, John, and Goetz Wolff
  1982   World City Formation: An Agenda for Research and Action. *International Journal
            of Urban and Regional Research*, 6: 309-344.

Gans, Herbert
  1962   *The Urban Villagers*. New York: Free Press.

Geertz, Clifford
  1973   *The Interpretation of Cultures*. New York: Basic Books.
  1988   *Works and Lives*. Stanford: Stanford University Press.

Goudsblom, Johan
  1967   *Dutch Society*. New York: Random House.

Handler, Richard
  1985   On Dialogue and Destructive Analysis:
            Problems in Narrating Nationalism and Ethnicity. *Journal of Anthropological
            Research*, 41: 171-182.

Hannerz, Ulf
  1969   *Soulside*. New York: Columbia University Press.
  1980   *Exploring the City*. New York: Columbia University Press.
  1983   Tools of Identity and Imagination. In: *Identity: Personal and Socio-Cultural*. Anita
            Jacobson-Widding, ed. Uppsala: Almqvist & Wiksell International.

1989   Culture between Centre and Periphery: Toward a Macroanthropology. *Ethnos*, 54: 200-216.
1991   Scenarios for Peripheral Cultures. In: *Culture, Globalization and the World-System*. Anthony D. King, ed. Binghamton, NY: MRTS.
1992   *Cultural Complexity*. New York: Columbia University Press.
forthc. a   The Cultural Role of World Cities. In: *The Age of the City*. Anthony Cohen and Katsuyoshi Fukui, eds. Edinburgh: Edinburgh University Press.
forthc. b   Stockholm: Doubly Creolizing. In: *To Make the World Safe for Diversity*. Åke Daun, Billy Ehn and Barbro Klein, eds. Botkyrka: Swedish Immigration Institute.

Jansen, A.C.M.
1991   *Cannabis in Amsterdam*. Muiderberg: Coutinho.

Kahn, Joel S.
1989   Culture: Demise or Resurrection? *Critique of Anthropology*, 9(2): 5-25.

King, Anthony D.
1990   *Global Cities*. London: Routledge.

Lambooy, J.G.
1988   Global Cities and the World Economic System: Rivalry and Decision-making. In *Capital Cities as Achievement*. Léon Deben, Willem Heinemeijer, and Dick van der Vaart, eds. Amsterdam: Centrum voor Grootstedelijk Onderzoek.

Levitt, Theodore
1983   The Globalization of Markets. *Harvard Business Review*, 61(3): 92-102.

Lewis, Oscar
1965   'Further Observations on the Folk-Urban Continuum and Urbanization with Special Reference to Mexico City. In: *The Study of Urbanization*. Philip M. Hauser and Leo F. Schnore, eds. New York: Wiley.

Machlup, Fritz
1980   *Knowledge and Knowledge Production*. Princeton: Princeton University Press.

Niekerk, Mies van, and Hans Vermeulen
1989   Ethnicity and Leisure Time: Surinamese Girls in Amsterdam. In: *Dutch Dilemmas*. Jeremy Boissevain and Jojada Verrips, eds. Assen/ Maastricht: Van Gorcum.

Olsen, Donald J.
1990   *Time and the City & Urbanity, Modernity, and Liberty*. Amsterdam: Centrum voor Grootstedelijk Onderzoek.

Ortner, Sherry
1984   Theory in Anthropology since the Sixties. *Comparative Studies in Society and History*, 26: 126-166.

Otterloo, Anneke H. van
1987   Foreign Immigrants and the Dutch at Table, 1945-1985: Bridging or Widening the Gap? *Netherlands' Journal of Sociology*, 23: 126-143.

Redfield, Robert, and Milton Singer
1954   The Cultural Role of Cities. *Economic Development and Cultural Change*, 3: 53-73.

Sanjek, Roger
1990   Urban Anthropology in the 1980s: A World View. *Annual Review of Anthropology*, 19: 151-186.

Sansone, Livio
1991a   From Creole to Black: Leisure Time, Style and the New Ethnicity of Lower-class Young Blacks of Surinamese Origin in Amsterdam: 1975-1991. Unpublished ms.
1991b   Marginalization and Survival Strategies among Young Lower-class Blacks of Surinamese Origin in Amsterdam. Unpublished ms.

Schama, Simon
1987   *The Embarrassment of Riches*. London: Collins.

Simmel, Georg
1964   *The Sociology of Georg Simmel*. New York: Free Press.

Soja, Edward W.
1991   *The Stimulus of a Little Confusion*. Amsterdam: Centrum voor Grootstedelijk Onderzoek.

Swaan, Abram de
1991   *Perron Nederland*. Amsterdam: Meulenhoff.

Turner, Victor
1977   Process, System, and Symbol: A New Anthropological Synthesis. *Daedalus*, 106(3): 61-80.

Tyler, Anne
1985   *The Accidental Tourist*. New York: Knopf.

Vries, Jan de
1988   Power and the Capital City. In: *Capital Cities as Achievement*. Léon Deben, Willem Heinemeijer, Dick van der Vaart, eds. Amsterdam: Centrum voor Grootstedelijk Onderzoek.

Wallace, Anthony F.C.
1961   *Culture and Personality*. New York: Random House.

Webber, Melvin M.
1968   The Post-City Age. *Daedalus*, 97: 1091-1110.

Wetering, Wilhelmina van
1987   Informal Supportive Networks: Quasi-kin Groups, Religion and Social Order among Surinam Creoles in the Netherlands. *Netherlands' Journal of Sociology*, 23: 92-101.

Wheatley, Paul
1971   *The Pivot of the Four Quarters*. Edinburgh: Edinburgh University Press.

Time and the city
Is there an urban history?

Donald Olsen

We historians like to think that our discipline knows no boundaries. We share the arrogance of the Hamburg-Amerika Line in the years just before 1914 when it put an eagle with outstretched wings at the bow of its new transatlantic superliners with the motto, *'Mein Feld ist die Welt'*. Just as Herodotus in his travels through the known world asked questions about every subject that came into his head, from the behaviour of the Egyptian gods to the marital practices of the Scythians, and included all the answers that he received, whether consistent or contradictory, in his history, we assume the right to incorporate the subject-matter of all other disciplines in ours.

Everything, we insist, has a history: not just war and politics but commerce, agriculture, science, religion, art, philosophy, education, sex, cookery, gardening, whatever you name will have specialized scholarly journals and professional societies devoted to uncovering its history. Well, if it keeps you amused, genuine philosophers, real economists, proper theologians might well respond to our efforts to encompass their disciplines in ours. But by and large we not only enjoy our research into such esoteric fields, but claim that in a very real sense we understand philosophy better than philosophers, economics better than economists, religion better than theologians, because of the special insight historical perspective grants.

The magical word is 'context,' by which we mean that unless one places event, institution, idea, or artifact into the specific time and place in which it happened, existed, or was created, one cannot really understand it at all. (It is, for example, the absence of any sense of temporal, spatial, or cultural context that makes Lewis Mumford's attempts to construct a general urban history, for all the occasional brilliance of his insights, ultimately so preposterous.)

But if in theory historians have always claimed the whole of human experience for their realm, in practice they have until recently followed more in the footsteps of Thucydides than of Herodotus in limiting their inquiries mostly to politics, diplomacy, and war. Social history would be dealt with summarily in a descriptive chapter covering everything from sport to costume to table manners, as Macaulay, for instance, devoted the third chapter of his *History of England* to a panoramic picture of English life and society in 1685 before proceeding thereafter to conventional political narrative.

In the past generation the situation, as you know, has been radically altered. Following the lead of the *Annales* school in France, historians have tried to bring social history from a peripheral to a central role in their investigations, relegating political history to a subordinate position as consisting merely of *les évenements,* and worse, of events involving only a tiny minority of the population. So, instead of the history of parliament we have the history of the family, instead of the history of philosophy we have the studies of *mentalités,* instead of diplomatic narratives studies of child-rearing, housework, courtship, petty crime.

As part of the new emphasis on 'history from below,' urban history has expanded from being the concern of amateurs and local patriots to a 'growth industry,' with its own journals, book series, organizations, and conferences. Its practitioners share with other social historians the conviction that theirs is not merely a legitimate branch of history but is one that may provide the key to an understanding of history as a whole. (For though the emphases and subject-matter of historical research have shifted radically, they persist in the old conviction – even an article of faith – as to the unity of history, that all its parts are somehow linked to form a coherent whole, in which no segments moves independently of any other.)

My own work fits into the tendency I have described, if somewhat uneasily, for I fish in a small bywater of the main stream of urban history. While most urban historians have sought answers to the question: what have cities done to people? my own question has been, instead, what have people done to cities? Yet the evidence I have used, and the subjects I have treated would certainly place me in the company of those writing history from below: landowners and developers rather than mayors and town councillors, anonymous speculative builders rather than famous architects, leases and restrictive covenants rather than laws and decrees, the floor-plans of private dwellings rather than the policies of government.

Such evidence I find endlessly fascinating: I know few more satisfying pleasures than untying the red tape around a bundle of solicitors' letters and watching eighteenth-century sand fall into my lap, or unrolling an estate plan showing some executed or abortive project of urban beautification. And, as in the past few weeks, finding in the streets and canals of today's Amsterdam the living records of past ages has kept me in a state of voluptuous bliss.

But do my inquiries and those of other urban and social historians consist of more than individual and collective self-indulgence? 'You would have wished that philosophers had written history,' Voltaire wrote Catherine the Great, 'because you wish to read it as a philosopher. You are only looking for useful truths, and you have hardly found, you say, anything but useless errors.' (Vous voudriez que des philosophes eussed écrit l'histoire [ancienne] parce que vous voulez la lire en philosophe. Vous ne cherchez que des vérités utiles, et vous n'avez guère trouvé, dites-vous, que d'inutiles erreurs.') Voltaire was here anticipating Fernand Braudel in suggesting that 'les évenements,' or 'one damn thing after another,' the mere recording of successive events, are not in themselves worth the attention of the serious historian. Has the new social history, the new urban history provided us with 'useful truths,' ingredients with which to create a more satisfying and valuable understanding of human history as a whole? Can it?

The five delightful weeks I have so far spent in Amsterdam, going up and down its streets, passages, and canals, conversing with scholars who are working to uncover its secrets, and struggling to learn enough Dutch to read a little of the impressive scholarly literature on the city have left me dazzled, stimulated, and enlightened, but also worried. My worries can be stated crudely thus: may our faith in the unity and coherence of history, in the overwhelming importance of temporal context, in the interconnectedness of things, and in the prospect of discovering some ultimate meaning in it all, perhaps not be justified? May the discoveries in the new and expanded fields of social and urban history, however interesting, prove ultimately to be not very important? And may this perhaps result from the fact that the new subjects of the new history: the family, *mentalités*, child-rearing, housework, courtship, petty crime, estate management, urban neighbourhoods, and, alas, cities themselves, may not have a history, at least not in the sense that the Netherlands, the British Constitution, religion, philosophy, and science have histories. I am beginning, that is to say, to wonder if, contrary to my earlier beliefs, Herodotus may not have been wrong, Thucydides right. Or, more devastatingly, that Aristotle may have been correct in asserting that poetry was more true than history, since Homer, for example, contained truths about human behaviour and the nature of things that would have eternal validity, whereas Herodotus had done no more than record a succession of unrepeatable and mostly insignificant events, which Catherine the Great might later justifiably dismiss as 'useless errors.'

The up-to-date history that I have been reading in recent years – dealing with subjects like popular culture, sex and marriage, women's role, ethnic minorities, the 'moral economy,' amusements, eating habits, and so forth –

produces evidence and arrives at conclusions that have this in common: on the one hand, a persistence of beliefs and practices, material circumstances and social institutions, over immense periods of time, century after century, Renaissance, Reformation, Scientific Revolution, Industrial Revolution, and French Revolution pass by virtually unnoticed; on the other hand, immense variation, not just from country to country and region to region but often village to village. (The former would almost seem to justify all those maddening sentences in Lewis Mumford that begin, 'between the thirteenth and the eighteenth century...'). Changes, where observed, more often took the form of temporary fluctuations than of long-term movement in any observable direction. It is, that is to say, 'la longue durée' with a vengeance, not only different from, but unconnected with old-fashioned, élitist 'history from above,' with its Defeat of the Spanish Armada in 1588, its Protestant Wind bringing William III to save the liberties of Englishmen in 1688, and its Battle of Blenheim and Treaty of Utrecht bringing to an end the period of French Hegemony.

What I fear may be emerging is a situation in which we have old-fashioned history, perhaps the only 'real' history, where kings and parliaments, philosophers and scientists – consisting almost entirely of white, upper-class males – make decisions and arrive at discoveries at particular times and places, thereby producing long-term and widespread consequences; alongside this, but unconnected, or at best very loosely connected with it – and with one another – we have the history of women, of peasants, of childhood, and, perhaps, of cities – occasionally affected by high historical events like the Protestant Reformation and the Thirty Years' War, but seldom if ever affecting the history in return – in which any really significant changes – like, say, the coming of a money economy or the invention of the nuclear family – either took place at a time before historical records exist or sometime in the 1960s. All this has been fascinating to learn, and I look forward to learning more, but I wonder if all this constitutes 'history,' if by history we mean the study of significant change, what Voltaire and Catherine the Great meant, I think by history 'en philosophe.' The new history, urban and otherwise, has yet to establish its claim to being a unifying, explanatory discipline rather than merely a way of providing amusement and harmless employment for its practitioners and devotees.

I apologize for going on at such length on a subject that may strike non-historians as being as parochial and trivial as the debates among structuralist and deconstructionist literary critics appear to me. But I thought it necessary as background to an account of what the past month spent viewing, studying, and enjoying Amsterdam has done to my own thinking about cities, about time, and about history.

Let me begin with time and the city. Cities rarely build or rebuild themselves in accord with the needs and values of the contemporary age. As a rule each generation occupies, none too happily, the city bequeathed it by its parents. Thus, for the most part, the Victorians lived in Georgian London, and hated it. (This, parenthetically, is one reason why the novels of Dickens should be used with great caution as sources for *Victorian* London. Not only are they usually set in the 1820s or early 1830s – that is to say *before* the accession of Queen Victoria in 1837 – and usually 10 or 20 years earlier than their period of composition, but the parts of London in which the action occurs are almost invariably far older, 18th-century, 17th-century, or even earlier.) A significant proportion of the leaders of the economy, thought, and politics of Amsterdam continued to occupy, as Dr. Wagenaar has shown, their 17th-century houses along the canals well into the 20th century.

There are, of course, significant exceptions. The discovery of gold in California and Australia respectively turned San Francisco and Melbourne into instant metropolises in the 1850s; a second wave of prosperity and speculative fever made Melbourne rebuild itself almost wholly around 1888, while the earthquake and fire of 1906 made San Francisco do the same two decades later. The Great Fire of 1666 forced the City of London to become an instant emblem of modernity in the years that followed, while the operations of Napoleon III and the Emperor Franz Joseph made late 19th-century Paris and Vienna wholly appropriate expressions of the requirements and values of what was then 'today.' But today quickly becomes yesterday and the day before yesterday, and economic depression or stagnation can prevent adaptation to changed circumstances. The Melbourne of the 1880s and post-Earthquake San Francisco remained nearly intact until the building madness of the 1960s, while Vienna's Ringstraße and Haussmann's boulevards remain to this day very nearly what they were a century ago.

Then there is Amsterdam. What are we to make of it? If the growth and transformation that occurred in the course of the 17th-century took somewhat longer to accomplish than that of London after 1666 or Melbourne in the 1880s, it was by contemporary standards an astonishing performance. And yet, as I intend to argue next Thursday, Amsterdam chose not to be a city of its own time, but turned itself into a 17th-century city that rejected the 17th century: at least the 17th century as it is usually thought to have been. If, as Simon Schama has argued in *The Embarrassment of Riches*, the Netherlands were the 'great exception' in 17th-century Europe, Amsterdam was at once the most amazing and the least representative metropolis of the age.

But then London, too, fails to fit the textbook expectations of what the 17th-century city ought to have been like, and the closer we examine the other cities of the period the more we shall be impressed by variation and diversity, the less certain we shall be that there was a 'spirit of the age,' that 'the 17th century' may be no more than a chronological expression, that abstract concepts like 'the Age of the Baroque' or 'the Age of Absolutism' or 'the Scientific Revolution' or 'the General Crisis' may reflect the intellectual fashions of the 20th century but have nothing very useful to say about the 17th.

Irrespective of whether or not Amsterdam embodied the values or essential character of the age in which it took its present form, its subsequent development had at best a partial and spasmodic relationship to the broader currents of European history. Admittedly, the economic stagnation of the 18th century did not stop building in Amsterdam as much as the collapse of 1893 was to preserve central Melbourne as if in amber for the next 70 years. Even in the period from 1795 to 1870 *some* alterations were made in the existing fabric of Amsterdam, and some new buildings were erected. And if the outward expansion of the city after 1870 was at first of very limited extent, it gave Amsterdam the opportunity to participate in contemporary fashions of urban layout as well as of architectural style.

But for what they are worth, my very preliminary impressions of the architectural and urbanistic record of Amsterdam between 1600 and 1902 suggest that the city does not have a 'history,' at least not a philosophical history that would have satisfied Catherine the Great. Like the new 'social history' or 'history from below,' it displays distinctive local variations, the independence of local practices from more widespread developments, and within itself the persistence over a long period of forms and patterns combined with superficial and directionless fluctuations. This is perhaps an unnecessarily complicated way of saying that Amsterdam has remained unmistakably itself throughout the past four centuries, and that even its outermost extensions down to 1940 have characteristics that distinguish them from the suburban growth of other cities. Amsterdam seems somehow to have maintained until recently a degree of independence from general history, and may possibly be said not even to have had a 'history' of its own. This is said, let me assure you, in admiration and envy: 'Happy the city that has no history.'

Of course what I have just said is not true: but it may contain a half-truth or a quarter-truth that is worth thinking about. In any event, let me give some examples of what I mean, drawn mostly from my superficial and probably inaccurate observation of building types and architectural forms. The almost universal building type in Amsterdam down to the close of the 19th century was a modified form of what had been the standard European urban medieval house: narrow, multistoried, usually no more than three windows across, with a shop or workshop at ground level, and a steeply-pitched gable facing the street. In Amsterdam as in other cities the façade, at least, by the 17th century, was coming to be brick rather than timber, but the constructional forms in the new material followed the lines of the traditional wooden city house.

It is my impression that Amsterdam, along with other Dutch cities, maintained an essentially medieval type of house as the standard dwelling longer than most other European cities. In Vienna, the individual burgher house had by the end of the 18th century been almost totally superseded by the 'palace' – either a genuine monumental royal or noble residence or an imitation palace divided into suites of separate apartments. Both would be characterized by a broad, impressive façade onto the street and an ornamental carriage entrance leading to a central courtyard. In Paris the narrow street-house of medieval origin continued to be built down to the end of the 18th century, but the gable was either turned so that it did not face the street or disguised by a false wall so that only a flat cornice would be visible. But both the nobility and the greater bourgeoisie, instead of building enlarged versions of the medieval house for their own occupation, had long before abandoned it for the *hôtel particulier*, separated by a broad walled courtyard from the street. In London the terrace house persisted into the 20th century but there, as in Paris, the street gable was abolished in favour of a flat, continuous roof line, which increasingly came to accord with the cornices of adjacent houses.

I stress this point, for if there was a single aesthetic principle that governed the architectural taste of Renaissance and post-Renaissance Europe it was the dominance of horizontal over vertical elements, and in particular the importance of the seemingly flat roofline. (I say seemingly, because of course there was always a sloping roof, but it was kept decently hidden behind the parapet or balustrade.) In cities like Vienna that cornice or balustrade might serve as a base along which heroic statues in the antique taste might stand, point, and gesture, but they clearly had nothing to do with the shape of the roof that lay behind them.

In Amsterdam things were far different. Whether as step gables or neck gables of whatever shape, and however different to external ornamentation, the tops of street façades of houses large and small continued, for the most part, to express the shape of the steeply inclined gables they covered. The flat cornice, sometimes surmounted by a central pediment, began to appear in the 1630s, and – particularly in larger and wider houses – became common by the eighteenth century. Common but never universal; even along the most fashionable canals, decorated gable ends that must to foreign eyes have seemed at best old-fashioned, at worst aesthetically offensive, continued to be built throughout the eighteenth and into the nineteenth century. Even the flat cornices and balustrades tended to suggest, rightly or wrongly, that a steeply pointed gable lay behind them, by the placement of a decorative cartouche or coat of arms at their centre; even the most correctly classical pediments rarely extended to encompass the whole of the façade, but were only as wide as the central bays: as if to suggest that they were really there as a substitute for the most usual gable end.

All of this served to stress the identity and separateness of the individual house at the expense of the terrace as a whole. Actually I am probably mistaken in using the English word terrace at all to indicate a row of adjacent town houses: is there in fact an equivalent word in Dutch? Certainly the fact of a terrace in the English sense of a row of houses forming a unified composition is rare in Amsterdam; I can think of Sarphati's East and West End of the 1860s, but I don't think anything of the sort can be found along the 17th and 18th-century canals. Occasionally two adjacent houses might form one single composition, as in the Trippenhuis, but in general the Amsterdam burgher did not wish to have his residence subordinated to some more comprehensive whole. (That the acquiescence of London householders in such architectural schemes indicates a lesser degree of individualism in the 18th-century England seems unlikely; yet I wouldn't like to give up the hope that such a sharp contrast in architectural taste may prove to have *some* broader significance.)

Unlike eighteenth-century London, the lines of windows, string courses, and parapets of adjacent houses in Amsterdam accord with one another only by accident, even along the best canals. Low, narrow houses crouch between their tall, broad neighbours, giving a sense of happy diversity to the typical Amsterdam canal or street scene. But what strikes this post-Romantic age as an enchanting mixture of the picturesque with the classical must have struck a French connoisseur or an English man of taste in the eighteenth century as yet another instance of Dutch boorishness.

During the 19th and early 20th century Amsterdam was, if possible, even more selective in what it chose to adopt from international architectural styles. The stark and unadorned, so-called Revolutionary style of the 1790s and after seems hardly to have touched Amsterdam, which likewise seems to have had no counterpart to the Regency style of early 19th-century England, or, for that matter, of the Italianate style that succeeded it. In all these connections the extreme rarity of stucco facing is remarkable. Elsewhere in Europe stucco, as a cheap and easily-ornamented alternative to stone, dominated early 19th-century building. Critics, in particular English critics, condemned it as deceitful, insofar as it pretended to be something that it was not, and masked the load-bearing walls themselves. But speculative builders and their customers clearly revelled in its smooth, plain surfaces, and for decades preferred it to the roughness of naked brick. But in Amsterdam aesthetic and philistines alike remained content, as they had been in the past, with traditional brick surfaces.

The Gothic revival seems to have made even less of an impact on Amsterdam than it did elsewhere on the Continent. It was, in any event, mainly a craze of the English-speaking world. The Queen Anne Revival that swept England in the 1870s and 80s certainly had its counterpart in Amsterdam and elsewhere in the Netherlands, but here it was more a continuation and exaggeration of a still-living, or merely dormant local building tradition, not the abrupt reversal of aesthetic direction that is was in London.

It was in the early twentieth century, though, that Amsterdam seems most emphatically to have pursued its own aesthetic path, most totally to have ignored outside fashions. The rarity, apart from a few splendid villas near the Vondelpark, of examples of Art Nouveau or Jugendstil is not surprising: for nowhere were these movements either generally adopted or long-lasting. More remarkable is the almost total absence from Amsterdam of examples of the new styles that dominated the first decades of the twentieth century in Britain, the United States, and most of the European Continent: all reflecting the revival of Classicism and a new appreciation of the merits of eighteenth-century architecture. Whether in the historically accurate work of Beaux-Arts architects like Stanford White in the United States, the 'stripped classicism' of Lutyens and his followers in England, or the florid and undulating classicism that enlivened Paris in the years just before 1914, the Classical Revival promised to provide the dominant style of the 20th century. (One would not gather as much from reading most histories of 20th-century architecture, but an examination of the major buildings that were actually constructed will, I think, confirm the observation.) But here, quite as remarkable as the abundance, ubiquity, and precocity of works of the Amsterdam School, is the almost total absence of examples of the elsewhere dominant Classical Rivival. Amsterdam clearly marched to the sound of a different drummer.

What does all this do to the claims of urban history to be genuine 'history' rather than a mere chronicle of disparate, random phenomena? It suggests, I think, that to attempt to incorporate Amsterdam into a general history of cities as built environments, artifacts, or works of art may do violence to the meaning of the evidence. Even to retreat from the claim of the existence of a single urban history to one of many urban histories presents difficulties, given the early establishment of the dominant patterns of urban design, building types, façades, and internal plans, and their persistence century after century, changing either in a random manner or in ways and times unconnected with broader historical changes. Attempts to relate urban and architectural developments to such phenomena as the Reformation, the Enlightenment, the French Revolution, the Industrial Revolution, and the First World War have had, at best, limited success.

I use Amsterdam only as an example, if the example that has necessarily dominated my thoughts for the past month. My general point, which I throw out for your consideration, is that urban history has so far failed to meet Voltaire's criteria for history worthy the attention of a philosopher, or man or woman of sense. Needless to say, I very much hope to be satisfactorily refuted, for I intend to continue my own inquiries into urban history and would like to think that I can hope thereby to be doing something more than merely contributing to my own amusement.

Urbanity, modernity, and liberty
Amsterdam in the seventeenth century

Donald Olsen

The city as an historical source

The capacity of the built environment – above all that of the city – to reveal significant truths about its builders is a scholarly commonplace. 'No other source can inform us (...) in the same totally undeceitful manner as can the material city', according to Wolfgang Braunfels.[1] Jean Reynaud assured the readers of the *Encyclopédie nouvelle* in 1841 that the city was 'the symbolic shape of the society which it contains and of which it is (...) the garment'. Each city constituted 'an inscription marking on the earth, in sharp and positive letters, the history of the world at the point where it rises'.[2]

Yet the inscriptions on most cities are neither sharp nor positive, but blurred and obscured by the passage of time. While the ordinary source, wether written or monumental, can be fixed in time, a city, by its very nature, is a palimpsest, subject to additions, alterations, and excisions from one age to another.[3] Still, there have been cities which physical catastrophe, sudden prosperity, or altered political circumstances made instant emblems of an age: Lisbon or San Francisco after their earthquakes, Melbourne after the discovery of gold in Australia, Berlin after German unification. Amsterdam, through the happy survival of its seventeenth-century structure and much of its seventeenth-century fabric, not only was but is a sharp and positive inscription of Dutch civilization from its golden age, whose 'symbolic shape' it represents in all its sober splendour. In no other city has so much of the seventeenth century been preserved for our pleasure and instruction.

Amsterdam as a legible text

The pleasure is immediate and overwhelming; the instruction less certain. If, as Simon Schama reminds us, 'the Dutch Republic was the Great Seventeenth-Century Exception',[4] Amsterdam was equally exceptional as a city. It diverged politically, economically, and intellectually, as well as aesthetically, from the rest of Europe. Capitalistic, individualistic, tolerant, republican, cosmopolitan, pragmatic, rationalistic, and scientific, Amsterdam in its golden age might seem on the surface to anticipate the twentieth-century. Yet Peter Burke warns against the temptation to exaggerate 'the modernity of the Amsterdam élite [of the seventeenth century], their combination of rationalism, Protestantism, capitalism and science.'[5] Neither the ruling minority nor the city it ruled anticipated the future course of European urban development.

A thoughtful contemporary observer would have been justified in viewing the Amsterdam of Rembrandt and Vondel not as a portent of the future, but as an unaccountable throwback to a barbarous past. However well-fed its citizens, however solid and stately the buildings arising along its new canals, Amsterdam would have seemed an anachronism, destined to be swept away, if not necessarily by a triumphant revival of dogmatic Catholicism, certainly by dynasticism, absolutism, and mercantilism: that is to say by the centralized territorial state. It was rather the last great medieval city than the first modern city: more the successor to Venice and Florence than the precursor of Manchester and Chicago.

'What impressed contemporaries about Amsterdam [in the seventeenth century] was that it was a city entirely dedicated to making money', Mark Girouard tells us. 'The squares were as crowded with commercial activity as everywhere else. Even (...) the Dam square (...) contained a fish market, a crane and a public weigh-house. Commerce was inescapable, (...) every available piece of space and all the available manpower were made to pay their way.'[6] Such surprise was either hypocritical or ill-informed. The *amount* of money being made in Amsterdam might well have elicited astonishment. Holland was an island of growth and prosperity in an age marked by depression and hunger. But the concentration of its energy and the dedication of its space to the pursuit of wealth ought to have struck contemporaries not so much as unique as old-fashioned. However beautifully, however splendidly the Dutch capital has met the practical and aesthetic needs of its residents from that time to the present, Amsterdam represented the culmination of a medieval urbanistic tradition, not the best modern notion of what a city ought to be.

The medieval city

To describe Amsterdam as medieval will seem strange to one who thinks, with the late Lewis Mumford, that 'the medieval city in Europe may be described as a collective structure whose main purpose was the living of a Christian life.'[7] But such a view confuses the actual individualistic, profit-oriented towns of the Middle Ages with the ingenious efforts of medieval intellectuals to fit untidy reality into their theories of society.[8]

If cities had become, by the twelfth century, the most dynamic and creative elements of medieval civilization, they remained a theoretical anomaly. Graeco-Roman antiquity had used the city to embody its conception of order, to convey its notion of what mattered in life. The early middle ages instead used the monastery, the high middle ages the cathedral as symbolic representations of their very different ideas on the subject. The quickening revival of urban life that occurred around the year 1000 did not bring back the ancient city: the new and revitalized towns of the middle ages were responses to practical military needs or immediate economic opportunities, not conscious expressions of political programmes or theoretical principles.

The outward guise of the medieval city reflected both the necessity of defence and the urge to profit. The expense of erecting surrounding fortifications made space within too valuable to be squandered on inessentials. Spired churches and a soaring town hall might express civic pride, but for the most part capital went into productive investment rather than into private or public display.[9] The tall, separate house, devoted to production and trade, was the standard building unit. Historically the single-family house began as a combination of street-level shop with workrooms and dwelling-space arranged behind and above. Such an arrangement of space and priorities subordinated domestic activities to the requirements of production and exchange. Whatever open spaces – usually few enough – the town possessed would be occupied by one market or another in the course of the week. Unlike either its ancient predecessors or its modern successors, the medieval town was designed for *use*, not as a statement of value, or an attempt to inform or impress.[10]

Each town strove to achieve and maintain its independence precisely in order to be able to devote all its space and all its energy to the creation of wealth.[11] Along with the pursuit of gain and the defence of independence went personal, economic, and intellectual freedom for the citizen.

Let it seem strange to cite freedom and toleration as specifically medieval virtues, let it be said that I am thinking of the great trading towns rather than medieval society in general, and of the twelfth century more than the thirteenth. Even there and then intellectual freedom and religious toleration existed more in practice than in theory, given the economic advantages of trading with infidels and heretics over a strict emphasis on theological orthodoxy. But so, too, was Amsterdam's toleration in the seventeenth century more one of practice than of theory. Whatever the limitations on religious freedom even in the thirteenth century, they were less far-reaching and effective than those imposed by the Counter Reformation, or Calvin's Geneva.[12]

The liberties and individual rights of the medieval town found visual expression in its architecture. The gabled single-family houses represented the independent merchants and craftsmen who made up the citizenry. The structural and decorative elements of the Gothic worked harmoniously with the political and economic aspects of contemporary urban society. Rightly or wrongly, nineteenth-century theorists came to associate the Gothic with freedom, classicism with despotism. For Viollet-le-Duc, the 'structural efficiency' of Gothic architecture 'reflected a rational, democratic society. (...) The Gothic was the building system of free, thinking men.'[13] He saw the pointed arch as 'symbolic of republican, civic spirit', insofar as it 'permitted efficient, piecemeal construction and thus presumed political freedom...'.[14] Friedrich Schmidt would choose a Northern Gothic as the style for the new Vienna Town Hall in the 1880s as reflecting the independence of the free medieval commune.[15]

The medieval and the modern

To oversimplify in pursuit of clarity, a list of contrasting qualities can be used to distinguish the medieval (thirteenth-century) from the modern (seventeenth-century) city. The qualities in the medieval column are those of *actual* cities (notably the more successful Italian towns), while the modern column represents in particular the seventeenth-century urban *ideal*, and the direction in which cities were then moving (notably the capitals of dynastic states). Given the absence of systematic urban *theory* in the thirteenth century, and the practical difficulties the seventeenth century had in realizing its urban ideal, the comparison, if not strictly logical, still seems worth making:

MEDIEVAL (13TH CENHTURY)	MODERN (17TH CENTURY)
Bourgois	Aristocratic
Republican	Royal
Particularistic	Centralized
Secular	Religious
Capitalistic	Mercantilistic
Free	Authoritarian
Diverse	Uniform
Gothic	Classical
Vertical	Horizontal
Money	Land (preferred investment)

The mixture of political, economic, ideological, and aesthetic qualities is deliberate, and central to the argument that seventeenth-century Amsterdam was the last and greatest of medieval cities. Rome and Vienna can be viewed as portraying what the European city might have become had there not been:

1. The Revolution of 1688
2. The Revolution of 1789
3. The Industrial Revolution
4. 'The Rise of the Middle Classes'

Amsterdam represents another 'might have been': the European city had there not been:

1. The Counter Reformation
2. The triumph of the territorial state
3. Centralized absolutism
4. 'The Rise of the Aristocracy'

Amsterdam as anachronism

That Amsterdam – and the rest of Holland – were politically and economically conservative, if not reactionary, is generally recognized. 'The Dutch were not remarkable for many innovations, but rather for the more effective and intensive use of methods already known elsewhere,' writes E.H.D. Haley of the economic practices that were enriching Amsterdam.[16] 'As one reviews the unfolding capitalism of Amsterdam', writes Violet Barbour, 'it is evident that its strength lay in extension and intensification, not in experiment or innovation.'[17] Amsterdam gave medieval economic institutions and practices 'more precise formulation, greater flexibility and extension, and used them effectively over a wider field (...) her golden age was rather the climax of a period of transition than the beginning of a new economic era.'[18]

Huizinga points out that 'the Netherlands prospered under an antiquated economic system, one, moreover, that the most neighbouring countries were trying to discard for a more efficient one (...) the Netherlands achieved greatness under a system of pre-mercantilism and medieval 'liberty'...'.[19] The merchants and bankers of Amsterdam paid as little need to religious objections to their pursuit of profit as had the merchants and bankers of medieval Venice. 'Continued complaints by the church were ignored,' according to Haley, 'nor did the great capitalists pay any attention to the attacks which the synods occasionally made on the taking of usury...'.[20] Medieval particularism and medieval tolerance proved as compatible with economic growth as with military victory.

Dutch political institutions were similarly antiquated. While 'the sixteenth and seventeenth centuries were a period in which most men thought in terms of princes and courts', in the Netherlands 'central institutions were fewer and weaker, there was less of a paid state bureaucracy, and more opportunity for the rulers of cities like Amsterdam to hinder the development of a consistent state policy in their own local interests'.[21] Amsterdam behaved like a medieval city state, dominating the loose alliance of theoretical equals that formed the United Netherlands. Simon Schama shows how Dutch nationalism was being created in the course of the century, but a nation *state* still lay in the future.[22] What then existed was, according to Huizinga, 'thoroughly conservative, holding fast to old traditions and established laws. A love of liberty was kept alive, but the concept of political freedom was again that of the Middle Ages: a chain of limited privileges...'.[23]

The spirit of the seventeenth century

Europe in the seventeenth century seemed intent on making Amsterdam and all that it stood for not only anachronistic but obsolete. The new territorial, dynastic states were achieving their goals and enhancing their power by the systematic suppression of feudal, ecclesiastical, and municipal particularism within their boundaries. The spirit of the new age demanded the replacement of independent city states by centralized monarchies, of economic individualism by the wise direction of national resources, of Gothic particularism by classical coherence, of the proliferation of religious error by the imposition of religious truth, of medieval liberties by modern order. To bring about such changes and give them tangible expression, the city would need to be transformed, in shape, guise, and essence.[24]

The medieval city had been, in practice if not in theory, a profoundly secular enterprise, successful to the degree that it kept itself independent of ecclesiastical, aristocratic, and royal control. A modern city was one whose priorities more nearly reflected the political will of its sovereign than the economic interests of its inhabitants. Throughout Europe kings were striving to subordinate church, town, and aristocracy to their authority. In exchange for outmoded medieval liberties they offered them wealth and outward splendour in accordance with their new role as instruments of royal power, emblems of dynastic glory. The style of such splendour might vary from the florid Austrian or South German baroque to the more austere forms of classicism favoured by French or English taste. But such variations within a classical vocabulary mattered less than the common rejection not only of the specific forms of the Gothic, but of its underlying individualistic spirit.

Accompanying, and sometimes supporting the rise of the territorial dynastic state was an intellectual climate that favoured clarity, uniformity, and symmetry, qualities also dominant in the aesthetic theory and artistic production of the century of Descartes and Racine, Newton and Dryden. All aspects of human thought, experience, and creativity strove to conform to the rules of logic and the beauty of mathematics. The reform of language, of music, of poetry, of the stage was paralleled by the subjection of economic behaviour to rational control, so that the labours of artisan and merchant could be made to contribute to the prosperity of society and the power of the state. Uniting the exertions of statesman, mercantilist, jurist, philosopher, tragedian, lexicographer, grammarian, surveyor, theologian, and scientist was a vision of order, coherence, and unity.

Absolutism was the political expression, mercantilism the economic expression of an age 'intoxicated with the power of man'.[25] Art and science, economics and politics shared a 'determination to mold nature in man's image and display the power of the human spirit'.[26] All stressed the subordination of the parts to the principle governing the whole. Just as the baroque gave visible expression to absolutism, so mercantilism offered it an appropriate economic policy, one that subordinated the interests of the individual and the locality to the requirements of state and society.

In philosophy, science, and the arts, the vision of order, coherence, and unity was to an astonishing extent made real. A verse tragedy, a philosophical treatise, a royal palace, even something as vast and complex as the French language itself turned out to be amenable to rational direction, capable of being made something that the mind could comprehend and the judgement approve. But market forces everywhere proved mightier than mercantilistic controls, traditional practices than royal edicts, individual greed than rational altruism, immediate necessity than farsighted calculation. Every age inevitably displays a sharp contrast between its professed ideals and its actual behaviour, but the discrepancies between theory and practice were particularly blatant in the seventeenth century, and nowhere more than in its cities.

The seventeenth-century city

Yet the urban ideal of the age, breathtaking in its audacity, helped determine much of what was to happen to cities in later centuries. It revived the ancient notion of the city as a monument, a concrete manifestation of the beliefs of its rulers, a representation in space of the ideas the régime existed to promote, an expression in stone of the principles that underlay the culture of the age. No longer was the city to be merely a fortress, a workshop, and a market; now it was to do what the Gothic cathedral had attempted in the thirteenth century, and what the palace and the garden were achieving in the age of rationalism and absolutism: sum up and express the aspirations and convictions of contemporary civilization.

Had such a city actually been built it would have been vast and various, yet governed by a single organizing principle, so that its message would ultimately have been one. Each part would have justified itself by its contribution to the larger whole, and the whole something that could be comprehended by the eye and approved by the intellect. It would have resembled an extended baroque palace, informed throughout by the same qualities of symmetry, balance, subordination, dramatic contrast, rhythmic variety that characterized its component buildings. Broad avenues, regularly disposed, would terminate in stately churches and public buildings, each richly adorned with inscriptions and figurative sculpture that explicitly and implicitly encouraged, exhorted, and proclaimed. Appropriate classical forms and mythological references would express the taste and learning of the regime, the mathematical regularity of the street plan and the uniformity of the façades the rule of law and the universality, impartiality, and firmness with which those laws were enforced.

The population would be diligent, submissive, and industrious, working to increase the wealth and uphold the glory of the dynasty, and attentive to the teachings of the one true church. There would be fixed boundaries, with gated walls to repel its enemies and exclude the idle and the disaffected. Just as the licensing of the press, the stage, and the pulpit would ensure that correct doctrine was taught and error suppressed, architectural regulations would impose proper standards of taste: order, measure, and degree in the physical surroundings would encourage dignified conduct and rational thought. Just as the rules of architecture, of poetry, and of etiquette reinforced one another, so the structural and plastic vocabulary of classicism would support the economic and social order of mercantilism and the moral order of Christianity. A dignified, stable, and weighty environment would induce feelings of awe, respect, wonder, submission, and happiness.

Of course no such city was ever built, just as no prince was able to achieve a genuinely absolute monarchy. Rome and Turin, Nancy and St. Petersburg would attain some of the outward attributes of the baroque ideal, but sheer considerations of expense kept most cities, even capitals, in their existing disorderly state. Yet certain forms of extravagance the age could afford – the palace, the garden, and the stage – give a fair notion of the ideal to which its cities aspired. If Louis XIV could not rebuild Paris to his liking, he could create at Versailles a controlled environment adequate to his glory and appropriate to his aims. A neatly clipped, well watered, carefully maintained Dutch garden, with geometrical tulip beds and rows of rigorously pruned trees, subdued nature by reason to form a world of order and delight. In his designs for masques performed before Charles I, Inigo Jones realized completely the aesthetic aspirations and moral convictions of his sovereign; in the Banqueting House and the Piazza at Covent Garden he could at best insert two islands of beauty into the stormy and chaotic London that surrounded them.

If the age of the baroque lacked the resources to create a baroque city, the vision of a city of controlled magnificence was certainly present. What was new in early modern Europe was the notion that cities of size and importance had significant functions that were other than economic and military. For the first time since the collapse of the Roman Empire cities were beginning to serve as symbolic expressions of the power of the regime and (in Catholic countries) the validity of the teachings of Holy Church, while at the same time providing amusement for the ruling classes.

Amsterdam in its Golden Age

Amsterdam had the means, but lacked the will to approximate the contemporary urban ideal. Van Campen's Town Hall, with its rich iconographic contents, came closest to meeting international requirements for an urban monument that would both promote and incorporate the values of the age. That the rest of the city chose not to imitate the didactic qualities of the Town Hall, much less the baroque extravagances of Rome or the sober classicism of Paris, can only mean that it found the 'values of the age' either irrelevant or repugnant.

Amsterdam rejected both centralized planning and profitless display.[27] It showed little enthusiasm for grandiose schemes for expansion; the outer walls were extended only just far enough to accommodate assured demand for building space. Ed Taverne has demonstrated that the new canals resulted not from the imposition of a comprehensive plan, but as pragmatic responses to immediate economic, demographic, and strategic requirements – just as had the inner canals of the medieval city.

The layout of the new streets and waterways did not reflect Renaissance theories of urban design, much less the more dramatic proposals of baroque town planners.[28] No ambitious programmes for buildings or open spaces, but instead a ring of residential suburbs for the well-to-do along the Heren-, Keizers-, and Prinsengracht, and for the workers in the Jordaan.[29]

That from such cautious practical motives were created some of the most enchanting urban environments of that or any age has misled scholars into assuming farsighted urbanistic planning. Lewis Mumford is too good a socialist and proponent of town planning not to take for granted that Amsterdam's admirable qualities stemmed from an overall plan: he hails it as 'one of the greatest examples of the town planner's art.'[30] Wolfgang Braunfels sees 'the new baroque sense of Form' in Amsterdam's 'city-plan'.[31] Steen Eiler Rasmussen writes that 'Amsterdam has been planned as a city of canal vistas, built in rings, one beyond the other'.[32] Certainly the careful, regular plotting along the straight-sided segments of the canal quarter, and the generous width of quays and waterway – as broad as 150 feet from house to house on the opposite sides –

and the classical ornaments on the buildings would have been unthinkable in the middle ages.[33] Yet the whole constituted an adaptation of traditional forms and methods to modern needs, not the rejection of the utilitarian for the representational that baroque theory would have demanded.

The Amsterdam house

The seventeenth-century Amsterdam house was a modified version of the standard urban medieval dwelling: narrow, multistoried, usually no more than three windows across, with a steeply-pitched gable facing the street.[34] Brick came to replace wood, but the older shape persisted.

Unlike the French move to pure classicism, or the triumph of Palladianism in England, the Dutch continued the sixteenth-century practice of putting classical ornament on traditional constructional forms. However classical the external ornamentation, the tops of street façades continued, even into the eight-eenth century, to express the shape of the steeply-inclined gables they covered. The flat cornice, sometimes surmounted by a central pediment, began to appear in the 1630s, and – particularly in larger and wider houses – became common by the eighteenth century. Common but never universal: even along the most fashionable canals, decorated gable ends continued to be built throughout the eighteenth and into the nineteenth century. Even the flat cornices and balustrades tended to suggest, by the placement of a decorative cartouch or coat of arms at their centre, that a steeply-pointed gable lay behind them.

Separateness and verticality

If the baroque was 'a search for the intimidating and overwhelming,' Amsterdam was the achievement of the friendly and cozy. One of the ways baroque architects suggested 'weight and oppressiveness was by a heavily depressed pediment. A shallow pediment gives a sinking rather than a rising effect, emphasized by a base-line which projects beyond the corner of the building'.[35] The proportionally tall and narrow pediments of Amsterdam create precisely the opposite effect. They rarely extend even so far as the width of the building, much less beyond it, and often serve as a kind of substitute for a gable end, thereby increasing the element of verticality in the façade.

The notorious steepness of Amsterdam's staircases, both within and without, similarly emphasized verticality. Baroque architecture, as Wölfflin points out, went to the opposite extreme: 'The design of staircases showed how much satisfaction was found in low, spreading forms. The aim was to 'salire con gravità', ascend with gravity (...) and often the steps were so shallow that they were uncomfortable to walk on.'[36] No one could have made such a complaint of the steeply-pitched stairs in Amsterdam.

Along with an exaggerated verticality went an emphasis on the separateness of each constructional element. The Renaissance theorist Alberti had taken for granted that the load-bearing bricks of a building would be decently coated with a smooth 'revetment'. He advised 'at least three coats of plaster (...) the role of the outermost is to display the charm of the finish, colour, and lineaments (...). The more coats of plaster there are, the smoother the surface (...). The last coat should gleam like marble...'.[37] Wölfflin explains the attractions of a smooth stucco façade to the baroque architect: 'a *wall* was now regarded as a single uniform mass, not as something made up of individual stones (...) the general practice was to cover brick with stucco'.[38]

Not so in Amsterdam, in the seventeenth century or since. Unlike the fashion elsewhere in Europe, builders there made no attempt to give superficial unity to their façades by applying stucco facing: each individual brick retained its separateness. Their practice represented a continuation of 'High Gothic standards [whereby] the individual elements, while forming an indiscerptible whole, yet must proclaim their identity by remaining clearly separated from each other.'[39] Amsterdam architectural taste has maintained to this day something that Huizinga regarded as one of the 'essential traits of the declining Middle Ages (...) the tendency to see each thing as an independent entity (...). To this the spirit of the Renaissance is opposed.'[40] At no period have the Dutch lost their affection for undisguised brick walls.

Similarly, the identity of the individual house was never submerged into a larger architectural composition, as classical theory demanded. The Amsterdam householder was no more subservient to aesthetic than to political or religious authority. Unlike the practice in seventeenth and eighteenth-century London, the lines of windows, string courses, and parapets of adjacent houses in Amsterdam accord with one another only by accident, even along the best canals. Low, narrow houses crouch between their tall, broad neighbours, and lend a sense of happy diversity to the typical street scene. Amsterdam had no counterpart to the unified terrace of square, whereby in the place des Vosges or place Dauphine in Paris, the Piazza at Covent Garden in London, the individual house was made to seem part of a larger unit. The Dutch language has no equivalent to the English 'terrace', meaning an architecturally unified row of town houses. Until Sarphati developed his East End and West End in the 1860s, no such arrangement seems to have been tried in Amsterdam.[41] Occasionally two adjacent houses might form a single composition, as in the Trippenhuis, but in general the Amsterdam burgher did not wish his residence subordinated to a comprehensive whole.

In one important respect, the dwellings along the new canals did represent a break from standard medieval practice: the separation, in the grander houses, of residence from business. The ground floor no longer contained either shop or workshop, but was devoted, like the upper stories, to domestic purposes.[42] But the resulting daily move from house to office and back in no way constituted a rejection of capitalistic or urban values, any more than did the seasonal move to a summer villa along the Vecht or in the dunes.

Indeed, the unashamed if dignified assertiveness of the great merchant houses that adorn the canals represents yet another defiance of contemporary values. Just as Amsterdam refused political subservience to a prince, it refused social subservience to an aristocracy. More fundamentally, it failed to share the otherwise universal preference for land as an investment.[43] Its leading families, successful in their commercial investments, were happy to use a portion of the profits for domestic display. Peter Burke finds in 'the works of architecture and sculpture commissioned by the Amsterdam élite (...) less magnificence, less display and less desire for the conspicuous glorification of the family' than was the case in Venice.[44] Yet when compared to the dwelling-houses of London merchants, those of Amsterdam are notable for their degree of assertive pomp.

Conclusion

In its architectural and urbanistic practices, as in its economic and political policies, seventeenth-century Amsterdam was by contemporary standards the reverse of modern: traditional, old-fashioned, backward-looking, in a real sense medieval. Yet it became the richest, most powerful, and most beautiful city of Europe, with the liveliest intellectual and artistic life of the period. Amsterdam achieved wealth, power, and beauty by ignoring theory, rejecting modernity, pursuing an anachronistic building tradition, and following outmoded economic and reactionary political policies. Is there a lesson here for us today?

Fernand Braudel has stressed the uniqueness of the towns of medieval Europe, 'marked by an unparalleled freedom. They had developed as autonomous worlds and (...) had outwitted the territorial state.'[45] Yet the coming of the modern age brought such urban freedom to a close. 'Everywhere in Europe, as soon as the state was firmly established it disciplined the towns with instinctive relentlessness (...). Except in the Netherlands and England obedience was imposed...'.[46]

Amsterdam, from the time of its initial defiance of Philip II to the disrespectful behaviour of its *provos* and squatters in recent decades, has perhaps done more than any other city to propagate the myth or demonstrate the reality of freedom. The liberty it claimed for itself it has in turn granted its residents political, religious, intellectual, and artistic. Even the apparently dominant Reformed Church was unable to impose the kind of doctrinal and

moral discipline it would have wished. The Regents, while in control politically, permitted a degree of economic freedom unmatched elsewhere. The city
where Descartes and Locke and Spinoza thought the unthinkable and wrote
the unsayable enjoyed unparalleled intellectual freedom. Its painters and
architects pursued their creative paths unrestrained by the elsewhere operative
rules of classicism.

The freedom Amsterdam represented was not absolute: neither freedom to
be idle or disreputable nor to ignore the requirements of the community, but
a liberty consistent with the maintenance of a decent, orderly, humane society.
Its architecture expressed the individual personality of its householders,
tempered by the restraints necessary for urban life and by a judicious balance
of traditional and contemporary taste. Amsterdam gave to the artist and the
builder no more than to any other individual the right 'to do his own thing',
yet granted everyone immensely greater latitude for self-expression than was
permitted by the elsewhere ubiquitous notions of *bienséance.*

What was thought, said, and done in Amsterdam was totally antithetical to
the dominant moral, political, religious, and aesthetic standards of the time.
Such blatant defiance of the *Zeitgeist* suggests that Amsterdam enjoyed freedom
not merely from church and state but from *history*: that a body of sufficiently
strong-minded individuals, particularly in an urban environment, can defy the
spirit of the age and go its own way if it so chooses.

The capacity of history to astonish has rarely been demonstrated more
strikingly than by the events of late 1989 and early 1990. The Revolution of
1989 has forced us to question our assumptions as to what is historically
possible, what the human will can achieve, wether we are in fact the slaves of
historical necessity. Like the experience of Amsterdam in the Golden Age, it
suggests that history is unpredictable, that human freedom is not an illusion,
that humanity may be able to control its destiny. As we enter the 1990s we are
more willing than we have been for two centuries to entertain the possibility
that 'liberty' may be at least as useful an historical abstraction as 'the city', 'the
seventeenth century', 'the Middle Ages', and 'Modernity'.

But surely, we shall be told, such freedom was and is illusory. We all know
what Tolstoy has to say about historical inevitability. Whatever they may have
thought at the time, Descartes and Rembrandt and van Campen were, it will
be argued, as much the prisoners of historical determinants as the most abject
subject of Louis XIV. But *what* historical determinants? The more we search for
them the more they evade us; the closer we approach, the less tangible they
become. Certainly the failure of Amsterdam to fit into any general theory,
historical or aesthetic, of the seventeenth century, suggests the unlikelihood of its
ever having existed. Yet there it stands, solid and resplendent, confounding our

sense of historical probability. Either our notion of the course of modern history or Amsterdam will have to go, and Amsterdam stubbornly refuses to vanish.

Amsterdam, as it took its present shape in the seventeenth century, at the very least complicated the task of the historian struggling to make sense of the past. That it dissolves the distinction between medieval and modern, renders nearly meaningless the adjective 'urban', and reduces 'the seventeenth century' to a mere chronological label can only drive the seeker for tidy historical explanations to despair. But for those who can delight in instances of historical contingency, and applaud the human capacity to create something that is at once unlikely and beautiful, Amsterdam will exert a special attraction.

All this may, of course, simply mean that Historical Necessity is more devious in its operations than we thought. If so, it adds to the challenge to those who search for meaning in history. Until that challenge is met, we shall be justified in viewing seventeenth-century Amsterdam as a refutation of historical inevitability, a demonstration of the artificiality of schemes of periodization, an indication of the fragility of conventional notions of causation, a triumph of urban form, and a monument to human freedom.

Notes

1.   Wolfgang Braunfels, *Urban Design in Western Europe: Regime and Architecture, 900-1900* (Chicago: university of Chicago Press, 1988), p. 10. I should like to express my gratitude to the many individuals who made my sojourn in the Netherlands in the spring of 1988 so enlightening, stimulating, and agreeable. In particular I would mention Prof. Dr. G.H. Jansen of the University of Utrecht, Prof. Dr. Ed Taverne of the University of Groningen, and, at the University of Amsterdam, Prof. Dr. A. de Swaan, Prof. Dr. W.F. Heinemeijer, Drs. G. Andriessen, Prof. Dr. L. Brunt, Prof. Dr. B. Kruijt, Drs. I. Teijmant, Drs. P. Nijhoff, Dr. A. Reijndorp, Drs. H. Schijf, Drs. D. van der Vaart, Drs. M. Wagenaar, Drs. J.M. van der Weiden, I. van Winkel, Prof. Dr. H. van der Wusten, Dr. P.L.L.H. Deben. I owe special thanks to my three student research assistants: Froukje Boer, Ineke Verweij, and Hein Mulders.

2.   *Encyclopédie nouvelle*, VIII (1841), 682, 684, quoted in David van Zanten, *Designing Paris* (Cambridge, Mass.: MIT Press, 1987), p.58. 'Until the Industrial Revolution, the urban complex may have been a semiotic system ... [which] asserted itself as one of communication and information.' Françoise Choay, *The Modern City: Planning in the 19th Century* (New York: George Braziller, 1969), p. 7.

3.   G.H. Martin, 'The Town as Palimpsest', in H.J. Dyos, ed., *The Study of Urban History* (London: Edward Arnold, 1968), pp. 155-69.

4.   Simon Schama, *The Embarrassment of Riches* (Berkeley: University of California Press, 1988), p. 224.

5.   Peter Burke, *Venice and Amsterdam* (London: Temple Smith, 1974), pp. 77-8.

6.   Mark Girouard, *Cities and People* (New Haven: Yale University Press, 1985), pp. 151-2.

7.   Lewis Mumford, *The City in History* (New York: Harcourt Brace Jovanovich, 1961), p. 267.

8.   'To find a city as teeming, raw and rough as Manchester was in the 1830s one has to go back to Florence and Ghent in the 1330s. The Manchester cotton lords were as thrusting, ambitious, powerful and successful as the merchants who dominated the medieval textile towns.' Girouard, p. 258.

9.   'Perhaps the most striking feature of the medieval city was the scarcity of public places and buildings. Streets and squares were under the jurisdiction of the municipal, seigneurial, or royal authorities, and the right to eminent domain was not unknown.
      Nevertheless, one has the impression that the public sphere was limited and residual; worse still, it was constantly threatened by private encroachment.' Philippe Contamine, 'Peasant Hearth to Papal Palace: the Fourteenth and Fifteenth Centuries', in George Duby, ed., *A History of Private Life,* II (Cambridge, Mass.: Harvard University Press, 1988), p. 438.

10.   The later middle ages, with declining opportunities for profitable investment, did, to be sure, see a weakening of such pragmatic and bourgeois priorities. Venice in particular had become, by the seventeenth century, notorious for its addiction to pleasure. It was precisely as their economic importance declined that the cities of northern Italy became genuinely pleasant places to live and to visit.

11.   'The cramped, fragmented nature of the public sphere reflected, in the very topography of the city, the weakness, lack of resources, and limited ambitions of the state. Streets were generally so narrow that an avenue of 20 or 22 feet across was considered impressive. Cities were mazes of twisting, tiny streets, impasses, and courts; squares were small, and there were few broad vistas of buildings set back from the street ... traffic was always clogged.' Contamine, p. 439.

12.   For the degree to which economic and other freedoms reigned in the early medieval town, see A.P. Hibbert in M.M. Postan et al., eds., *Cambridge Economic History of Europe,* III (Cambridge: Cambridge University Press, 1963), pp. 181-98. He argues that the high degree of regulation practiced by towns and guilds in the fourteenth and fifteenth centuries was a response to the contracting opportunities during the long late-medieval economic depression. In the twelfth and thirteenth centuries, by contrast, there was a 'sense of 'freedom' in urban policy ... tolerance towards strangers, towards merchants and craftsmen from outside the town ... no oppression of craft producers ... no marked restriction of entry into trading and industrial association ... [an] absence of regulation, absence of that meticulous regimentation of economic life so pronounced in the later Middle Ages.' *Ibid.,* pp. 181-2. The parallels to seventeenth-century Amsterdam are evident.

13.   Van Zanten, p. 155.

14.   *Ibid.,* p. 156.

15.   Peter Haiko and Hannes Stekl, 'Architektur in der industriellen Gesellschaft', ed. by Hannes Stekl (Salzburg: Wolfgang Neugebauer, 1980), pp. 265-7.

16.   E.H.D. Haley, *The Dutch in the Seventeenth Century* (New York: Harcourt Brave Jovanovich, 1972), p. 40.

17. Violet Barbour, *Capitalism in Amsterdam in the 17th Century* (Ann Arbor: University of Michigan Press, 1966), p. 140.

18. *Ibid.*, p. 142.

19. J.H. Huizinga, *Dutch Civilisation in the Seventeenth Century* (London: Collins, 1968), pp. 21-2.

20. Haley, p. 91.

21. *Ibid.*, p. 74.

22. Schama, pp. 51-125.

23. Huizinga, *Dutch Civilisation in the Seventeenth Century* (London: Collins, 1968), pp. 21-2.

24. 'Territorial states, which had superseded a dilapidated feudalism, took the lead from the towns.' Victor-L. Tapié, *The Age of Grandeur: Baroque Art and Architecture* (New York: Frederick A. Praeger, 1960), p. 18.

25. Carl J. Friedrich,k *The Age of the Baroque 1610-1660* (New York: Harper & Brothers, 1952), p. 44.

26. *Ibid.*, p. 86.

27. 'The Dutch merchant and owner of capital acted not from feelings of national interest ... but mainly for the sake of quick gain and secure investment, although there was some loyalty to the province and still more to the city. What mattered was flexibility, rather than being tied to the general interest.' Renee Kistemaker and Roelof van Gelder, *Amsterdam: the Golden Age, 1275-1795* (New York: Abbeville Press, 1983), p. 57.

28. Ed Taverne, *In 't land van belofte: in de nieuwe stad* (Maarssen: Gary Schwartz, 1978), pp. 112-75 *passim*. 'In feite werd het systeem der vorige middeleeuwse stadsvergrotingen gevolgt ...' p. 152.

29. 'Net zo min als er behoefte bestond aan het stichten van nieuwe steden, veroorloofde men zich de luxe van grote pleinen of ruime marktvelden in de nieuw aan te leggen stadswijken die, door het ontbreken van openbare gebouwen als kerken, hallen, scholen, stedelijke gestichten en instellingen, met recht beschouwd zouden kunnen worden als de voorlopers van onze huidige slaapsteden.' *Ibid.*, pp. 113-14.

30. Mumford, p. 501.

31. Braunfels, p. 105.

32. Steen Eiler Rasmussen, *Towns and Buildings* (Liverpool: Liverpool University Press, 1951), p. 91.

33. *Idem.*

34. 'Gabled Renaissance houses with their corbel-steps seem half-gothic, and even when the façades of the 17th century were decorated with classic pilasters and cornices, the spacious windows were retained and huge gables shot into the air above the crowning cornices, with loft openings and projecting joisting beams.' *Ibid.*, p. 93.

35. Heinrich Wölfflin, *Renaissance and Baroque* (Ithaca, New York: Cornell University Press, 1968), pp. 43-4.

36. *Ibid.*, pp. 44-5.

37. Leon Battista Alberti, *On the Art of Building in Ten Books,* Joseph Rykwert et al., trans. (Cambridge, Mass.: MIT Press, 1988), p. 175.

38. Wölfflin, p. 46.

39. Erwin Panofsky, *Gothic Architecture and Scholasticism* (New York: New American Library, 1957), p. 50.

40. J.H. Huizinga, *The Waning of the Middle Ages* (London: Edward Arnold, 1924), p. 244.

41. For Dr. Sarphati's failure to extend such a pattern of English urban design over a larger area, see H. Schijf, 'Wonen op stand in negentiende-eeuwse Amsterdam', *Sociologisch tijdschrift,* XIV (1988), 604-5, 607-11.

42. Lawrence Stone asserts that the contemporary housing developments in the western suburbs of London were 'unlike Amsterdam', whose canal houses 'served their merchant and banker owners as places of residence, storehouses, and shops'. 'The Residential Development of the West End of London in the Seventeenth Century', in Barbara C. Malament, ed., *After the Reformation: Essays in Honor of J.H. Hexter* (Philadelphia: University of Pennsylvania Press, 1980), p. 208. In fact Amsterdam paralleled and even preceded London in the separation of residence from business and achieved, in the outer canals and the Jordaan, neighbourhoods that were more socially homogeneous than anything in London's West End in the first half of the seventeenth century.

43. 'The middle classes (...) bought either land or office (...). This hunger for land (...) became a major phenomenon in European society from the Age of Discovery (...) landed property was at a premium from Spain to Russia'. Tapié, p. 18. Yet in seventeenth-century Amsterdam, where 'the availability of capital for investment was fairly widely diffused,' there was 'little outlet for it in the purchase of land, unless it was in the drainage of polders like the Beemster, which reflected the rise of property values near (...) Amsterdam.' Haley, p. 38.

44. Burke, p. 87.

45. Fernand Braudel, *Capitalism and Material Life 1400-1800* (New York: Harper and Row, 1973), p.396.

46. *Ibid.,* p. 405.

On the authors

LÉON DEBEN, WILLEM HEINEMEIJER and DICK VAN DER VAART were editors of the book on *Capital Cities as Achievements* refered to in the introduction. Léon Deben is director of the Centrum voor Grootstedelijk Onderzoek and associate professor of urban sociology at the University of Amsterdam. Willem Heinemeijer is professor emeritus of human geography and now holds the Wibaut chair. Dick van der Vaart is secretary of the Centrum voor Grootstedelijk Onderzoek and is engaged in urban research at the University of Amsterdam.

MANUEL CASTELLS is Professor of Sociology and Director of the Institute for Sociology of New Technologies at the Universidad Autónoma de Madrid. He is also Professor of City and Regional Planning at the University of California at Berkeley. Before being appointed to Berkeley in 1979 he taught sociology for 12 years at the University of Paris. He has also been a visiting professor and an invited lecturer at more than one hundred academic institutions in thirty-two countries, including M.I.T., Harvard, Columbia, Chicago, Stanford, Wisconsin, Oxford, Berlin, Milan, Copenhagen, Louvain, Moscow, Chile, Beijing, Hong Kong, and Hototsubashi (Tokyo).

He has published 15 books, including *The Urban Question* (French, 1972 translated into eight languages), *The City and the Grassroots* (Winner of the 1983 C. Wright Mills Award), and *The Informational City* (1989).

Castells visited Amsterdam in April 1992. The text is a synthesis of two lectures previously published in the autumn of 1992 in the CGO 'yellow series.'

JOHN O'LOUGHLIN is Professor of Political Geography at the University of Colorado, Boulder. He gave the lecture during his stay in Amsterdam in May and June 1992. The lecture was previously published in the CGO 'yellow series.'

EDWARD W. SOJA teaches Urban and Regional Planning at the University of California, Los Angeles. He is author of several books and articles on African development and, more recently on the economic and spatial restructuring of the Los Angeles basin. He is the author of *Postmodern Geographies* (1989) and 'Inside Exopolis' in M. Sorkin (ed.) *Variations on a Theme Park: Themes from the New American City* (1991).

Soja was visiting professor in Amsterdam in the spring of 1990. The lecture – previously published in the CGO 'yellow series' – went out of print soon after its publication.

LYN H. LOFLAND is Professor of Sociology at the University of California, Davis. She has written about cities and public life in her classic study *A World of Strangers*. Lofland visited Amsterdam in the autumn of 1992. The lecture has not been published before.

ULF HANNERZ is Profesor of Social Anthropology at Stockholm University and Director of the Swedish Collegium for Advanced Study in the Social Sciences, Uppsala. He is member of the Royal Swedish Academy of Sciences and the author of *Soulside: Inquiries into the Ghetto Culture and Community* (1969), *Exploring the City: Inquiries toward an Urban Anthropology* (1990), *Cultural Complexity: Studies in the Social Organization of Meaning* (1992) and other books and articles.

Hannerz was a guest of the University of Amsterdam in October-November 1991. The first of the two lectures published here was given at the Autumn School of the Netherlands Graduate School of Housing and Urban Research at Kijkduin on October 30, 1991. The second lecture was given at the University of Amsterdam on November 12, 1990. The lectures were previously published in the CGO 'yellow series,' be it in a slighly different order.

PAUL CLAVAL is Professor of Urban and Political Geography at the Université de Paris IV Sorbonne. Claval was visiting professor in Amsterdam in the spring of 1993. The lecture, now edited by Sheila Gogol, has not been published before.

DONALD J. OLSEN holds the Eloise Ellery Chair of History at Vassar College, Poughkeepsie, New York. He published *The City as a Work of Art* (1986) which has been translated into major European languages including Dutch (1990).

The essay *Time and the City: is there an Urban History?* was given as a lecture in the spring of 1988. An earlier version of *Urbanity, Modernity, and Liberty: Amsterdam in the Seventeeth Century* was presented in 1988: the final version appeared in 1990 in the CGO 'yellow series' and was soon sold out.